ON AUTHORITY
AND REVELATION

harper ✝ torchbooks

A reference-list of Harper Torchbooks, classified by subjects, is printed at the end of this volume.

SØREN KIERKEGAARD

ON AUTHORITY
AND REVELATION

*The Book on Adler, or a Cycle of
Ethico-Religious Essays*

INTRODUCTION TO THE TORCHBOOK EDITION BY
FREDERICK SONTAG

TRANSLATED, WITH AN INTRODUCTION AND NOTES, BY
WALTER LOWRIE

HARPER TORCHBOOKS ❦ THE CLOISTER LIBRARY

HARPER & ROW, PUBLISHERS, NEW YORK

CONTENTS

INTRODUCTION TO THE TORCHBOOK EDITION

by Frederick Sontag

"Kierkegaard is a dangerous man," said a friend of mine in concluding a discussion about that controversial author. In many ways it is easy to imagine that Soren Kierkegaard would have relished such a comment, since he did everything in his writings to make it impossible for us to assimilate them without extreme caution. Whatever else can be said, Kierkegaard cannot be read either easily or lightly, and that is the way he wanted it to be. Time and again he tells us that each reader must work out his own solution, that his author's bag of tricks is employed, not to reach a conclusion, but simply to make each listener become aware, be ever on the alert and never at rest.

It is impossible to read far into Kierkegaard without gaining the distinct impression that there are times when the author is laughing at you, defying you to believe him; then he may suddenly switch to some serious point, without indicating any absolute line of demarcation between the supercilious and the profound. Soren Kierkegaard speaks time and again about the difficult relationship of author to reader; and, when he raises this issue, we should always listen carefully, since it is perhaps the only basis upon which that flood of writing can be understood. Two of his own comments on authorship are perhaps crucial:

> . . . an author . . . who writes in order to be misunderstood, . . . to count it to his credit that Professor Heiberg had not understood him.[1]
>
> . . . an author who, so far as I am acquainted with him, is sometimes rather deceitful—not, however in such a

[1] *The Concept of Dread*, trans. W. Lowrie, Princeton University Press, Princeton, 1946, p. 17.

way that he might say one thing and mean another, but in such a way that he carries the thought to extremes, so that, if it is not grasped with the same energy, it appears the next moment to be something different.[2]

If one does not match in reading, Kierkegaard's own energy in writing, then all is lost.

If it is true that we need to be on our guard against the "tricks" Soren Kierkegaard may play upon his readers, we need even more to resist any dogmatic or final interpretation which may be given to us of Kierkegaard's views—including (as will be the theme of this Introduction) Kierkegaard's own self-interpretation. He has warned us that his successors would make a mockery of his words by giving them an overly-scholarly treatment, claiming to explain all his thought in some synthesis. Time and again he writes parodies on pedantic inquiry which thinks that a little more research can yield a final answer. It is a touch of irony that his own words have been transformed into finished doctrines in precisely the manner that he gave his energy to attempt to prevent. Since S.K. denies that a system is possible where men are concerned, it ought not to be possible to "systemize" his own writings—in spite of the fact that he contradicted himself by attempting his own self-summary in his closing days. The only interpretation of Kierkegaard which is to be rejected, then, is one which claims authority for itself.

Our problem in hermeneutics is that we are dealing with an author who: (1) insisted on the importance of his personal life for his writings; (2) left us a Journal which may be as much poetry as it is fact; (3) denied the possibility of uncovering a final key with which to piece together all the views; (4) while at the same time producing in his last days his own interpretive key to his writings; (5) but the key which he gave us is neither entirely consistent nor fully adequate to cover the whole authorship. Certain decisive transformations do take place during the period of his writing,

[2] *Repetition*, trans. W. Lowrie, Princeton University Press, Princeton, 1946, p. 7. (Harper Torchbook edition, New York, 1964.)

but whether they are precisely as he describes them, whether they have the significance which he (and others) attribute to them—this is the dialectical issue which each reader must face individually.

In entering into this necessary combat with S.K. over his own interpretation, the issue at hand is whether *Authority and Revelation* can provide a valuable and perhaps revolutionary clue. What would happen, we must ask, if you look at Kierkegaard's Collected Works with *Authority and Revelation* as an alternative "point of view"? And there is some evidence that this might be a valuable thing to do. Clearly S.K. changes in his later days, although understanding the nature of this change is, of course, the question at issue. In 1846 the first copy of what he then called *The Book on Adler* was finished, but he did not publish it. This is the year in which the *Postscript* is completed, the authorship which was to have ended now suddenly begins again on a new key, the pseudonymous works are acknowledged publicly as his own, he announces a decisive change in himself, begins to speak directly, and starts the fantastic controversy with *The Corsair* which is to dominate his later years. What did the discoveries which S.K. made in writing about Adler have to do with all of this, and why did the manuscript remain (together with *The Point of View*) unpublished until after his death?

The Point of View, which shares a similar history, has been simply accepted as accounting for these decisive changes in S.K. and as being the perspective within which to understand Kierkegaard's authorship as a whole. It is his own direct account, it is true, and yet he has time and again warned us that indirect techniques are the only authentic means and that direct statements may be a necessary deception which stand in need of careful correction. Let us accept S.K.'s oft given advice and remain skeptical even of his own direct summary. Following his example, let us try an experiment and apply S.K.'s own analysis of Adler to Kierkegaard himself and to his works. *The Book on Adler* comes at such a crucial period in S.K.'s productive life, and is surrounded by such fascinating circumstances, that it must at least be taken with greater seriousness than it usually has been. To accomplish this: first, an account of the important themes which emerge in *Authority and Revelation;* then, a brief review of S.K.'s writings to see what light may be shed by applying S.K.'s words on Adler to Kierkegaard himself.

I. THE INDIVIDUAL

Before turning directly to appraise any single work, however, we must first pay some attention to Kierkegaard himself. (The one person he never lets the reader forget is S.K.) Whether or not we accept his own particular interpretation of the relation which exists between an author and his writing, we are forced to consider this issue because S.K. himself has raised it so many times. Romantic exaggeration is ever present whenever Kierkegaard speaks about himself, so that it is quite possible that the personal element has been overstressed. Nevertheless it is there, and S.K. has forced us to pay attention to him in paying attention to his work. The personal, self-referential element is inescapable. It is often said that the story of his life is the story of his authorship, but that is too easy and too obvious a view and we must beware of it. First of all, we should ask, what do we mean by "the story of his life"? If we mean his own words written in his *Journals* (which he wrote expressly for publication) and elsewhere, then we must consider whether this account is simple prosaic fact or perhaps more romantic poetry.

His short life (1813-1855), if inwardly stormy, was outwardly quiet and comfortable. His father was a wealthy merchant who eventually left Kierkegaard well provided for, so that he never needed to work and never did. Copenhagen society was conservative and traditional, and S.K. left its security for only a few short trips. Inside Denmark he was a well-regarded and soon famous figure, known to Danish royalty and acquainted with every famous figure of his day. Marx was writing *The Communist Manifesto* during this same period; but, if Kierkegaard rebelled, it was an inner and not an outer rebellion, as befitted his own stress on inwardness. He lived if not in splendor at least in solid comfort, until in his last days he had exhausted his inheritance. He did not teach or preach, although he talked increasingly about so doing. He did write, and his writings have had great impact, but his own life was not particularly outgoing. He complained at being a genius in a provincial town, but he enjoyed the esteem and flattery which accompanies such a situation.

This is not the place to recount the details of his father's pre-marital affairs, of Kierkegaard's early and brief engagement which S.K. himself quickly broke, or even of his crucial religious experiences, although they have an interesting similarity to Adler's. Probably too much has been made of these events, although the constant stress upon them comes from Kierkegaard himself. Outwardly he possessed a great deal quietly, so that we must never confuse a perhaps genuine inner suffering with what was evidently an outer happiness. Those who knew him seemed surprised by the feelings which his writings reveal, and at least some of them considered him a gay and vivacious personality. In 1834 he began to write, and for ten years his work poured forth as an uncontrolled torrent, beginning with no less than six books in the first year. Apart from his writing, Kierkegaard did not lead an active life. In his later years he provoked a public storm against himself by attacking Bishop Mynster, an old family friend, after the Bishop's death. He took exception to a reference by Bishop Martynson in the funeral oration listing the late Bishop as a "witness to the truth." Kierkegaard burst into a public attack upon the late and revered Bishop, and also upon the church. This was only one expression of the violent outbursts which were to mark his last years. Certainly the church always stands in need of challenge, but the occasion of this attack seems hardly rational. An interesting fact concerning *Authority and Revelation* is that it was Bishop Mynster who suspended Adler from his pastoral duties, charging that his mind was deranged.

[xi]

Kierkegaard's public and violent denial of Bishop Mynster's right to be called "a witness to the truth" came after he had written his book on Adler. Similarly the even more famous controversy with *The Corsair* arose just as the *Postscript* was finished and Adler was on Kierkegaard's mind. *The Corsair* was a controversial political journal given to attacks upon the establishment, but S.K. was the one prominant figure whom the editor (Goldschmidt) did not abuse precisely because of his respect for Kierkegaard. S.K. demanded that he be included in their ridicule, but in order to force them to do so he had to reveal the connection of P. L. Møller with the *Corsair*. Møller had wanted a university chair, but Kierkegaard's revelation of his secret editorial connection with this questionable journal ruined the man's career, and he soon left the country a finished man. S.K. got the abuse he asked for (although for the most part it was caricature), but he had to destroy another man's career in order to receive any treatment worth complaining about.

He died having spent his father's fortune, refusing on his deathbed to be reconciled with his brother, attacking a family friend after his death over a statement made in eulogy of the departed; in spite of all this having succeeded in attracting nothing but respect—except in the instance of having ruined Møller's career. None of this detracts from S.K.'s clearly genuine religious insight or his psychological profundity, although perhaps it tells us something about the religious personality, but it does force us to distinguish (and on his own terms) Kierkegaard's outer self from his inner self. Outwardly S.K. had little to complain about, except what he brought upon himself through his own violence. It is clear that he was inwardly torn, but to attempt to understand the inner Kierkegaard as it emerged on paper by reference to the outer circumstances is to misunderstand his own words on the subject, although he is partly responsible for the confusion in this matter. Perhaps it is precisely because he had so little to complain about that he was forced to provide his own grounds for complaint.

By way of contrast, A. P. Adler (1812-69) was a priest

on the Island of Bornholm who, although an intellectual, was reportedly well loved by his parish. S.K. often talked of becoming just such a country parson and intended to close his writing career in order to do this in the year in which he wrote *The Book on Adler;* in fact he never did. Unlike S.K., Adler was a devotee of Hegel (as was Bishop Martynson). Adler based his writing upon a claim to special revelation, and clearly this claim occupied S.K.'s mind during the time that Kierkegaard too felt that he had undergone a decisive religious transformation. The striking parallels—and the differences—could not have escaped Kierkegaard, and perhaps they account for his intense interest in Adler. The suspension of Adler from his priesthood was in fact a minor affair, but perhaps in this minor incident S.K. learned far more about himself than in any conscious attempt to write his *Point of View*.

II. "THE BOOK ON ADLER"

The details surrounding S.K.'s production of this manuscript are fully recounted in the Translator's Preface which follows. Our interest now is to set down the insights which, according to Kierkegaard, Adler's case produced in him. Then these can be compared with the central doctrines in S.K.'s other writings, to help the reader to decide whether this encounter with Adler has unintentionally provided us with an insight into S.K. himself and his total authorship. Kierkegaard's uncertainty over publishing this manuscript, its many drafts and numerous prefaces, its timing at a transitional period in S.K.'s writing, in the lull before the storm which he drew down upon himself—all this ought to move us to a close analysis of this work for a possible disclosure at a moment of crisis, Kierkegaard's favorite situation for insight. It is an old saw that our criticisms of others tell as much about us as they do about their intended targets. Not that what S.K. finds in Adler is also true of him in a literal sense, but his criticisms might have provided the occasion for his (and our) insight.

One other way to see the possible radical impact of the

doctrines contained in *Authority and Revelation* is to consider what S.K. would appear to be saying if we were familiar with only *A & R* and knew nothing of his other writing. In the following we will attempt to understand how S.K.'s earlier doctrines appear when considered from the "point of view" of *A & R*. If considered in isolation, the views put forth in *A & R* would yield us a quite different Kierkegaard, just as we would see a different man if we knew S.K. from his devotional and purely religious writings alone, his "edifying discourses." The problem of understanding S.K., then, is that of putting together all the different perspectives; but we must beware of assuming in advance that all the pieces can be made to fit together into some consistent whole, made understandable on a single basis. Perhaps, as S.K. tells us, no synthesis is possible, in which case we will have to remain skeptical of any "explanation" offered which claims to resolve every conflict into one resolution—including Kierkegaard's own. In understanding S.K., the understanding must never be allowed to depend upon any one solution.

After completing the manuscript in one draft in 1846, Kierkegaard wrote two prefaces for it in the next year and a third and longer one in 1848. He tells us that the book is intended for theologians, which is interesting since S.K. seldom wrote either formal theology or explicitly for theologians. Immediately Kierkegaard tells us that Adler is the subject of the book only in the sense that his case throws light upon dogmatic concepts, and that he intends to pay as much attention to the age as to Adler. Kierkegaard is often intentionally a confusing writer, and yet he begins by deploring Adler's "confusion" (p. xvi). Then Kierkegaard admits that Adler was just what he (S.K.) needed; Adler's going astray was very opportune.

"Revelation" is the subject of this book, and this too is interesting, since it is a theological concept to which S.K. seldom gave much direct attention. When he did, as in the doctrine of the incarnation, it was to stress its paradoxical nature, the impossibility of its being totally assimilated rationally, and to emphasize that it leaves man faced with the absurd as the only condition of his faith. Revelation, S.K. now says, suffers from confusion in his own age, and he equates the investigation of this with the concept of "authority" (p. xvi). If revelation has only been considered heretofore as it produced paradox, Kierkegaard hardly considered the concept of authority at all before this, and indeed it is somewhat at odds with S.K.'s constant stress upon the absolute aloneness of the *individual* in matters of faith. Kierkegaard says that the age has confused the concept of authority, but he himself almost ignored it up till now— until Adler "woke him from his individualistic slumbers."

S.K. declares that he has read and reread Adler's works, because they provide a transparent medium for seeing the confusion of his age. Kierkegaard now claims that Christianity's greatest enemies are not the irreligious, but those who are under religious influence and whose religious attitudes are confused. Previously S.K. has talked about absolute individuality and a lack of passion; now he changes his analysis of the faults of his age:

> For the misfortune of our age . . . is disobedience, unwillingness to obey. And one deceives oneself and others by wishing to make us imagine that it is doubt. No, it is insubordination: it is not doubt of religious truth but insubordination against religious authority which is the fault in our misfortune and the cause of it.
>
> Disobedience is the secret of the religious confusion of our age (p. xviii).

Reading this it is hard to remember that the author is the same man who always claimed to be tormented by tremendous doubts and who constantly spoke of subjectivity and anguish. Adler affected S.K., and he tells us that he had to "take a step backward to get the point of view" (*Ibid.*). S.K. begs us to read his book on Adler, remembering that it is important to his main effort, but the importance has not always been discovered. It will be an edifying book, S.K. adds mysteriously, for him who understands it.

In the third preface, Kierkegaard begins to speak of

Christianity as capable of solving the problems of the age, whereas it had previously seemed to him that Christianity was itself an utterly unsolvable problem. Christianity can explain in time what otherwise in the temporal order would have to remain a riddle, S.K. now tells us. Far from being itself a riddle, S.K. asserts here that Christianity can solve riddles. This is not, of course, a worldly understanding and it requires a leap into the religious. Then, S.K. turns significantly to the concept of the martyr, which is to obsess him in his last years. True martyrdom stems from obedience:

> And this sacrifice is the sacrifice of obedience, wherefore God looks with delight upon him, the obedient man, who offers himself as a sacrifice, whereas he gathers his wrath against disobedience which slays the sacrifice— this sacrifice, the victor, is the martyr; for not everyone who is put to death is a martyr (p. xxiv).

Ruling religiously is a form of punishment and involves suffering, but now Kierkegaard draws a very important distinction between selfish, self-induced suffering and suffering which is submissive, which does not seek its own ends:

> . . . in a *worldly* sense one makes a fuss over sufferings, one suffers in order to conquer—and then perhaps he doesn't conquer at all. In a Christian sense . . . he does not suffer in order to conquer, but rather because he has conquered, which simply gives him pleasure in putting up with everything and exalts him above sufferings, for once he has conquered he can surely put up with a bit of suffering (p. xxvi).

How interesting that this is written by a man who spent his last years complaining loudly about the suffering he had to endure, and who had spent most of his life as an author feeling sorry for himself in print. Adler has indeed induced a new maturity, but it did not prevent S.K.'s exaggerated acts. To see and to do are not the same, and Kierkegaard closes his preface by once again proclaiming that he himself is "without authority." Producing books does not make a man an author, S.K. is convinced. An author should be able to complete his work, and yet the last part cannot be written. If he goes ahead and writes the last part (as S.K. did in *Point of View*), then "he will make it thoroughly clear by writing the last part that he makes a written renunciation to all claim to be an author" (p. 3-4), since a genuine author knows that no project can really be finished and completed and placed in final perspective. To find a conclusion really means to discover that one is lacking and then to feel this lack keenly. "Every poetic conclusion is an illusion" (p. 4); this statement comes at a time when S.K. is preoccupied with an authorship that he intended to leave incomplete with the *Postscript*, but then reversed himself and added a conclusion.

Kierkegaard now begins his important analysis of the "premise author" versus the "essential author," the former being outer directed and the latter inner directed. The premise author tries to raise an outcry, thinking this a good thing for its own sake, but he must wait for something outside himself to enlighten him. He needs to communicate, and if he has great talents he may raise many doubts. S.K. has previously supported attention-getting techniques because they make men aware; now he says abruptly:

> But everyone should keep silent insofar as he has no understanding to communicate. Merely to want to raise an outcry is a sort of glittering idleness (p. 9).

This is somewhat startling, coming from a man who claimed he had no understanding to impart but took it as his socratic task only to wake men up. S.K. had reserved teaching for God alone (c.f. *The Fragments*), but now he wants the author who cannot instruct to keep silent. Once he claimed that exaggeration was the road to enlightenment, now he wants precision:

> . . . every premise author is devouring. He is devouring precisely because, instead of keeping silent, he utters doubts and makes an outcry.

[xvii]

The art of all communication consists in coming as close as possible to reality, i.e., to contemporaries who are in the position of readers ... (p. 9).

Passion has been Kierkegaard's password, but now he adds a word of caution, perhaps as a result of observing its excesses in Adler:

It is one thing to depict a passionate man when with him is ... a life view which can control him, and it is quite a different thing when a passionate man ... becomes an author, runs amuck, and by the help of books assaults us at it were with his doubts and torments. (p. 10).

It is one thing to be a physician who knows all about cures and healing ...—it is one thing to be a physician beside a sickbed, and another thing to be a sick man who leaps out of his bed by becoming an author, communicating bluntly the symptoms of his disease (p. 11).

Who is Kierkegaard writing about here? He claims that he wants to deal only with the writings and leave the author out of consideration, but he finds he cannot do this with Adler, and he has made it impossible for us to do it with himself. S.K. complains of anyone who writes too hastily: "Nowadays one takes for a revelation any strong impression, and the same evening puts it in the newspaper" (p. 13). Kierkegaard claims only to be a serviceable critic, a lonely person, and warns us against confusing an apostolic existence with genius.

Kierkegaard fears a growing sensuality, a dangerous temptation to cleverness in his time, and yet he claims to have no talent to write for "the instant" (oddly enough the title he chose for his published attacks against the church). What he has written, he feels, applies to and can be read at all times. Seldom has S.K. spoken so loosely about the particular setting of the written analysis or divorced it so from the individual and the circumstances. Kierkegaard continues to upbraid Adler for changing his mind and announcing at a later time something different from what he once stated (p.

20 footnote), and S.K. adds that one cannot treat the later saying as though it were the contemporaneous interpretation. This remark is extremely interesting in view of the fact that S.K. changed his mind about himself as an author and tells us in the *Point of View* that what he came to think in the end was actually what he had thought in the beginning—although it certainly does not seem to be so if one believes his early writings when taken alone.

Adler is an "extraordinary" man and Kierkegaard also certainly thought of himself as one, if not precisely in the same sense. Thus it is interesting when S.K. dwells so long on the problem of "the extraordinary." Such a person may be the cause of the most frightful corruption, and he cannot render service to the Establishment by attacking its very life, S.K. asserts. If such a man receives a revelation, fear and trembling now comes over any attempt to communicate it directly. Yet no authority can now come with such silence. If God has called him to be an apostle, his silence transforms this into the role of genius.

Divine authority is the decisive thing that makes one an apostle, and offense, which S.K. used to say came from the non-rationality of the concept of the incarnation, he now sees as coming from the confrontation of genius by divine authority. Be he lowly or great, the offense is that a mere man possesses divine authority. We cannot, of course, always discern this at the time: ". . . nowadays it is all too easy to understand that Peter was an apostle, but in those days people found it far easier to understand that he was a fisherman" (p. 25). The true apostle will not find it at all strange that many fail to recognize his authority. Only the genius who mistakes himself for an apostle will rant and rave over his lack of attention and use extreme means if necessary to bring attention to himself.

Yet Kierkegaard sees that a touch of genius must go with apostleship, to give the man the tools with which to translate his message (". . . Paul too had a revelation; only that in addition he had an unusually good head." p. 26). Whereas before questions have always been quite complex and agonizing for S.K., now suddenly at this point they become crystal clear:

> The question is quite simple: Will you obey, or will you not obey? Will you bow in faith before divine authority? Or will you be offended?

Then this man, who has engaged in infinitely subtle dialectic, goes on to berate those who take refuge in the problems of exegesis or who treat Scripture so scientifically that it might as well be anonymous writings. Such tactics are merely evasive, he is convinced, and they divert us from the real issue of obedience. Adler collided with the church because he clung to his individuality, and so did Kierkegaard. Strangely enough, in *The Book on Adler*, S.K. seems to be on the side of the church and its authority. The fundamental principles must be defended against reflection gone astray:

> And so it is with relation to the spiritual life, the most injurious thing when reflection, as it too often does, goes amiss and instead of being used for advantage brings the concealed labor of the hidden life out into the open and attacks the fundamental principles themselves (p. 30).
>
> But when the established order does not hold the reins tight, then finally every man who will not obey becomes a reformer (p. 33).

Consider all this as coming at a time when S.K. has just made public his pseudonymous authorship, has insisted on causing an uproar in the press, and is about to attack the church himself. The most interesting people are of more than one mind about themselves! In criticizing Adler, Kierkegaard sides with Bishop Mynster, and here has nothing but mild praise for the man he is shortly to attack from his own death bed. How quick and violent is the shift of an irrational mood to its opposite! S.K. asserts that a truly extraordinary individual is above any established order; but this is a dreadful responsibility if you have heard your call amiss. And you cannot complain about resistance from the

established order, since the genuine apostle will actually
want a suitable resistance, a firmness against which alone
he can define himself. If everyone agrees with him, then he is
nothing extraordinary.

A truly extraordinary man is concerned with nothing but
his relationship to God, and S.K. is sure that being victorious in the world is something he will be unconcerned about,
a joking matter (p. 40-41). 'Conquering' is an inward affair,
a matter of the spirit, and Kierkegaard parodies worldly
attempts to have things one's own way in one of his most
graphic phrases:

> . . . in case Jesus Christ did not conquer by being cruci-
> fied, but had conquered in the modern style by business
> methods and a dreadful use of his talking gear . . .
> (p. 42, footnote).

Reflection and intelligence, the two marks of the modern
age, will become for the *extraordinarius* merely tools at his
disposal. Profundity will not be in words, in utterance, in a
statement, but will be only in a mode of existence (p. 48).
Such a special individual will be a shock to the established
order, but the accomplishment of a divine task is necessarily
slow, and one has a remedy for the impatience of reflection
only in faith, humility and daily consecration (p. 50). Yet
this labor goes on in silence; he who has a revelation has
shut himself up within himself and keeps silent—only his
mode of life can betray him, not words.

In Chapter II Kierkegaard moves on to consider the fact
of revelation, which he considers crucial for the modern
age that thinks of itself as historical. For the Christian
fact (the incarnation of God) has no history, is not a part
of historical study or sequence, since it stands immovably as
a paradox. Faced with such a fact time is of no importance.
To have studied the matter for eighteen hundred years
brings one no closer to a solution than if the event had happened yesterday (p. 63). Thus Adler is instructive, since his
appearance and his claim to revelation offer a contemporary
example of what the Christian must always face. Adler's case

removes the illusion of the aid of historical study by being an immediate event which demands decision without the benefit of historical study. Whether Adler himself is mistaken or not, his case offers a challenge to all, since it confronts Christianity with a paradox in a contemporary setting. Without such cases, we might be tempted to think of Christianity as an historical matter. Christianity is a contemporary affair and a case like Adler's reminds us of this fact.

"Adler is quite properly a sign" (p. 67). We must decide about him, whether he is God's elect or simply demonically shrewd, and this is precisely the decision which must be put to any age, without the benefit of allowing them to treat is as a scholarly problem. More than that, however, is the fact that an intellectual age confuses words *about* Christianity with the experience *of* it, so that when the formulae come alive in an individual who is already familiar with the doctrines, it is a strange experience. Overwhelmed by living through in fact what before he knew only as words, he looks about frantically for the strongest words he can find to describe his experience: revelation. If we did not think of Christianity as a matter of knowledge, we would not get into this situation. But treating it as we do in terms of books and doctrines, Christian experience affects us in a way that is both strange and familiar; we reach for extraordinary expressions to describe it, since the experience has made the words we already know seem weak and inadequate by comparison.

S.K. goes on to analyze Adler's claim to revelation in Chapter III, where we see that what he cannot abide is Adler's conceit in publishing his experiences and the tumult with which he surrounds it. An enthusiast, a man awakened religiously he may be, but the problem came in over-stepping the bounds of privacy. In claiming more by a public fuss he calls attention to the individual himself, rather than to the experience itself or to Christianity. The fact that he has been moved dramatically and personally must be distinguished from a claim to a new revelation of doctrine; yet the personal force of the experience tends to obscure this distinction, as S.K.'s "easter experience" perhaps did for him. ". . . There is a decisive qualitative difference between being rescued in a miraculous way, and being entrusted by revelation with a new doctrine." (p. 86).

Until now Kierkegaard has been trying to draw some important distinctions: the qualitative line between a genius and an apostle, the words of Christianity versus the experience of it, a personally miraculous experience versus the revelation of a new doctrine, a private experience versus a public communication. Important as all this is (for Kierkegaard as well as for Adler), he never excludes the possibility of the private revelation of new doctrine. He draws crucial distinctions but does not rule out any individual case or set any objective standards—until he comes to the end of the first section:

> It is true that Christianity is built upon a revelation, but also it is limited by the definite revelation it has received (p. 92).

These are important words coming from S.K., who has stressed Christianity's subjective existence and its subjective appropriation. Now there is a definite norm to which all experiences must conform and by which each may be tested.

Whatever Adler's personal situation or conviction, his views may be judged by an external criterion; and S.K. pronounces him to be a "confused genius." There is, evidently, some clear and objective standard which can be referred to and by which the inner tortures of a struggling religious passion may ultimately be judged. Passion, inwardness and subjectivity have been S.K.'s key words. These are not set aside, and none of Kierkegaard's interest in the personal struggle over religion is now diminished. It is just interesting to see, as he develops his criterion with Adler, that when all the inner struggle is over its fruits may be (in fact are to be and must be) judged by some already established norm. However creative and subtle the person, Christianity knows only one original revelation, and all later works are to be subjected to its rule.

A side light, to be sure, but an interesting one, is S.K.'s strong objection to Adler for having published too many books in one year. The parallel in circumstances to Kierkegaard's own fantastic publication rate is quite amusing and one can easily see why S.K. was so sensitive on this point. His objections to rapid and voluminous publication seem to apply to himself too, although S.K. does not overlook this fact and seems to think he has a way of protecting himself from this same criticism. The reasons are rather minute, and the reader is advised to "judge for yourself" whether S.K.'s excuses are valid or sophistical. The objections against excessive length are particularly humorous in view of Kierkegaard's own doctrine of 'repetition' and his own excessive use of words (pp. 94-97).

How is one to distinguish the genius from the apostle among the writers in Christendom? Kierkegaard often discusses genius and clearly considers himself equal to any in those ranks. He thought that "reflection" had to be opposed in his day, and he felt that it took intellectual powers equal to the finest to do this. As time goes on he seems to stress the religious, to become more convinced of the essential rightness of his own approach and the essential wrongness of other current views of Christianity. This being the case, S.K. is bound to think more and more about the signs of genuine discipleship (although he previously completely disclaimed *authority* for himself). Then along comes Adler, openly claiming what Kierkegaard has heretofore said must be held in secret, and all the while S.K. has been gaining momentum toward *revealing* himself directly. Kierkegaard has stresed inwardness and indirection; Adler is direct and outer, just at a time when S.K. seems to be tending in this direction himself.

Kierkegaard has prided himself on the poetic quality of his writing; now he declares that Paul (the model apostle) ranks rather low as a stylist (p. 105). Plato and Socrates had often been S.K.'s models, even providing the basis for the analysis of Christianity in the *Fragments*. Now Plato is put in another class, ruled qualitatively distinct from the genuine apostle. The genius is what he is by reason of himself (S.K.'s pride in his own authorship has been obvious), but an apostle is what he is by reason of his divine authority. A genius straightens out his early apparent paradoxes (just as S.K. comes to see his authorship perfectly clearly in his last years), but an apostle is a man called and sent by God (not really dissimilar from the earlier analysis of Abraham in *Fear and Trembling*). Aesthetic grounds appraise the genius; divine authority is the only decisive factor for the apostle. S.K. has been basking in his own cleverness, but now he sees clearly that one obeys Paul only because he has divine authority, whether or not Paul is clever. Kierkegaard has drawn this distinction many times before, but seldom has he rested the religious claim on God's authority.

Christianity's current confusion comes from its uncertainty about God. This leads, in the ensuing rebellion, to a forgetfulness of what divine authority is. Earlier Christianity had been diagnosed as lacking inwardness and passion; now the confusion of our age is said to come, not from superficiality, but from a failure to submit (p. 108). Doubt is the culprit here, and yet it is S.K. who has given us the definitive analysis that has tended ever since to make excruciating doubt a necessary prerequisite to faith. Doubt degrades God, Kierkegaard now says, pulls him down to ordinary levels, whereas what He needs to be is above doubt. Instead of obeying, men engage in cross-examination, and here the criteria tend to be cleverness and profundity.

At this point S.K. reaches a climax in his argument. Listen and see if, when taken on its own, it does not sound for all the world like Karl Barth:

> Authority . . . is something which remains unchanged, which one cannot acquire by having understood the doctrine in the fullest sense. Authority is a specific quality which comes from another place and makes itself felt precisely when the content of the saying or of the action is assumed to be indifferent (p. 110).

[xxv]

Kierkegaard goes on to say that to preach is precisely to exercise authority and that preaching means the enunciation of what the age has forgotten. Perhaps seeing this as the prerequisite for preaching and denying authority for himself kept S.K. from leaving everything to go and preach. The religious revolution within Kierkegaard leads him away from the ministry rather than toward it, as it does for so many others who discover its divine demands.

Before, the demands of religion had all been said to be inner; now they require that external authority be given to the individual. It is often said that Barth rebelled against an early existentialism. It is interesting to speculate as to whether he might have learned his rebellion from Kierkegaard, just as S.K. might have learned it from Adler. Between God and man Kierkegaard now stresses an eternal, essential, qualitative difference. The qualification, "an apostle", belongs in the sphere of transcendence (p. 112), a sphere S.K. has not heretofore said much about. Profundity comes in for casual treatment too. The profound (and how much this has characterized all of existential theology!) entices men as if it could make them believe. But this is merely confusing. Doubt only makes men embarrassed to obey, and thus it essentially works against Christianity, not for it.

S.K.'s new line of thought is that it is an affectation to want to believe in Christianity on account of profundity, and according to him all modern speculation is "affected." It has done away with obedience and authority but still wants to believe orthodoxy. Genius projects itself and is active in the world, accomplishing perhaps more than ten businessmen, but there is nothing transcendent about this work. The genius lives withdrawn from the world in self-satisfaction (p. 121); the man called by revelation has become an instrument of God, to go out into the world, to labor, to suffer. And precisely here S.K. rants against the clever writer, at ease in his study, publishing collections of his cleverness. At this point what could be a more devastating criticism of S.K.'s own career? He may have begun intending to talk about Adler (but remember that Adler actually was an active and beloved pastor), but it is hard to believe that his final description fits anyone better than himself.

For simple men silence is the expression of inwardness. But in expression S.K. now demands "connection and continuity" (p. 124), and he pronounces Adler to be "deranged" because his writings lack these qualities—and yet Kierkegaard has ruled a "system" out as impossible. Before, S.K. has always lauded genius; now he qualifies this praise by asserting that dizziness is the essential character of genius, propounding dizzy aesthetic views. ". . . dizziness results when the eye has no fixed point on which to rest," (p. 127) the remedy for which is spiritual discipline and limitation. Contrast this with S.K.'s usual characterization of the believer as one suspended over 70,000 fathoms of water. Kierkegaard evidently now feels that philosophy only confuses the religious life (p. 145), whereas before Socrates had served as his model in the *Fragments*. Yet a decisive change (such as Adler's conversion away from Hegel) should not be given immediate outer expression, S.K. is convinced (p. 152), and Kierkegaard now recommends the slow outer reflections of inner experience.

In the last chapter Kierkegaard begins to return to his early theme of inwardness as the essential mark of religiousness, and he pauses to observe a somewhat stylistic effect in his own writings and in Adler's. But then he moves on to a crucial distinction:

> to be shaken . . . is the more universal foundation for all religiousness; the experience of being shaken, of being deeply moved, the coming into being of subjectivity in the inwardness of emotion, the pious pagan and the pious Jew have in common with the Christian. And one does not become a Christian by being moved by something indefinitely higher, and not every outpouring of religious emotion is a Christian outpouring (p. 163).

Specifically Christian concepts have been defined by a revelation given once and for all, so that, to qualify as Christian, such a passionate experience must be more than profoundly inward. It simply must fit designed Christian categories. One must acquire skill and schooling in Christian concepts, S.K. is now convinced. An awakening is required, yes, but so is conceptual and terminological firmness and definiteness (p. 165).

All this has in interesting similarity to the famous distinction which S.K. draws near the end of the *Postscript* between Religiousness A and Religiousness B (which is specifically Christian). But a careful examination reveals that the distinction in *A & R* is much more clear-cut; here it is objectively oriented and non-dialectical. Perhaps it is Adler, who was on Kierkegaard's mind at the writing of the *Postscript*, who induces this crucial distinction; and then perhaps in thinking directly about Adler it all comes home to S.K. with even greater clarity. For now he accuses Adler of confining religion to subjectivity: ". . . he confounds the subjective with the objective, his subjectively altered condition with an external event . . ." (p. 168). The famous originator of the view that "objectively Christianity has no existence" now says something quite different!

Every believer must be conscious that Christianity has not arisen in his heart, that it has an objective determinant.

> Christianity exists before any Christian exists, it must exist in order that one may become a Christian, it contains the determinant by which one may test whether one has become a Christian, it maintains its objective subsistence apart from all believers, while at the same time it is the inwardness of the believer (p. 168).

It must be stressed that S.K. has not here abandoned inwardness as a condition, just as he never overlooked the existence of objective doctrine in the earlier *Postscript*. It is just that the solidity of Christianity's objective existence is here much more clearly stressed, and the objective and subjective sides brought into more equal proportions. Again, there is little in the above statement which Barth could not endorse; so that, if Barth could be said to have developed the late Kierkegaardian "right," Tillich has held on to the Dane's early "leftish" views, while still attempting the systematization.

Now S.K. recommends that one remain silent about any inner change, that one act and labor rather than be productive in a literary way (p. 170)—which certainly is not what S.K. did himself. Instead of concluding by emphasizing subjectivity Kierkegaard finishes with a rather startling phrase: "the point of departure is from above, from God" (p. 192). And in summarizing Adler he seems to be prophetic about his own soon-to-come excesses and the violation of his own restrictions:

> . . . as a pagan he became a Christian priest, and that when he had undeniably come somewhat closer to being a Christian he was deposed (p. 178).

All of S.K.'s earlier energy is devoted to the problem of becoming a Christian. Now he sees in startling clarity that, if too much energy is sent inward, the violence of propulsion may ironically not only send one to the mark but also far beyond it. Did S.K. heed his own advice and remain content to stop with faith, or did the violence of his inner subjectivity, when made public, propel him way out beyond it?

III. PASSION VERSUS SUBMISSION

Although in a sense some reference has already been made to Kierkegaard's other doctrines and other writings, if we are to understand S.K. from the "point of view" of *Authority and Revelation*, then a brief review and comparison with his complete writings should be revealing. Let us proceed in rough chronological order.

The Journals[3] cover the whole period of his authorship, but not his whole life, and they are in the strictest sense intellectual journals, not comments on people and places and events but commentaries on religious and intellectual con-

---

[3] Trans. A Dru, Harper Torchbooks, New York, 1959.

cerns from a personal perspective. Although S.K. tells us that he had no expectation of leading a happy earthly life, that he was torn asunder inwardly (p. 40), all this must be contrasted with the outer stability in which he lived comfortably, cared for by servants and secretaries. It is here in the *Journals* that he complains about the lack of passion in the age (p. 77) and denies that after his death anyone will be able to find the final words that will explain everything (p. 85). In Adler perhaps S.K. saw a startling example of passion without external restraints, and, if established categories can be applied, then perhaps more can be explained than when just the inner life is considered. He talks of silence, of becoming a priest, of not making himself intelligible to anyone, of his ideal to live for marriage, just at the moment when he is about to fix himself in the opposite of these intentions. He is aware of a metamorphosis, at about the time he has written on Adler and is struggling through numerous revisions and prefaces. Perhaps it is Adler who made Kierkegaard aware of himself and determined him to speak out, as Adler had done, and for which S.K. criticized him. Then in an entry in 1849 (p. 153) Kierkegaard perhaps explains the strange discrepancy between his written words and the facts of his life:

> What does being a poet mean? It means having one's own personal life in quite different categories from those of one's poetic work, it means being related to the ideal in imagination only, so that one's own personal life is more or less a satire on poetry and on oneself.

Yet Adler lived what he proclaimed and spoke directly of his experiences. Is it he who moved Kierkegaard to forget indirection and in his last days to forsake the role of the poet for that of the martyr?

Either/Or[4] is S.K.'s first big book, and with attention drawn to the fuss he created in his later life its importance tends to be forgotten or countermanded. It is here that

[4] Trans. Swanson, Oxford University Press, 2 vols., London, 1946.

Kierkegaard meditates upon an external mode of life in complete contradiction to an inner life (p. 4), and then he will spend some time after the Adler affair trying to prove that this was not the case with him. In his own introduction to *Either/Or*, S.K. perhaps gives the best clue both to it and to himself. These two radically opposed views of life (the aesthetic and the ethic) he suggests (p. 11) might be the work of one man, so that one need not try to straighten everything out in life in order to put it all on a single plane. Such a life is never finished, it simply ends, and no single standpoint can ever explain it, only that one person was capable of living in several ways. In the late pages of Vol. II (p. 200) S.K. says that the tears a man sheds for himself bear no fruit, but to feel oneself guilty and to cry in repentance is a genuine act. The second volume closes with essentially a sermon on S.K.'s favorite theme "against God we are always in the wrong." Here it is impossible not to note that he sheds many tears for himself in his closing days, and instead of ending on a note of guilt and wrongness before God he ironically closes his days by asserting his absolute rightness. In this case the earlier ending seems more profound than the later and actual finale.

The Edifying Discourses,[5] surprisingly enough, are what yield perhaps the best insight when placed next to *A & R*. Kierkegaard insists that these are discourses, not sermons, because he has no authority to preach (p. 1). So the concept of "authority" does not appear earlier in his writings, but only in these unpreached sermons which are essentially devotional meditations. To one familiar with the Kierkegaard of *Fear and Trembling*, a first reading on any *Discourse* may come as a shock. Here there is no anxiety, no tension, no strain or shouting. These are meditations, and the author both seems to know God and to be calm in his relationship to Him. Not to say but to do is a frequent theme (p. 67), and the rarest kind of greatness is often described as the

---

[5] Trans. Swanson, Harper Torchbooks, ed. P. Holmer, New York, 1958.

person who knows that of himself he can do absolutely nothing (p. 151). Here Kierkegaard sees that inwardly no outer circumstance can be essential, that internally man strives only against himself (p. 166), and thus ought to attack no one else.

When compared with *A & R* and the more vociferous "dialectical" writings, this question arises: *If these works reveal two such different views on the nature of the religious life, could it be that the experience with Adler broke the wall which separated the calmness of the devotional works from the storm of the "dialectical" writings?* The calmness and clarity which were always present before, but only in the isolated devotional sphere, have now become the standard for all the religious life and also for theology. Adler's excesses perhaps taught S.K. the need for external norms within which to contain the stress and strain of inward struggle. The lesson Kierkegaard learned from Adler was the necessity of bringing these two sides of the religious life together. In Adler perhaps S.K. saw his earlier extreme subjectivity detached from the theological tradition, as it never actually was for Kierkegaard. The *Discourses* reveal a man very sure of God within traditional Christian formulations. S.K. did not go to Adler's brink of heresy, but when he saw how far astray independent subjectivity could go— even to madness—he recoiled to bring the inner religious life back under *Authority and Revelation*.

Repetition[6] is one of Kierkegaard's most fascinating little books. Because he claims that it was "misunderstood," he writes some of his most insightful comments on authorship, already quoted. In considering his later direct outbursts, and his criticism of Adler's quick announcement, perhaps his views on irony and silence are most illuminating:

He did not have the strength to carry out the plan. His soul lacked the elasticity of irony. He had not the

[6] Trans. W. Lowrie, Princeton University Press, Princeton, 1946; Harper Torchbooks, New York, 1964.

strength to take irony's vow of silence, not the power to keep it; and only the man who keeps silent amounts to anything (p. 27).

Was Kierkegaard mistaken, did he forget his earlier advice, when he decided in his last days to speak out and to do so with violence? Did he carry this view forward to apply it to Adler in judgment, only then to be unable to restrain himself? Kierkegaard stressed man's frail humanity, and it is all too human to be unable to heed one's own advice, to discern most clearly in others a flaw also ours.

In *Fear and Trembling*[7] one of the most interesting comparisons suggests itself, Abraham versus Adler. Like Abraham, Adler thought he was acting on direct divine instruction, the individual higher than the universal, involving a suspension of normal modes of judgment. With Adler Kierkegaard wants to find a norm against which his excesses may be measured, and S.K. finds that the original Christian revelation provides a check. On the other hand with Abraham S.K. is more radical, defining faith as beginning where thinking leaves off and then advising his age to stop with faith. But "faith is this paradox, and the individual absolutely cannot make himself intelligible to anyone" (p. 115). Only the individual can decide; no one outside can decide whether he is a knight of faith or is in temptation, since religion is inwardness which is incommensurable with material reality. Such a radical interpretation of faith can be allowed to stand with Abraham, who maintains himself within the tradition, but Adler stepped outside; and Kierkegaard suddenly saw the necessity to establish limits. But to do so is to change his doctrine of the radical subjectivity of faith, so that Adler taught S.K. something which Abraham could not do.

In the *Philosophical Fragments*[8] Kierkegaard actually does mention the concept of authority, but interestingly enough only to deny that any human being can ever truly be an

---

[7] Trans. W. Lowrie, Princeton University Press, Princeton, 1945.
[8] Trans. Swenson, Princeton University Press, Princeton, 1936.

authority for another (p. 7). Error is something only the individual can discover for himself alone (p. 9), and in the case of Christianity it cannot be checked by knowledge, since "no knowledge can have for its object the absurdity that the eternal is the historical" (p. 50); ". . . belief is not a form of knowledge, but a free act, an expression of will" (p. 68). Rational tests for faith here seem impossible, since its core is an unassimilable paradox, which can exist as an object for faith alone (p. 80). Had S.K. applied this standard to Adler, he could not have denied him his position. Yet Kierkegaard knew that Adler's views were the product of a deranged mind and thus had to be rejected. The authority of the original divine revelation is introduced, and essentially God provides the ground for judgment. Actually the seed of this doctrine is present in the *Fragments*, but men are not allowed to assume the divine standpoint for purposes of judging the faith of another man. However, Adler went too far, and God's point of view, wielded by man, had to be introduced as a check.

In *The Concept of Dread*[9] Kierkegaard considers the "religious genius," which is interesting in itself, since much of *A & R* is based upon a radical distinction between the two. But in the earlier work S.K. describes him, this religious genius:

> The first thing he does is to turn towards himself. For by the fact that he turns toward himself he turns *eo ipso* towards God . . . (p. 96).

This of course fits Kierkegaard's early near-equation of the subjective and the religious, but Adler's subjectivity actually carried him away from God, and S.K. ended by establishing objective norms and denying that genius could be called religious.

The Concluding Unscientific Postscript[10] was intended to conclude S.K.'s published works, but at its conclusion he

[9] Trans. W. Lowrie, Princeton University Press, Princeton, 1946.

[10] Trans. Swenson and Lowrie, Princeton University Press, Princeton, 1944.

changed his mind. This is interesting in relation to Adler, since the *Postscript*'s almost constant theme is "subjectivity," and we know that Adler was on S.K.'s mind at the same time. "God exists only for subjectivity in inwardness" (p. 178). The conformity of thought and being is actually realized only in God, so that no existing individual in the process of becoming can judge with authority. What happens to alter this important doctrine, since according to it S.K. is assuming the role of God in his later writings? In the devotional works he had always known God with calmness and clarity, so that Adler's subjectivity may have frightened Kierkegaard into introducing the traditional theological divine perspective.

The *Postscript* taken literally provides no standard with which to test Adler's demented doctrines. To believe against the understanding is described in the *Postscript* as martyrdom, so that according to this Adler would be a martyr. Reading S.K.'s early radical subjectivity, it is easy to see why Adler should have thought that he would find a defender in Kierkegaard and came to him to plead for support. It is equally easy to see why S.K. should have found being faced with Adler so unsettling. Inwardness cannot be directly communicated and Kierkegaard has just said that indirect communication is the only true way (p. 246). And yet there stands Adler who must be directly dealt with and objectively ruled out of bounds. Christianity is said not to be a doctrine (p. 339), but Adler is crazy and subjective and not within the bounds of doctrine. A sane man who actually stays within traditional bounds (as S.K. did) can be allowed to espouse radical doctrines, but a crazy man cannot be allowed to be radical and so Adler forces a change upon Kierkegaard. In the *Postscript* S.K. denies external authority; in *A & R* it becomes a needed concept.

In *The Point of View*[11] Kierkegaard discusses his relation to all of his works, as he had said in the appendix to the *Postscript* he could not do. There he told us that he could

[11] Trans. W. Lowrie, Oxford University Press, London, 1939; Harper Torchbooks, New York, 1962.

never claim the pseudonymous words as his own, since their anonymity prevents anyone from claiming a personal relationship to words so written. Having made the claim that no word can be uttered in his own name he ends the *Postscript* with the plea: "And, oh, that no half-hearted man would lay a dialectical hand upon this work, but would let it stand as it now stands!" (Feb. 1846) and his *Journal* records his intention to give up being an author and prepare himself to be a pastor. As fate would have it, however, it is Kierkegaard himself in *The Point of View* hardly two years later who will not let the *Postscript* stand, who insists on claiming all his pseudonymous words personally and who violates his norm of indirect communication with a sometimes violent direct discourse. Why? Although Kierkegaard did not intend to reveal himself in the process of writing about Adler, could it be that the indirect communication contained there (in *A & R*) is still better (as the early S.K. would believe) than his own later direct summary?

In *The Point of View* the psychological concepts are ignored, not accounted for, and many times before S.K. had claimed only to be a psychologist. So *The Point of View* actually does not account for all of the authorship. Without recounting the doctrines of *The Point of View*, it is enough to see that they run counter to almost all that S.K. has previously said about communication. Of course, the work is not all of a piece, and at moments of lucidity S.K. seems to realize the impossibility of what he is trying to do so bluntly and so overtly. Then he returns again to his themes of duplicity from first to last, of the maintenance of ambiguity as making a final explanation impossible, and that a desire to prevent all misunderstanding is a sign of youth, not maturity. What drove S.K. to these personal and verbal extremes? Adler's doctrines were not taken seriously by any large numbers of people and in that sense could not have been a threat to Kierkegaard, and yet he acts like a man who has been challenged to the core. It was he who challenged the *Corsair*, not *vice versa*, and it was he who attacked a dead Bishop who could not return the challenge; but Adler was alive and crazy. Yet it may have been he who gave Kierkegaard's radical doctrines their most decisive challenge by conforming to them while yet being deranged.

IV. GOD VERSUS MAN

The edifying discourses continue to be written right through Kierkegaard's career, but *Training in Christianity*[12] comes late and may be given some special significance. At this time the self-induced outer storm is in progress, but here in this work the religious life is still quiet and, if anything, deeper. A contrite heart and a consciousness of sin are the narrow way into Christianity outlined here, whereas in the public press S.K. is now talking of popular persecution and protesting his own ultimate rightness. The *Two Discourses*[13] come in 1851, well after S.K.'s Easter experience that his sins were not only forgiven but "forgotten," and in these *Discourses* he gives an entirely different account of how a Christian authorship should end. This account is one so radically different from the facts of his last years, which ended in a near riot at his funeral, that it is hard to compare the two; and yet it is so significant that a word from the *Discourses* should not be overlooked as a contrasting summary:

> A gradually progressing work as a writer which had its beginning in *Either/Or* seeks here its definite point of rest at the foot of the altar, where the author, who personally knows best his imperfection and guilt, does not by any means call himself a witness for the truth, but only a peculiar sort of poet and thinker who, "without authority," has nothing new to bring (p. 4).

The quietness, the inwardness, the return to self-description as a poet and thinker—all are striking, after the violence

---

[12] Trans. W. Lowrie, Princeton University Press, Princeton, 1941.
[13] In *For Self-examination*, trans. W. Lowrie, Princeton University Press, Princeton, 1944.

of his claim to religious authorship in *Point of View* only a few years before. Yet like *The Book on Adler, Point of View* was not published in S.K.'s lifetime, so that it is possible that Kierkegaard himself could never quite bring the two works, and the causes which induced them, into clear focus. The ending for his authorship quoted above is so fantastically in contrast to the facts and the strong words of his last years that it is hard to accept. And yet perhaps the uncontrolled violence and extremes of the last years gave S.K. an insight into himself, so that his words and not his deeds (as befits a poet) are still to be accepted as his truest record.

In the preceding, S.K. has denied that he can be a "witness to the truth," and yet in reading *Attack Upon "Christendom,"*[14] it is hard to hear the strong words there without the distinct impression that Kierkegaard at least at times fancied himself as a witness. In the first place he speaks out now in direct judgment, whereas before he has used indirection as the modest method of the mere poet. Yet as he begins to define a "genuine witness" it is hard to think that he does not have himself partly in mind.

A witness must be unacquainted with enjoyment and initiated into suffering; S.K.'s words tell us time and time again that this applies to him, and yet outwardly it does not appear to be the case. A witness must live in poverty and abasement, unappreciated, derided, etc.: S.K. spent his fortune; he would abase himself in his religious writings, but not in his poetic works, and in his later years he worked to bring insults upon himself. Kierkegaard says that his only task is the Socratic task (p. 283), to revise the definition of Christianity and to prove that others fit it even less than he. But if Christianity is inwardness and subjectivity, he cannot tell from any outward sign whether the good Bishop or any one else is or is not the genuine article. Adler has forced him to more overt definitions, but the result of this seems to be a violent public outburst.

Kierkegaard is a puzzle to his biographers and to the

[14] Trans. W. Lowrie, Princeton University Press, Princeton, 1946.

theologians, because there are so many of him. He might be easier to understand if such decisive and drastic changes had not taken place in his later years. But when he acts against his earlier advice and changes so radically, claiming his own interpretation to be the truth, then all is reduced to chaos. If Adler at least helped to induce this reaction, then one thing we can see in the later writings is an over-compensation for the shortcomings of the early doctrines, which are now made so vividly clear to S.K. in a startling example. Adler fits S.K.'s example too well and yet he is deranged. In turning, Kierkegaard perhaps turned too far too fast, as fits his own description of life. In a crazy example he may have been brought closer to the truth than in the subtle dialectic, a conclusion at least a majority of the many Kierkegaards might agree with. After all, in Christian doctrine it ought not to be so shocking if one's crucial lessons are learned through strange people—even through a crazy minister or an overly self-centered philosopher.

Does all this make a "system" of Kierkegaard's writings? Hardly. There are too many built-in impediments for that, so that just when one seems to have an answer another statement takes it away. But among the tedious lines, the romantic exaggeration and self-absorption, there is many an instructive phrase which any individual reader can find. Kierkegaard may formally have changed his mind and his methods; but, in doing so, in a strange way he was in the long run more consistent with his deeper insights than if he had continued on the same theme, or had not upset the apple cart by resuming his authorship in a new vein. Perhaps S.K. was strong and clever enough to keep the weakness in his own views covered, from himself as well as others; but, when he saw them defenselessly exposed in another, he was unstrung. Kierkegaard was radical in his subjectivity, but he himself objectively never moved from orthodoxy. In considering Adler's defiant self-confidence in his own wild views, S.K. brought the clear, calm objectivity which had always been in his devotional literature together with the necessity of subjectivity and inwardness in the genuine religious life. But this clue came too late and S.K. did not see fully enough how the lessons learned in Adler might apply to him.

In the early writing through the *Postscript*, it is clearly man who struggles with God by struggling with himself. In the devotional writings, and finally in *A & R*, it is God once again who seems to have man on his own terms—although S.K. could not leave it that way in his own last public years, but instead asserted himself more blatantly than he ever had before. Yet, as Kierkegaard says of Abraham, a man is great in proportion to the greatest of that with which he strove, and he who struggles with God becomes the greatest of all. The struggle of God versus man is the classic religious theme. (As the nineteenth century closes, man seems to be winning.) It is just that he should have ended, to borrow one of his curtain speeches, by being brought to rest at the foot of the altar prepared to confess his guilt. Instead, he ends shaking his fist at the world and announcing that God has certified his rightness. He had forgotten one of his favorite sermon themes, "As Against God We Are Always In the Wrong," with which he closed his earliest large book, *Either/Or*. Had he remembered this, he might have ended exactly where he began, a very Kierkegaardian thing to do—although, like any reader of his, certainly more edified for all that he had gone through.

Pomona College
Claremont, California
July, 1966

PREFACE

By the Translator

THIS BOOK THE VICTIM OF A PERVERSE FATE

Never, I believe, has a major work by a great author been
pursued by a fate so perverse as has obscured for more than
a century *The Book on Adler*. The first fair copy was written
in 1846, but at first S.K. was reluctant to publish it because
it dealt with a priest against whom he felt no animosity, and
public criticism of him might seem like hitting a man when
he is down—for Adler had already been deposed. Yet to
the end of his life (for nearly nine years) he still treasured
the thought of publishing this book, and in the meantime
made more corrections in the first draught than have usually
been devoted to any book. His first thought was to publish
it in his own name. Later he proposed to ascribe it to his
pseudonym Johannes Climacus (*Papirer* VII B 21, 22), the
reputed author of his last work, *The Concluding Unscientific
Postscript*; but when he reflected that Climacus was not a
convinced Christian, he sought another pseudonym, either
Petrus Minor, or Thomas Minor, or Vincentius Minor, or
Ataraxius Minor, changing the title to (VII B 26):

THE RELIGIOUS CONFUSION
OF THE PRESENT AGE

illustrated by Magister Adler as a phenomenon,

a mimic monograph,

by Petrus Minor.

Edited by

S. Kierkegaard.

Therefore the second preface (VIII B 27) was written by S.K.
as editor, whereas the first (only the beginning of which is

reproduced here) was written by him as the author (VIII B 270).

In 1848 the epidemic of revolutions in Europe, which involved Denmark in a disastrous war with Germany, revealed to S.K. how timely this book was. Thereupon he resolved to publish it in his own name, but to ignore Adler in the title, calling it "A Cycle of Ethico-Religious Treatises," to this end dividing it into many more and smaller chapters; and for this he wrote a new preface (IX B 9-13), the longest he ever wrote, which here is reproduced as No. 3, and also the Postscript (IX B 24) which concludes this book. But all this effort came to naught, and he had to content himself with publishing the longest section of the big book which contains no mention of Adler. This he published in Denmark in 1849 as one of the *Two Minor Ethico-Religious Treatises*, which was ascribed to the vague pseudonym H.H. and accompanied by the shortest preface he ever wrote: "Doubtless these two small treatises will be able to interest only theologians"—an echo of the first sentence of his first preface.

But the untoward fate of this book did not end with S.K.'s strange reluctance to publish it. Ill fate has pursued it for more than a century. It has never been published in Denmark, except in the twenty volumes of his *Papers*; and nowhere else has it been published, except in the excellent translation by Haecker in German, which is deemed worthy of inclusion in the new edition of S.K.'s works which is about to replace the scandalous translation of the notorious Schrempf, which subjected S.K. to an indignity from which no great author, so far as I know, has ever suffered; for every volume was accompanied by a *Nachwort* which showed what a fool S.K. was, while the whole edition was accompanied by a biography in two volumes which confirmed this opinion. Schrempf had been convinced by S.K. that he was not a Christian. Thereupon he resigned his pastorate in the Lutheran Church quite honestly, though he had no other means of supporting his family but by making atheistic speeches and translating Kierkegaard—

and thereby taking his revenge by denouncing him. During nearly half a century (from 1906 to 1950) while S.K. was the principal intellectual interest in Germany there was no other complete edition of his works. In the new edition by Jacob Hegner of Cologne and Olten the first volume contains *The Book on Adler* in Haecker's translation. This volume is entitled *Einübung und Anders* and is enriched with admirable notes by Niels Thulstrup, Secretary of Kierkegaard Society of Denmark. Haecker had called this book *The Concept of the Elect*, in order to avoid all mention of Adler; but now the original title is restored and his is made a subtitle although it indicates only one of the many subjects with which the book deals, and by no means the most important of them. Admirable as Haecker's translation is, it has the defect that it takes no account of the thousand corrections S.K. proposed, not even omitting the phrases he had cancelled in the text, and that it appears without the Postscript which was written later, and without any preface—though S.K. had written four!

The Book on Adler does not deserve the perverse fate which has pursued it for more than a century. Though it is not to be reckoned among S.K.'s most important works, it is very important nevertheless as a corrective of the prevalent misconceptions about him. Perhaps the fact that it reveals his intimate thoughts so clearly was one of the reasons which made him reluctant to publish it during his lifetime. For that reason he left *The Point of View for my Activity as an Author* to be published after his death as "A Report to History"; and now that it has been published and translated into English, men (for sheer incredulity) do not suck from it all the profit they ought. His political and social views are expressed in *The Present Age*, but to that people have paid hardly any attention. *The Book on Adler* reveals him more fairly than did *The Attack upon Christendom*, of which, as he said, if it were to succeed as an attack, it must be "onesided and exaggerated." Nothing but his *Journals* reveal him more clearly: and of that his critics have not made enough use, and in English we have not nearly enough extracts from the *Journals*. Padre Cornelio Fabro has undertaken to introduce S.K. into Italy by the publication of three big volumes of selections from the *Journals*—almost as many as need to be translated. If S.K.'s *Journals* had been generally known before his pseudonymous works were published, he surely would have been better understood—or perhaps, to use his own words, "more passionately misunderstood."

Among the many misunderstandings is the common complaint that S.K.'s greatest defect was his "subjectivity," his blindness to anything objectively given in Christianity. This will not be said by anyone who reads in this book what he affirms about "revelation," about the Scriptures, and about the divine authority of an apostle. It may be said truly enough that, though he relied upon the objective authority of the Church, he did not feel for it a warm affection as the Body of Christ. But who did among the Protestants of his day and generation—unless perhaps Grundtvig, S.K.'s *bête noire*, who talked with warmth about the "Congregation" (*Menigheden*), with perhaps the same sort of sentimentality which led Josiah Royce, a belated Hegelian, to talk about "the Beloved Community"? There were as yet no High Anglicans and no High Lutherans, Christianity was "a geographical expression," men felt no loyalty to the Church of Christ, but only loyalty to their denomination.

ABOUT MAGISTER ADLER

S.K. was aware that the title he first gave to this book had, to say the least of it, no sales-value, that instead of attracting readers it would repel them. He protested that "only in a certain sense is it about Adler," and to indicate that it dealt with more than "Adler as a phenomenon" he chose as his third title a general description of the contents which makes no mention of Adler.

But by changing the title one cannot get rid of Adler. Except for his escapade this book would never have been written. Adler is the warp upon which this whole fabric is woven, and the interesting patterns of the brocade have no consistency apart from the longitudinal threads supplied by him.

Today Adler would be totally forgotten were not his name embalmed in this book. I was perhaps too scrupulous in feeling that I ought to read Adler's works, or at least the six books upon which S.K. comments. But Thulstrup informed me that no copies were anywhere to be found: "You must read them as I did in the Royal Library, where the copies which S.K. owned and annotated are preserved. You can imagine that I found no great pleasure in reading them. This author evidently needed the attention of a psychiatrist." I learn from Niels Thulstrup's admirable commentary to the latest German edition that Adolph Peter Adler was born in Copenhagen in 1812, a year earlier than S.K., that like S.K. he came of a well-to-do family, that like S.K. again he could boast of the degree of Magister Artium at a time when it was equivalent to Ph.D., that like S.K. he studied for a year in Germany, but unlike S.K. he was strongly addicted to the Hegelian philosophy, and in pursuit of this interest published four learned or at least pedantic works. In spite of his learning he was content in 1841 to accept the pastorate of two parishes in a simple rural community, where, according to the testimony of Bishop Mynster, he was diligent in the performance of his duties and was loved by his flock. But in 1842 he had a "vision of light" which turned him against Hegel. Jesus Christ bade him burn his earlier books and manuscripts and dictated to him the greater part of a big book which he entitled *Several Sermons* and published at his own expense in 1843. In 1844 he was suspended by Bishop Mynster on the ground that his mind was deranged, and in 1845 he was deposed, after he had replied evasively to several questions put to him by the Bishop and had admitted that "revelation was perhaps too strong an expression." He was given a small pension which, as S.K. said, allowed him leisure to write books against the Church. The first was a pamphlet, *Documents pertaining to my suspension and deposition*, which was published in 1845. In 1846 he published four books on one day: (1) *Several Poems*; (2) a very big book entitled *Studies and Examples*; then two abbreviations of this, (3) *Attempt at a Systematic Presentation of Christianity in its Logic*, and (4) *Theological Studies*. These six last books S.K. bought on June 12, 1846, immediately after his return from Berlin, where he had gone soon after the publication of *The Postscript*; and with these books he was so constantly pre-occupied that till January 1847 he made no entries in his Journal. Adler after his volcanic eruption settled down to a quiet life in the country until his death in 1869.

Lately new light has been shed upon S.K.'s relations with Adler by two books which were published in 1953. In a collection of S.K.'s *Letters* edited by Thulstrup, Adler is mentioned in a letter to his brother, Bishop Peter Kierkegaard, dated June 29, 1843 (No. 85, p. 122): "You know that there is a Magister Adler here in town who has become pastor at Bornholm, a zealous Hegelian. He has come over here and will deliver several sermons in which he will certainly make a stir with regard to orthodoxy. He is a good head, fairly well experienced in several of life's *casibus*, but at this moment is a bit *exalté*. Meanwhile it is always posssible that this is a phenomenon worth watching."

"This time" was a year after Adler's "revelation" and likely just after the publication of *Several Sermons*. Likely Hans Brockner had in view this same time when in his *Memories of Søren Kierkegaard* (written in 1871 but only just now published) he refers in No. 20 to a visit Adler made upon S.K.: "About Magister Adler at the time his insanity began K. related to me several interesting traits. A. came to K. one day with a work he had published and talked to him for a considerable time about the religious literary works of both of them. Adler gave K. to understand that he regarded him as a sort of John the Baptist with relation to himself who, having had a direct revelation, was a messiah. I still remember the smile of K. when he told me that he had replied to Adler that he was perfectly content with the position to which Adler had assigned him: he regarded it as a very respectable function to be a John the Baptist and did not aspire to be a messiah. During the same visit Adler read to K. a good part of his work, partly in his ordinary voice, partly with a peculiar whistling voice. K. took the liberty of saying that he could discover no new revelation in Adler's work. Whereupon Adler said to him, 'When I shall come to you again and read the whole work in this voice (the whistling voice) you will see that it will open to you.' K. when he told me this story was much amused at this opinion of Adler, that a variation in the voice might make the book more significant.—In my first year as a university student I heard once from Adler an utterance about K. He talked about his clever conversation, but expressed the opinion that K. sometimes prepared beforehand for his conversations."

THE TEXT OF THIS BOOK

Ordinarily a translator is not required to make bricks without straw, to concoct a text as well as to translate it; he looks forward only to such joys and tribulations as are involved in the effort to render faithfully in another tongue the thought of a great author. It may be said of S.K. that his style is sometimes so obscure that it provides tribulation enough for the translator, but in the case of *The Book on Adler* the necessity of forming a text which takes account of the thousand and one corrections S.K. proposed in the course of three years, which occupy 144 pages distributed among six volumes of his papers, involves pure and unadulterated tribulation. Yet even this would not have been an intolerable labor, if Howard Johnson had not required me to give an account of all the changes I have made in the first fair copy and register in the appendix the sources which justify them. This involved a labor which almost broke my back;

yet it was not in vain inasmuch as it afforded me an opportunity to supply many omissions I had made in the first instance. But all this labor is only for the sake of satisfying the exigencies of experts: it can have no interest for the ordinary reader, who will be able, I hope, to ignore the small arabic numerals in the text which refer to the Appendix. My fear that I may have overlooked some of S.K.'s corrections is allayed by the consideration that he, when he excerpted from Chapter III the section which he finally published as "The Difference between a Genius and an Apostle," paid no attention to the corrections he had proposed during the course of three years and made only a few changes which occurred to him in the act of transcribing this passage.

The Appendix lists less than two hundred changes—what about the thousand and more which S.K. had proposed? Several of the more significant changes are justified in the footnotes; it is not necessary to remark upon the many erasures and additions which are noted on the manuscript itself; several hundred were stylistic changes which have no effect upon the translation; and—believe it or not—the rest are accounted for as cancellations of earlier corrections! Nothing so clearly shows his zeal to make this book perfect as these corrections of corrections—and for all that the book was never published! This effort of mine is the first that has ever been made to produce the text that he proposed. Yet, were he living now, I have no doubt he would propose a thousand more changes. In the Appendix I have called attention to one passage in which he had made nine corrections and which he subsequently discarded as a whole. There are other cases in which he made as many corrections in a passage he had *previously* discarded! On the whole, however, the text has evidently been improved by the alterations, although some passages which have been omitted I was sorry to lose. The omissions far exceed the additions—especially the omission of footnotes, among which there were some of inordinate length. The text as amended is forty-one pages shorter than the first fair copy which Haecker translated (about one fifth shorter), which in so big a book is obviously an advantage.

SO MANY PREFACES!

A humiliating misfortune which till now has dogged the story of this book is the fact that it is now published in Germany without any preface whatsoever, without even a preface by the translator, whereas S.K. showed his interest in it, his solicitude for it, by providing from time to time three prefaces (one might almost say four), two of which were the longest he ever wrote. My preface is still longer because it has to serve as an introduction to a very peculiar book which needs a great deal of explanation. So here we have four prefaces, three of them by S.K. He wrote the first in January 1847 as the *author* of *The Book on Adler*. It appears here in a shortened form because it was not completed by the quotation from the elder Fichte to which he refers in the latter part of the text. The second was written later in the same year as *editor* of the same book, though at that time he proposed to call it "The Confusion of the Present Age" and to assign it to a pseudonym. The third was written in 1848, and again as the *author* of a book essentially the same, though he then proposed to call it "A Cycle of Ethico-Religious Treatises." They are reproduced here in this order. The sources from which they were culled are mentioned in the first paragraph of this preface.

These prefaces make it abundantly clear that S.K. was not living in an ivory tower, as a poet or a theologian, unmindful of the social and political trends of his age. As "a thinker," as he preferred to call himself, he ruminated profoundly upon them, and with prophetic insight he traced their consequences into and well beyond our age, which has not yet outlived "the convulsive period."

Doubtless there were never so many prefaces written for one and the same book. But the reader may be reminded that in 1844 S.K. published a book entitled *Prefaces* which consisted solely of prefaces—eight of them. Seven of them need not be translated because they deal in a light vein exclusively with the current literary gossip in Copenhagen. But for *The Wind and the Rain* (the Summer Number of 1947) I translated the first, which deals with prefaces in general as a distinct branch of literature, and talks of the freedom and abandonment one feels in writing a preface. In the three prefaces he wrote for *The Book on Adler* one can divine the pleasure he had in letting himself go, without the relative constraint he felt in writing the text. In this case the prefaces were all of them written after the book was finished; but in the first preface to the *Prefaces* he takes notice of two different schools of thought: that of those who prefer to write the preface beforehand and that of those who would write it afterwards. In my practice I have sought to reconcile these opposed schools: I write a preface beforehand to define the lines the book ought to follow—and then, alas, because the book has fallen short of my ideal, I have to write a different preface afterwards. Thus in writing something like forty books I have had a good deal of experience in writing prefaces—I have written eighty of them, not to speak of prefaces I have written for other people's books. As a translator I knew of course beforehand the contents of this book and therefore could write the preface as well first as last. I will not divulge which school of thought I have followed in this instance.

WALTER LOWRIE

Princeton, 1954

PREFACES
By Kierkegaard

No. 1

S.K.'S PREFACE AS AUTHOR OF "THE BOOK ON ADLER"

Essentially this book can be read only by theologians, and among these again it essentially can interest only the individual in so far as he, instead perhaps of becoming self-important and setting himself up as my judge (with the objection, How could it ever occur to me to write so big a book about Magister Adler!), undertakes the labor of reading and then perceives in what sense A. is the subject of this book, and in what sense he is used to throw light upon the age and to defend dogmatic concepts, in what sense there is just as much attention paid to the age as to Adler.

January 1847.

S. Kierkegaard.

No. 2

S.K.'S PREFACE AS EDITOR OF "THE CONFUSION
OF THE PRESENT AGE"

I myself perceive only too well how obvious is the objection and how much there is in it, against writing such a big book dealing in a certain sense with Magister Adler. But truly it is only in a certain sense it deals with him, and I simply beg the reader not to let himself be disturbed by the plausibility of the first impression. If he will read the book as I have read it, and if at the same time he is a theologian, I venture to vouch that from it he will get a clarity about certain dogmatic concepts and an ability to use them which otherwise is not easily to be had. Furthermore I am confident that, if the reader will read attentively and at the same time possesses the theological equipment which enables him to pass judgment, he will agree with me that what the author accomplishes, and what perhaps it was important for our age that he should accomplish, could be accomplished in no other way. For much as I deplore the confusion of Magister Adler, and what at least for the time being we have lost in him, however seriously and slowly I have pondered over publishing this book, which for a year and a day has lain before me completely finished, I count that the author of it may be jealous of his good fortune, for Magister Adler was just what he needed—without him he could not have given his presentation the liveliness and the ironical tension it now has, nor the satirical background which now is to be had gratis. No physician can be better pleased with the normal development of a sickness than the author is with Magister Adler and his abnormal development; and perhaps never has a man by going astray come so opportunely into the hands of Petrus Minor.

The whole book is essentially an ethical investigation of the concept of revelation; about what it means to be called by a revelation; about how he who has had a revelation is related to the race, the universal, and we others to him; about the confusion from which the concept of revelation suffers in our confused age. Or, what comes to the same thing, the whole book is an investigation of the concept of authority, about the confusion involved in the fact that the concept of authority has been entirely forgotten in our confused age. Now the author might have dealt with the subject thus: he might have shown that this concept (revelation) lent itself to confusion (the possibilities), describing also how it has been confused, and he might seek to describe the whole age and its confusion. But upon the reader this perhaps would make the impression that the confusion described was after all only a possibility which did not actually exist, something the author had hit upon just to find something to do, so that after all he was only fighting the air. How very differently he proceeded, if not by Adler's aid, at least by the fact that Adler exhibits almost all possible confusions with respect to this concept, and at the same time declares that he has had a revelation.

Thus it is that by careful reading and rereading I have understood the author, and I wish that the reader would understand him in the same way. It can hardly be supposed that the author has found any special pleasure in reading Magister Adler's many books. Yet he had done that, presumably, because he had assured himself that it might serve his purpose; and likely in the course of his work he became more and more clearly conscious of his purpose, and so of the expediency of his plan. He has used Magister Adler as a foundation or made him a transparent medium for seeing the confusion of our age. Even where the treatise seems to concern itself merely with Adler's writings like a literary review, he has perhaps succeeded in adverting to some little trait which is characteristic of our age, or to a little quirk in the confusion which, even though it is misleading, serves to illuminate the concept more thoroughly. By this plan he has made it possible for the whole monograph to gain liveliness by having constantly the appearance of being a clinic, and besides that to gain an ironic duplication for the fact that Magister Adler, who admirably satirizes the whole age, is precisely one who has broken with the whole modern age, so that he satirizes himself without knowing it; and finally to gain the advantage of a contemporary instance. And as a good dish can be spoiled entirely by being served cold when it should be served hot, so it is in the spiritual sphere. A confusion always has the most interest *in presenti*—and here everything is *in flagranti*.

In case one should wish to affirm that Magister Adler, inasmuch as he has claimed a revelation, stands entirely outside this present age or is entirely isolated in it, I would reply: By no means. Precisely this confusion lies closer to our age than one might be disposed to believe, and Magister Adler, so understood, is, I could almost say, just as much in rapport with our age as Strauss, Feuerbach, etc., were with theirs. Without religion no generation can endure. But when the first rank, the levies which would abolish Christianity (by no means the most dangerous enemies), are through with their attack, there comes another rank of the missionaries of confusion, those which either will have a new religion or be themselves apostles. These are the most dangerous, precisely because they are under religious influence and are religiously confused, but also because they stand in relation to the deeper things in man, while the first enemies were irreligiously possessed. For the misfortune of our age—in the political as well as in the religious sphere, and in all things— is disobedience, unwillingness to obey. And one deceives oneself and others by wishing to make us imagine that it is doubt. No, it is insubordination: it is not doubt of religious truth but insubordination against religious authority which is the fault in our misfortune and the cause of it. But, dialectically, insubordination has two forms: either wishing to cast down the ruler or wishing to be the ruler—and so religiously: either wishing to be a Feuerbach or wishing willfully to be an apostle. Disobedience is the secret of the religious confusion of our age. This same spirit of disobedience is also, as the πρότον ψεῦδος (but rather hidden and unconsciously), at the basis of that which is the fundamental evil of modern Speculation, the fact that men have confused the spheres, confounded profundity of mind with authority, the intellectual and the ethical, the notion of being a genius and the notion of being an apostle. This book, though to many this affirmation will appear strange, is really an edifying book . . . for one who has the predisposition to let himself be edified by a reading which is in other respects laborious.

And herewith I would recommend this book, begging the reader to read slowly, in consideration of the fact that the author has often been obliged to take a step backward to get the point of view. I could wish that for once I might experience the good fortune of getting a good book well read. As editor it would have been easy enough to separate the whole into smaller parts, into little treatises at 4 farthings apiece; but against this the author has protested as though his life depended upon it—and that is reasonable enough. For my part too I have reflected that a regular plan is made impossible by a dismemberment, and that our little land is not well served by letting the rubric literature vanish entirely, so that Denmark would have only pamphlets and newspapers.

"My reader," may I simply beg you to read this book, for it is important for my main effort, wherefore I am minded to recommend it.

Of this I have assured myself in a peculiar way. For various reasons I have let this manuscript lie on my table. Then after having in the meanwhile written "discourses," I wanted to write a more dogmatic work. But precisely then I perceived that I was constantly obliged to presuppose this book. Therefore I resolved to publish it.

So now I part with this book. It is, what to many will seem strange, an edifying book—for him who understands it. And, what to many may seem stranger still, I could desire nothing better, for the sake of the small renown I have as an author, than to have written this book. For in relation to it there is an element of good luck which is rarely presented to one, for perhaps rarely has a man by going astray come so opportunely to hand as has Magister Adler to me.

1847.   S. KIERKEGAARD.

No. 3

S.K.'S PREFACE AS AUTHOR OF "A CYCLE OF ETHICO-RELIGIOUS TREATISES"

This whole work was written before, in part a long while before, the European war, the world historical catastrophe of the present year, which shows and confirms catastrophically the yawning difference between a negative and positive reckoning of time. Yet by the catastrophe this work is not antiquated but is brought within the present age, not put negatively outside but positively inside the time-reckoning, it has not lost but gained by the help of the catastrophe, which makes its publication still more evidently a duty. In its time it was afraid lest by publication it might come too early, now on the contrary it fears that it may come too late.

In order that for once I may signalize a bit with regard to what he who has been able and willing to see doubtless must have seen lying at the basis of my activity as an author totally understood, in regard, *ut ita dicam*, to my program as an author (which, it is true, comes not first as usual, but last)—this was and is my unaltered reckoning and aim; the catastrophe has only helped me to understand it better, while it also will help me to be better understood, or at least to be more passionately misunderstood. The question is not about one or two chambers, nor about the seating of committees or the unseating of ministers. For sure enough there is question about these subjects, again and again these questions are raised by thousands, there is really no question about anything else; but, behold, all this is what the age requires, not in the deepest sense what the age needs; it is simply unfortunate that the age requires what it doesn't need, what therefore is foolishness and a waste of time: in part, at least in certain instances, it is a lust for pleasure. No, ideally and essentially viewed, there is a question, or *the question* about Christianity; about Christianity, as to whether that is what men need; about Christianity, whether that is what men have abolished, whether a so-called Christendom, or rather a fallen Christendom, openly or more hiddenly, now by attack, now by defense, has abolished Christianity. Divine governance has lost patience, will not put up with it any longer, but will, as thoroughgoing as is its teaching, thoroughly make it evident how self-contradictory all this is, that men in general assembly or by casting their votes, or by handshaking, shall be, if you please, a surrogate for religiousness.

And therefore even the catastrophe, as hitherto it has manifested itself, is only an introduction, it belongs among rough drafts, not finished books; for only when one has got so far that he knows what the question is about, only then begins a new time reckoning. Throughout Europe people have in a worldly way, with ever-increasing velocity of passion, lost themselves in problems which can be solved only in a godly way, which only Christianity can solve, and *has* solved long ago. With amendments to the Constitution, with the fourth estate, with all men wishing to solve the problem of likeness and equality between man and man in the medium of worldliness, i.e. in the medium the nature of which is difference and inequality. Though all travel in Europe must stop because one must wade in blood, and though all ministers were to remain sleepless for ruminating, and though every day ten ministers were to lose their reason, and every next day ten new ministers were to begin where the others left off, only to lose their reason in turn—with all this not one step forward is made, an obstacle to it is sternly fixed, and the bounds set by eternity deride all human efforts, deride all presumption against its exalted and lordly privilege, with the pretense that the temporal will explain in time what in time must remain a riddle, which only Christianity can or will explain. The problem is a religious, a Christian problem, and, as I have said, it has already been solved. For give us eternity, a prospect of eternity every instant, its seriousness and its blessedness, its relief; give eternity again to every individual —then no more blood-shedding will be needed, and the ministers may be allowed to retain their respective reasons. Ah, but to get the conflagration quenched, the spontaneous combustion brought about by the friction of worldliness, i.e. to get eternity again—bloodshed may be needed and bombardments, *item* that many ministers shall lose their reason.

How long a time the merely convulsive period may last no man indeed can know. But one need not be a great psychologist to know how difficult it is to get the better of the situation with man's worldly and earthly understanding when, as now is the case with the whole generation, one has a supersti-

tious belief in the saving and beatifying power of the understanding, how difficult it is therefore, and how long drawn
out the transition may be before one lets the understanding
go and makes a leap into the religious. The worldly understanding is established all too firmly in the worldly man, or
he in it. It is like a wisdom tooth—it may take many efforts
and violent ones to rock it loose and to take the life out of a
thing so tenacious of life. Neither does it require a man of
great dialectic power to discover that for worldly passion the
notion may seem very deceptive and alluring that after all
it must be possible finally, if one keeps on calculating and
calculating, to bring about likeness and equality between man
and man in worldliness. In any case the finite dialectic will
be able to construct an incredible multitude of combinations.
The oft-repeated refrain will be: Treachery, treachery; no,
when one does it in another way, when one takes a little
more from here and puts a little more there, and then
distributes that more evenly, without forgetting the difference
in the harmony with the here and there, and here and here
and yonder and up and down—then one must necessarily
succeed in finding the likeness, the common divisor, the stencil,
for man's likeness and equality in worldliness (i.e in difference), likeness for the *worldly* human likeness and equality—
i.e. likeness for the different. The System [i.e. Hegel's
system] sought the "pure" man, and now this age must seek
the "equal" (or straight) man, for in worldliness we are
crooked, or crookedness, i.e. relativities. Worldliness is a
prodigiously variegated complex of more and less, a little
more and a little less, much, something, little, etc.; that is,
worldliness is differentiation. But the understanding in the
service of worldly passion will constantly imagine that it can
reckon this out and get likeness and equality in worldliness.
Every new construction becomes then—yes, in the now antiquated style it becomes a paragraph with the appropriate sign
—it now has become, *stili novi*, a new ministry. And then
when the new ministry goes out, or is convulsively thrust

out, has one then reached the conclusion that the misfortune did not lie in the accidental mistakes or defects of the combination but in the fact that what was needed was something entirely different, namely, religiousness? No, this conclusion one will not draw. There will immediately be a new combination and a new ministry in the offing, which having shaken the relativities kaleidoscopically in a somewhat different way imagines that it has found what it sought. And one will say almost quite systematically, "Well, no, in the way the former ministry wanted to do it it cannot be done, but if only one reckons rightly it must come out all right"—and there comes the new ministry which does less for the beer-sellers, more for the candle-makers, and then you take more from land-owners and bring the proletariat more to the fore, equalize priests and deacons, and above all make a humpback watch-man and a bowlegged blacksmith's apprentice into straight and equal men. The age would recall in many ways the age of Socrates (only that it is far more passionate and violent, for it is the sophistic of violence and of palpability), but it would be nothing that might recall Socrates.

With all this curriculum of §§ or the curriculum of ministers the human race has become more and more confused, like a drunken man, who, the more he rushes about, the more drunken he becomes, even if he gets no more to drink. And then when this provisional convulsive phase has been passed through, and the *political* ministers are gone, the race will be so tired out with sufferings and loss of blood that this thing of eternity might get permission at least to be taken into consideration, as to whether it might not, from the very first, heat passion anew and give it new powers. The reaction (conversely to that of the Reformation) will transfigure what seemed to be, and imagined itself to be, politics into a religious movement. To get eternity again requires blood, but blood of a different sort, not the blood of thousands of warriors, no, the precious blood of martyrs, of the individuals —the blood of martyrs, those mighty dead who are able to do what no living man can do who lets men be cut down by thousands, what these mighty dead themselves could not do while they lived but are able to do only as dead men: to constrain to obedience a furious mob, just because this furious mob in disobedience took the liberty of slaying the martyrs. For the proverb says, "He laughs best who laughs last"; but truly he conquers best who conquers last—so not he who conquers by slaughter—oh, dubious conquest!—but he who conquers by being put to death—an eternally certain conquest! And this sacrifice is the sacrifice of obedience, wherefore God looks with delight upon him, the obedient man, who offers himself as a sacrifice, whereas he gathers his wrath against disobedience which slays the sacrifice—this sacrifice, the victor, is the martyr; for not every one who is put to death is a martyr.

For tyrants (in the form of emperors, kings, popes, Jesuits, generals, diplomats) have hitherto in a decisive moment been able to rule and direct the world; but from the time the fourth estate has come into the picture—when it has had time to settle itself in such a way that it is rightly understood—it will be seen that in the decisive moment only martyrs are able to rule the world. That is, no man will be able to rule the human race in such a moment, only the Deity can do it with the help of absolutely obedient men who at the same time are willing to suffer—but such a man is the martyr. And when in an elder formation the decisive moment was overcome, then the ordinary worldly government took over; but from the moment the fourth estate came into the picture it will be seen that even when the crisis has been overcome it is not possible to govern in a *worldly* way. To rule in a worldly way, to be a ruler in the worldly sense, however much labor and responsibility is involved in it, is a *pleasure*, and therefore is posited upon the possibility that by far the greater number of men are not aware that they have no part in the life of the state or else are godfearing enough not to bother about it. So soon as the fourth estate comes into the picture it is possible to rule only in a godly way, religiously. But to rule religiously, to be religiously the ruler, is to be the sufferer, ruling religiously is suffering. These sufferers (the rulers), in case they are allowed to follow their own counsel, will naturally wish many a time that they were far away and could say good-by to the human race, either to lead their own lives in the solitude of contemplation or to enjoy life. But they do not venture to do so when in fear and trembling they bethink themselves of their responsibility before God. To be selected to be the ruler in a worldly sense is regarded as good fortune, but to be selected to serve as a ruler in a religious sense is, humanly speaking, rather like a punishment, in any case, humanly speaking, it is suffering, humanly speaking, it is the opposite of an advantage.

Discontented, unsatisfied, with the State, with the Church and with everything related to them (art, learning, etc., etc.) the human race, if allowed to follow its own devices, would resolve itself into a world of atoms—whereby nevertheless this progress will be made that now God will himself come directly into relation with the single individuals, not through abstractions, neither through representative persons, but God will himself, so to speak, undertake to educate the countless individuals of the generation, to become himself the school-master who looks after all, everyone in particular. Here thought comes to a stop. The form of the world would be like —well, I know not with what I should liken it. It would resemble an enormous version of the town of Christenfeld [an example of Christian Communism], and so there would be present the two greatest possible contrasts, striving with one another about the interpretation of this phenomenon. On the one hand *communism*, which would say, This is the correct worldly way, there must not be the slightest difference between man and man; riches, art, learning, rule, etc., etc., are of the evil one, all men ought to be equal like laborers in a factory, like cattle in a barnyard, partake of the same food, be washed in one common tub at the same stroke of the clock, be of the same dimensions, etc., etc. On the other hand *pietism*, which would say, This is the right Christian way, that one make no difference between man and man, we ought to be brothers and sisters, have all in common; riches, art, learning, etc., etc., are of the evil one; all men should be equal as it was once in little Christenfeld, all dressed alike, all pray at fixed times, marry by casting lots, go to bed at the stroke of the clock, partake of the same food, out of one dish, at the same time, etc., etc.

Ideally and essentially viewed, everyone who knows with God that he in truth believes in Christ, has "more than conquered," in spite of all the confusion and uproar of the world. He recognizes only one superior power, that of him who is able to pray more inwardly, with more fear and trembling, than he does; but such a superior is not his enemy but his mighty ally. Every opposition—that of power, talents, numbers—ideally viewed, is already overcome, even though *accidentally* he has experienced or may experience suffering for it. Accidentally, for in a *worldly* sense one makes a fuss over sufferings, one suffers in order to conquer—and then perhaps he doesn't conquer after all. In a *Christian* sense he has already more than conquered in advance, so that he does not suffer in order to conquer, but rather because he has conquered, which simply gives him pleasure in putting up with everything and exalts him above sufferings, for since one has conquered he can surely put up with a bit of suffering. In a worldly sense one must wait in the tension of uncertainty to see what follows after suffering, whether victory follows. In a Christian sense there is nothing to wait for, victory was long ago placed in one's hands by faith. This one learns from the Pattern. His last word in his suffering was not, Only wait a little and you will surely see that my cause triumphs. No, he said, "It is finished." What was finished? Suffering. But then he didn't talk at all about conquering? No, how could that occur to him—he knew indeed from eternity that he had conquered.

This is my interpretation of our age, the reflection of a lowly man who has in his nature something of a poet, who moreover is a thinker, but—ah, how often have I repeated this which for me is so important and decisive, my first utterance about myself—"without authority."

S. KIERKEGAARD.

October 7, 1848.

ON AUTHORITY AND REVELATION

(The Book on Adler,
or *A Cycle of Ethico-Religious Essays)*

INTRODUCTION

SINCE, as says the barber (and one who has no opportunity of keeping abreast of the age by the aid of newspapers may well rest satisfied with the barber, who in olden times when there were as yet no newspapers was what the newspapers are now: universal intelligence,[1] "our age is the age of movement," it is not improbable that the lives of many men go on in such a way that they have indeed premises for living but reach no conclusions—quite like this stirring age which has set in movement many premises but also has reached no conclusion. Such a man's life goes on till death comes and puts an end to life, but without bringing with it an end in the sense of a conclusion. For it is one thing that a life is over, and a different thing that a life is finished by reaching its conclusion. In the degree that such a man has talents he can go ahead and become an author, as he understands it. But such an understanding is an illusion. For that matter (since here we may hypothetically admit everything possible, so long as we hold fast the decisive point), he may have extraordinary talents and remarkable learning, but an author he is not, in spite of the fact that he produces books. Like his life, his book must be material. Perhaps this material may be worth its weight in gold, but it is only material. Here is no poet who poetically rounds out the thing as a whole, no psychologist who organizes the individual trait and the individual person within a total apprehension, no dialectician who prescribes the place within the life-view which he has at his disposition. No, in spite of the fact that the man writes, he is not essentially an author; he will be capable of writing the first part, but he cannot write the second part, or (to avoid any misunderstanding) he can write the first and also the second part, but he cannot write the third part—the last part he cannot write. If he goes ahead naively (led astray by the reflection that every book must have a last part) and so writes the last part, he will make it thoroughly clear by writing the last part that he makes a written renunciation to all claim to be an author. For though it is indeed by writing that one justifies the claim to be an author, it is also, strangely enough, by writing that one virtually renounces this claim. If he had been thoroughly aware of the inappropriateness of the third part—well, one may say, *si tacuisset, philosophus mansisset.*

To find the conclusion, it is necessary first of all to observe that it is lacking, and then in turn to feel quite vividly the lack of it. It might therefore be imagined that an essential author, just to make evident the misfortune that men are living without a conclusion, might write a fragment (but by calling it that he would avoid all misapprehension), though in another sense he provided the conclusion by providing the necessary life-view. And after all a world-view, a life-view, is the only true condition of every literary production. Every poetic conclusion is an illusion. If a life-view is developed, if it stands out whole and clear in its necessary coherence, one has no need to put the hero to death, one may as well let him live: the premise is nevertheless resolved and satisfied in the conclusion, the development is complete. But if there is lacking a life-view (which of course must be in the first part and everywhere, though the lack of it only becomes evident in the second part or the third, that is to say, the conclusion), it is of no avail to let the hero die, no, it avails nothing that the writer, to make quite sure that he is dead, even has him buried in the course of the story—with this the development is by no means complete. If death had that power, nothing would be easier than to be a poet, and poetry would not be needed at all. For in reality it is indeed true that every man dies, his life comes to an end; but from this it does not follow that his life has an end in the sense of a conclusion, "that it *came* to an end"—precisely this past tense shows that death is not the decisive thing, that the conclusion may fall within a man's lifetime,[2] and that to regard death as a conclusion is a deceitful evasion, for death is related quite indifferently to the premise of a man's life, and therefore is not a conclusion of any sort.

But the more the time for development is lacking, and the more individuals there are who lack a conclusion, all the more active men seem to be in multiplying premises. This in turn has the result that to get a conclusion becomes more and more difficult, because, instead of the decisiveness of the conclusion, there results a stoppage which, spiritually under-stood, is what constipation is in the animal organism, while the augmentation of premises is just as dangerous as over-loading oneself with food when one suffers from constipation, though for a moment it may seem an alleviation. Gradually the movement of time changes it into an unhealthy fermenta-tion. So the individuals whose life contains only premises may make use of this sickness of our age by becoming authors, and their productions will be precisely what the age demands. Under these circumstances an essential author would naturally prescribe a diet, but the premise-authors are[3] better off.

As opportunity makes thieves, so does this fermentation make "mad" authors (in the sense that we speak of "mad money" in times of serious inflation), for the lack of a con-clusion in our age obscures the fact that the authors lack it. The relative differences of premise-authors among them-selves, with respect to talents and such like, may be very great, but they have in common this essential mark, that they are not real authors. On the surface of such a fermentation there may be floating many clever pates, but even the most insignificant pates may aspire to writing at least a little premise-contribution for a newspaper. In this way there is prospect of advancement for the most insignificant pates, and consequently there is a great number, a multitude of authors, so that by reason of their number they may best be likened to sulphur-matches which are sold in bundles. Such an author, upon whose head is deposited something phosphorescent (the suggestion of a project, a hint), one takes up by the legs and strikes him upon a newspaper, and out there come three to four columns. And the premise-authors have really a striking resemblance to sulphur-matches—both explode with a puff.

But in spite of this explosion, or perhaps precisely because of it, all premise-authors, whatever their relative differences may be, have one thing in common: they all have a *purpose*, they all wish to produce an effect, they all wish that their works may have an extraordinary diffusion and may be read if possible by all mankind. This curious trait is reserved for man in such an age of fermentation: to have a purpose, for the sake of this purpose to be on the move in the sweat of their brow, and not really to know in themselves whither this purpose tends; for knowing *that*, one must also have the conclusion. This, as the proverb says, is to see that a town is called Little Run, but not to know whither it is running. Instead of having, each man for himself, a clear conception of what one wills *in concreto* before one begins to express one's views, one has a superstitious notion about the utility of starting a discussion,[4] one has the superstition that, while the individuals themselves do not know what they will, the spirit of the age should be able by its dialectic to make it clear what one really wills, so that by this these purposeful gentlemen may get to know what their purpose really is.[5] Everyone in his own way is busily engaged in kindling the fire under the boiler with these combustible premises—but nobody seems to think how dangerous this is with no engineer at hand.

The premise-author is easily recognized and easily described, if only one will remember that he is the exact opposite to the essential author, that while the former is outwardly directed, the latter is inwardly directed. Now it may be a social problem. The premise-author has absolutely no precise and clear notion of what is to be done, how the pressure can be relieved. He thinks thus: "If only an outcry is raised, then surely it will turn out all right." Now it may be a religious problem. The premise-writer has neither time nor patience to think it out more precisely. His notion is: "If only an outcry is raised in a loud voice that can be heard all over the land, and it is read by everybody and is talked about in every company, then surely it will turn out all right." The premise-author thinks that the outcry is like a wishing rod—and he has not observed that almost all have become outcriers.[6] It quite escapes the attention of the premise-authors that it would after all be more reasonable in our age, the age of outcry, if a man were to think thus: The outcry will certainly be made anyway, therefore it would be better for me to abstain from it and collect myself for a more concrete reflection. One smiles at reading all the romantic tales of a bygone age about how knights fared forth into the forest and killed dragons and liberated princes from enchantment, etc.—the romantic notion that in the forests such monsters dwelt, along with enchanted princes. And yet it is quite as romantic that in a whole generation everyone believes in the power of outcry to summon such monstrous forces.[7] The apparent modesty of wanting merely to make an outcry or to raise a discussion does not seem praiseworthy at all, seeing that experience again and again repeated must impress upon everyone the serious thought that he must look for real help in answer to his cry, or else refrain from doing anything to increase the confusion.[8]

Premise-authors are the opposite of the essential authors, for the latter has his own perspective,[9] he constantly comes behind himself in his individual productions; he strives forward indeed, but within the totality, not after it; he never raises more doubt that he can explain; his A is always greater than his B; he never makes a move on an uncertainty. For he has a definite world-view and life-view which he follows, and with this he is in advance of his individual literary productions, as the whole is always before the parts. Be it much or little he has hitherto understood by his world-view, he explains only what he has understood; he does not wait superstitiously for something from the outside to turn up suddenly and bring him to an understanding, instruct him suddenly

[7]

what he really wills. In real life it may make a comic effect when a man pretends to be another whose name he doesn't know and only learns later what he is called. Scribe has used this situation wittily in a passage in one of his plays. A young man introduces himself to a family, claiming to be a cousin who has been away for many years. He doesn't himself know what the cousin's name was, till an overdue bill made out to this cousin was presented to him and helped him out of his embarrassment. He takes the bill, and in an aside which is fairly witty he says, "It may always be well to know what my name is." Thus the premise-author, too, produces a comical effect by pretending to be somebody other than he is, by pretending to be an author, and in the end he must wait for something from outside to enlighten him as to what he really is, that is, spiritually understood, what he really wills. The essential author on the other hand knows definitely what he is, what he wills; from first to last he is attentive to understand himself in his life-view; he does not fail to observe that the expectation of an extraordinary result from a discussion he has started is skepticism, that the supposed reliability of the result really nourishes doubt.

Insofar as an essential author may be said to feel a need to communicate himself, this need is purely immanent, an enjoyment of his understanding raised to the second power, or else for him it would be an ethical task consciously assumed. The premise-author feels no need to communicate himself, for essentially he has nothing to communicate: he lacks precisely the essential thing, the conclusion, the meaning in relation to the premises. He does not feel the *need to communicate himself*, he is a *needy person*,[10] and like other needy persons he is a burden to the state and to the poor fund— thus essentially are all premise-authors needy persons who become a burden to the race for the fact that they want to be supported, instead of laboring themselves and nourishing themselves with the understanding they themselves earn. There can be no reason in existence unless every man may be assumed to have as much understanding as he needs, if he will honestly labor. If he has great talents and can also raise many doubts, so also he must have powers in himself to gain understanding, if he seriously wills it. But everyone should keep silent insofar as he has no understanding to communicate. Merely to want to raise an outcry is a sort of glittering idleness. It is easy to do that, it is easy enough to make oneself seem important thereby; it is easy enough to get on the poor list, and then it is easy enough to cry out to the state, "Support me." And every premise-writer cries out to the state, "Support me." But divine governance answers, "Thou shalt support thyself, and so must every man." Then the apparent modesty of merely prompting a discussion is seen to be a hidden presumption; for if the person in question is not capable of being an essential author, it is presumptuous to pretend to be an author. The essential author is essentially a teacher; and, if he is not and essentially could not be a real author, he is essentially a learner. Instead of being *nourishing*, as every essential author is (the difference being only with respect to talents and compass), every premise-author is devouring.[11] He is devouring precisely because, instead of keeping silence, he utters doubts and makes an outcry.

The art of all communication consists in coming as close as possible to reality, i.e. to contemporaries who are in the position of readers, and yet at the same time to have a viewpoint, to preserve the comforting and endless distance of ideality. Allow me to illustrate this by an example from an earlier literary production. In the psychological experiment "Guilty?/not guilty?" (in *Stages upon Life's Way*) there is depicted one who is taxed to the utmost, even to the point of despair, by the mortal danger threatening his spiritual life, and the whole thing is depicted as though it might have happened yesterday. In this respect the production is brought as close as possible to reality;[12] but now comes the comforting reflection that the whole thing is an experiment, spiritually understood, he is what in civil life would be called a very dangerous person; such a person as ordinarily is not allowed to go out alone and is usually accompanied by a couple of policemen for the sake of public security. So it is too in this production that to assure public safety there is included an experimenter (he calls himself a policeman) who very quietly shows how the whole thing hangs together, theoretically develops a life-view, which he completes and rounds out, while he illustrates it by pointing to the subject, in order to indicate the movements he makes in proportion as the noose is tightened. If this were not a mere experiment, if there were no experimenter at hand, no life-view developed—then such a literary production, whether or no it displayed talent, would be simply consuming. It would be agonizing to come in contact with it, because it merely made the impression of a real man who presumably the next instant might go mad. It is one thing to depict a passionate man when with him is depicted a *Gewaltiger* and a life-view which can control him,[13] and it is quite a different thing when a passionate man with the highest degree of personal reality becomes an author, runs amuck, and by the help of a book assaults us as it were with his doubts and torments.

If one would depict a man who thought he had had a revelation but later became insecure about it, and if one did this as an experiment, and if there was at hand an experimenter who understood his business thoroughly, and if a whole life-view was developed which made use of the subject of the experiment as a physicist might do—then that would be all right, perhaps much might be learned from the report of it. Perhaps the experimenter had assured himself by observation that such a thing might happen in his generation, and hence brought the experiment as close as possible to this age—but *nota bene* that he himself was in possession of the explanation which would be communicated. When on the contrary a real man in the perplexed condition of the subject of this experiment precipitates himself upon the public—then he is consuming in the highest degree. The abnormal man may be instructive when he is controlled and forced to take his place in a total life-view; but when he bluntly claims the authority of a teacher without being able to teach anything else but abnormality and its pain, one is painfully affected by the importunate reality of such an ex-author, who personally is in mortal danger and quite personally wants to claim our aid, or by the fact that he knows no way of escape, wants to make us uneasy, to make us suffer as he does. It is one thing to be a physician who knows all about cures and healing, upon which he lectures in his clinic where he recounts the history of a disease—it is one thing to be a physician beside a sickbed, and another thing to be a sick man who leaps out of his bed by becoming an author, communicating bluntly the symptoms of his disease. Perhaps he may be able to express and expound the symptoms of his illness in far more glowing colors than does the physician when he describes them; for the fact that he knows no resource, no salvation, gives him a peculiar passionate elasticity in comparison with the consoling talk of the physician who knows what expedients to use. But in spite of that there remains the decisive qualitative difference between a sick man and a physician. And this difference is precisely the same decisive *qualitative difference* between being a premise-author and an essential author.[14]

What here is said about premise-authors in a way so general that it may apply to perfectly insignificant pates and to superior talents as well, if they lack a definite life-view and lack a conclusion, has an application also to Magister Adler, an author against whom I am not conscious of any animosity, since in all honesty I even owe him thanks for the service he has rendered the pseudonymous authors whose natural protector I am, for the fact that he has hardly made any reference to them—at least he has not showed it in such a way that in quoting them and other such writers he has brought them into any intimate and annoying relationship with himself. And not only for this do I owe him thanks, but also in many ways as a reader. For it is certain that in his books there are many passages which one who is well-disposed cannot read without edification, that sometimes he is moving, not rarely entertaining by his liveliness, and does not altogether lack profundity, though he entirely lacks consistency in his thought. Magister Adler is equipped with many happy gifts, with many desirable presuppositions with respect to learning, and along with these he has one premise more which distinguishes him absolutely from all other premise-authors: he has a fact of revelation to which he can appeal. Far from me truly is every foolish jest. I shall certainly think of this claim with every possible concession and reserve; I do not presume to deny it or to affirm it. I regard myself simply as a learner. This at least is certain, that had he held fast to this fact of revelation as an unshakable fact, though others might consider him mad or else bow to his authority—had he done that, had he not indecisively, waveringly, higgled about it and privately interpreted it away, I would not have been justified in calling him a premise-author. But to press such a fact upon the attention of the public, and then in the end not to know himself what is what, what he himself means by it—that is to characterize himself as a premise-author, for that is to bluster in the most frightfully loud tones—and then to wait for the world to come to his assistance with the explanation that he had had a revelation, or had not had it. Such a phenomenon may have profound significance as a bitter epigram upon our age. In a wavering, doubtful and unstable age, where the individual is accustomed to seek outside himself (in the world about him, in common opinion, in town gossip) what essentially is only to be found in the decision of the individual himself—in such an age a man steps forward and appeals to a revelation, or rather he bolts out like a terrified man, with fright and fear depicted upon his countenance, still trembling from the impression of that moment, and announces that he has been favored by a revelation. *Pro dii immortales,* here

then at last there must be help, here at last there must be
firm ground to stand upon! Alas, he resembles this age only
too thoroughly—the next instant he does not himself know
definitely what is what, he leaves that unresolved—and
meanwhile he writes big and (perhaps) clever books. Lo, in
those remote times when a man was honored by high revelations he retired for three years, so that he might not be
taken by surprise, so that he might comprehend himself in
this incomprehensible experience before teaching others. Nowadays one takes for a revelation any sort of strong impression,
and the same evening puts it in the newspaper. Any strong
impression—indeed, to all eternity I should not regard myself as justified in saying that about the lowliest man who
appealed to a revelation, if he himself stood firmly by what
he had said; but Adler's conduct has justified me in saying
what he himself says in his latest works. Nevertheless, Magister Adler stands or falls with his fact of revelation, he may write
folios, and even though they were richer in ideas and happy
thoughts and many a profound hint than are the last books, an
answer is nevertheless due as to what is what, whether the
whole thing was a prank—or whether in that case he will
say that he repents it, since at one time he obtruded upon us
its reality—or whether it was a fact of revelation, whether he
then will assume that role, while other men with becoming
reverence for the person so eminently favored come forward
as inquirers, each one particularly in proportion to the talents
bestowed upon him, but only as a learner.

What has been briefly touched upon here and will be
treated more fully in a subsequent investigation sufficiently
shows that it is not my intention to appraise aesthetically or
critically particular passages in Magister Adler's books, or in
general to deal with his writings as a critic usually does.
Usually one deals with the writings and leaves the author out.
Here this cannot be done. My whole criticism and whatever
ability I may have as a critic is all within the assumption that
I am an insignificant individual. It is Magister Adler who

has put himself forward with his fact of revelation, and for me at least this is so decisive that I cannot forget it for an instant, nor for an instant can I regard myself as justified in using my measuring rod, and I cannot criticize revealed scriptures in the same way as I would books by men. Magister Adler is not simply an author, by reason of his revelation he is a phenomenon, in the midst of everyday life he is a dramatic person, and there can be no question of forgetting him while dealing with his writings, which commonly would be a duty. No, in dealing with his works it is necessary to be attentive to him, to him who by his fact of revelation is placed in a position so extreme that he must either be a charlatan—or an apostle. It will not do to carry the game so far as when one speaks of Denmark's Aristotle, though God knows he does not resemble him at all, but here in Denmark he resembles him more than others do—so that at last one plays the game that one was very near having a revelation, that in this country he came nearest to being an apostle. Since he has no other legitimation, the concept veers about, and it is he that is farthest precisely because he would obtrude himself.

As a phenomenon in our age (so that as much attention is paid to our age as to Adler) shall Magister Adler be the subject of discourse in this little book. His books should not be appraised aesthetically and critically as if they were by an ordinary author; no, he shall be treated by the lowly service-able critic with the respect due to his claim, and his writings shall be used only to see whether he understands himself in being what he gives himself out to be, and which *in any serious sense* he has not given any sign of wishing to revoke. Neither shall anything be said about the doctrine he expounds, as to whether it is heretical or not. All such questions must be regarded as unimportant in comparison with the qualitative decisive factor. On the contrary, the ethical accent of serious-ness shall be laid if possible upon that which must either give him divine authority (and in that case he must be re-quired to make use of this authority instead of being ambiguously clever in big books), or else it must be penitently revoked, since once he thrust himself forward by claiming it. It shall if possible be emphasized with the accent of seriousness that he has appealed to a fact of revelation.

Should anyone ask who am I who do this, here is my reply: I am a serviceable critic, a lowly person, who has only ethical justification, as every man has over against an author. In case the whole episode of Magister Adler is not to be treated as an insignificance which had best be ignored,[15] then it is disquieting that an author presses upon us as a riddle, not what we are to understand by the fact that he had a revelation (for that he has a right to do), but the riddle whether he himself thinks it was a revelation, or that it was just another sort of Hurrah boys. I am firmly convinced that the Apostle Paul, as can easily be seen from his writings, would not have taken it ill if anyone in a serious conversation had asked him whether he really had had a revelation; and I know that Paul with the brevity of seriousness would have expressed himself briefly and replied, "Yes." But in case Paul (may he forgive me for what I am about to say—it must be done to illustrate something), instead of answering briefly, were it yes or no, had entered upon a long and prolix discourse to this effect: "I see well enough now, in fact I already have said it, but perhaps after all revelation is too strong an expression, but something it was, something like genius it was . . ." Well, then the question would have been a different one. With geniuses I can hold my own fairly well. God preserve me—if it is in truth the greatest genius, then with aesthetic propriety I gladly express my reverence for the superior mind from whom I am learning; but that I show him religious subjection, that I should submit my judgment to his divine authority—no, that I do not do, neither does any genius require it of me. But when a man coolly wishes to explain away what was intended to be an apostolic existence into being a genius, without revoking the first claim—then he confounds the situation terribly.

To this a critic must hold fast, as I shall do in this little discussion.[16] Without praising my own wares I also venture to promise that he who reads attentively will find in this book illumination; for I am not unacquainted with my age and with what is fermenting in it, I follow along with it, though like one who sails in the same ship and yet has a separate cabin, not in the quality of anything extraordinary, as though I had authority, no, in the quality of an eccentric who has anything but authority.*[17]

Here this introduction should properly end. However, I still wish to add a word. It is not without sorrow, not without sadness, I write this review; I would rather leave it unwritten, if I had no need to fear that Magister Adler's works, which recently have been highly (and stupidly) praised in the *Northern Church Times*, might yet attract attention, and in such a case he must necessarily occasion great confusion in the religious field, precisely because he possesses a certain cleverness, and most men have not enough ability to distinguish *inter et inter*. The sad and sorrowful aspect of this, according to my conception, is due to the proportions of this land. In a little land like Denmark there naturally can be only a few who have time and opportunity to occupy themselves with the things of the intellect, and of this small number there naturally can be only some individuals who really have talents and also comprehend decisively that to them is appointed occupation with the things of the intellect as their only task. But all the more important it is that such an individual, precisely because the small proportions of our land hardly have room for a quick corrective, should check himself by the strictest

* The passage omitted here in 1847 referred to the "trousers" which had been made a subject of ridicule by *The Corsair*. This vulgar attack was made in 1846 and still rankled when S.K. wrote the first draft of this book. Later he proposed to abbreviate it as follows: Authority— well, yes, this might have been by the help of my trousers, for by my writings I have not attracted the attention of anybody, and, God knows it, my old gray trousers are entirely innocent of the fact that public opinion has paid so much attention to them.

discipline not to grasp at a glittering confusion instead of the truth. Magister Adler is such an individual,[18] it is not impossible that he might attract to himself the admiration of one or another less informed person, but by this nothing is gained; just because in a little land there are so few who can judge with competence and insight, either with superior or at least with equal justification, just for this reason everyone who by talents or favor is advantageously placed ought to keep watch on himself. But even if Adler with his last works has augmented the capital fund of cleverness which in our age is in so many ways accumulating with the contribution of so many clever sayings, this is of not much avail in comparison with the confusion of all the most important concepts upon which Christianity depends. There is also in the intellectual world a glowing sensuality, a dangerous temptation to cleverness, which precisely by the play of multiplicity conceals a total lack of clearness. And although every author has a responsibility, yet it seems that an author in a great literature like the German[19] or the French has less responsibility because he occasions less harm by swiftly vanishing in the multitude. It seems to me that Magister Adler should take this into account. I at least have sought to make this clear to myself in the consciousness of being such an individual. It is certain that in a small literature, precisely for the reason that it is small, one can realize tasks of a special sort which could not succeed in a great one where one author supplants the other; but it is also certain that the responsibility is all the more serious. When there are many springs it is not so dangerous that one of them is muddled, but in a little land, where in every direction there is hardly more than one spring, anyone who muddles it assumes a high degree of responsibility. And little as I love adherents and imitators, coteries and cliques, things that again thrive best in a little land but also do irreparable harm, all the more would I be glad if there were several other individuals who, on their own account and perhaps from entirely different points of view, were laboring for the cultivation of this field. But hitherto Adler has been of no profit; there is no concept he has explained, no new categorical definition he has supplied, no old and established one he has refreshed by new dialectical sharpness. Thus in no decisive sense has he been profitable, and to me in a way he has been a hindrance; for since he belongs to the religious field, and since he confuses *pro virili*, and since the proportions of this land are small, I have regarded it as my duty to interrupt my customary activity in order to correct a little bit the thinker whom I would have been more than willing to regard as my superior or as a fellow-worker—but *nota bene* one who was working on his own account.—Moreover, I myself understand very well how strange the whole thing looks. About an author who till now has not had many readers I write a book which presumably will not be read. As it is related of two princely personages who were very fat that they took their exercise by walking around one another, so in a little land the exercise of authors consists in walking around one another. However, I have chosen my problem in such a way, as I am accustomed to do, that in spite of the fact that it is an instant of time about which the investigation revolves, the treatment because of its more universal and ideal character will be fit to be read at all times. I have no talent nor competence to write for the instant.

¹Magister Adler's collision with the universal as teacher in the State-Church; a special individual who has a fact of revelation.

IT was in the year 1843 that Magister Adler published his *Sermons*, in the preface to which he announced with the utmost solemnity that he had experienced a revelation, that by this a new doctrine was communicated to him, and in the sermons themselves he distinguished (and thereby made everything definitely clear) between the discourses which were by him and those which were by the direct assistance of the Spirit.* He instructed us in the preface that the Spirit commanded him to burn everything he had formerly written. Thus he stood, or so he presented himself in the preface, as a picture of a new point of departure in the most decisive sense: behind him the conflagration, and himself saved from it with the new doctrine.

At that time,² strange as it may seem now, afterwards, he was a teacher in the State-Church, he had, if one will so say, happily and well become a priest, only then occurred the event which must put him in the position of the special individual *extra ordinem* by having a new point of departure from God. Dear as it may be to the State, and in the religious field to the State-Church, to see, if it were so, a new generation of functionaries all equipped with talents and other abilities³ quite different from those of the former ones, dear as it may be to the State, and in the religious field to the State-Church,

---

* In a sense this is confusing, inasmuch as the qualitatively heterogeneous sermons ought not to have been published together; in any case there is lacking here a dialectic middle term of comparison as to how he understands himself in the qualitative decisive difference: of being assisted by the Spirit or being without it.

to see the most distinguished and superior talents consecrate themselves to the service of the State and the State-Church, it follows as a matter of course that this joy has one condition, namely, that they really wish to serve the State, that within its presuppositions and recognizing them they will *ex animi sententia* use their glorious gifts; otherwise joy must be transformed into anxiety and disquietude for its own security, in any case into anxious sympathy for the individual or the individuals who are making their lives a failure. For the State, including the State-Church, is not selfish, not tyrannical (as the evil-minded or dissatisfied wish to think and to make others believe), it is, according to its idea, benevolent; when it accepts the service of the individual it means to do him a service by indicating to him the appropriate place for the expedient and advantageous exercise of his powers.

By the fact of his revelation, by his new doctrine,* by stand-

---

* That Magister Adler has said later in a way that there is nothing new in his doctrine does not alter the case. By his course of action he has confirmed it in the strongest and loftiest terms. It is a fact, as I learn from the printer, that he had the type remain undistributed at the press, presumably with the expectation that his *Sermons* might soon have a new edition. The fact that he says later irresponsibly that there is nothing new, as well as the fact that he, who by his course of action evidently aimed at a sensation, later tried to give as it were a certain humoristic turn to the matter—such behavior surely might give a newspaper writer who was disposed to advocate his cause occasion for total confusion. To my notion there is nothing more pernicious than these slovenly transitions and alterations. A man should know what he wills and stand by it: if he alters his position, he must do so officially. Otherwise all is confusion. By the help of an anachronism a newspaper writer shows up a man to his advantage by the help of the fact that he had blundered. One lets it seem as though it were not at a different time he had said this, one treats the latter saying as though it were the contemporaneous interpretation; and lo, the man who precisely by his duplicity characterizes himself as unstable becomes a hero and perfectly consistent—the State and the State-Church on the other hand are put to embarrassment. But Magister Adler has never solemnly (which by reason of the relation of the spheres calls for repentance) revoked what he most solemnly had said. On the contrary, he has let the first affirmation stand, and then in a gossipy way said this or that as it were about it not being something new, that neither was it quite a revelation,

ing under the direct outpouring of the Spirit, Magister Adler might easily become aware of being placed as a particular or peculiar individual altogether outside the universal, altogether *extra ordinem* as *extraordinarius*. Under such circumstances to wish to be in the service of the Establishment is a self-contradiction, and to expect of the Establishment that it shall keep him in its service is really to wish to make a fool of the Establishment, as though it were something so abstract that it was not able to concentrate itself in an energetic consciousness of what it is and what it wills. To wish to be in the service of the Establishment, and then to wish to perform a service which aims precisely at the life of the Establishment, is just as unreasonable as if one were to wish to be in the service of a man, and yet to admit openly that his labor and zeal were to serve this man's enemy. This no man would put up with, and the reason why one thinks that the Establishment might put up with it is that one has a fantastic-abstract conception of the impersonal character of the public and a fantastic notion of the public as a means of livelihood, in consequence of which the public is supposed to take care of every theological candidate. When the army stands drawn up with its front facing the Establishment, then to wish to be in the ranks and a *stipendiarius*, but to wish to take the inverse position, is a thing that cannot be done. The moment the march is to begin (as soon as life begins to stir) it will be evident that one is marching in the opposite direction. The *extraordinarius* has therefore to step out of the ranks. This is required as well for his high importance as for the seriousness of the universal; for an extraordinary man is too important to take his place in the ranks, and the seriousness of the universal requires unanimity and unity in the ranks, it needs to see who the extraordinary is, or to see that he is the

---

but something in some way remarkable, and such like. (But about this later in its proper place.) But in respect to ambiguous phenomena one cannot too often oppose the ambiguity, which precisely when it is not held together is calculated to confuse.

extraordinary. In this *discrimen* precisely shall the extraordinary acquire his competence: on the one hand the lowly one, a man all but lost, due to the fact of being pointed out as the individual in the peculiar sense, of being pointed out as a poor Peer Eriksen in comparison with the universal, so that no shrewd man dare be his friend or even walk with him in the street, so that his friend, if he were shrewd, would swear that he did not know the man, so that "they that passed by wagged their heads" (Matt. 27:39)—and yet to be the man from whom something new shall issue. This is the painful crisis, but it never will be easy to become an *extraordinarius*.*

So Magister Adler's collision with the universal it that of the special individual, with a revelation. Without wishing to deny straightway the possibility that this extraordinary experience might also occur to a man in our age, it certainly would be a very suspicious sign. But, if there is nothing new under the sun, neither is there any direct and monotonous repetition, there is constantly something newish or a new modification. Our age is the age of reflection and intelligence, hence it may very well be assumed that he who in our age is thus called of God would be *en rapport* with his age. He would then have at his disposition as a serviceable factor an eminent power of reflection. So this would be the difference: in olden times the man thus called would be the immediate instrument; in our age he would have as a serviceable factor this eminent reflection before which this lowly serviceable critic is obliged to bow. The man chosen in our age will be not merely an instrument in the immediate sense but will consciously undertake his calling in a sense different from that which has always characterized a divine calling: he will think of himself and understand himself in the fact that this extraordinary thing has happened to him.

* The long passage which follows, containing 13 paragraphs, is found in Papirer VIII B, pp. 61 ff. S.K. wrote it as a "supplement" to this book. The translator can find no place for it more appropriate than this.

How far it may be possible to conceive of a divine call within a human reflection, as a coefficient of it, I as a lowly serviceable critic am not bold enough to say; the answer would first be contained in the life of the extraordinary man, if such a one were to come. But to a certain point I can carry out the thought dialectically until reflection runs aground.

In case everything was in order about a man being called of God by a revelation, but he has as a serviceable factor an eminent reflection, he would then understand that to this call and to the fact of having a revelation there corresponds ethically a prodigious responsibility in all directions, not only inwardly (that he was sure within himself and understood himself in the fact that something extraordinary had happened to him, for that we can assume), but outwardly, in relation to the established order, because the extraordinary has in reflection the dialectic of being the highest salvation, but also of being able to be the greatest corruption. His responsibility in reflection would then be that he might not become the greatest misfortune to the established order, but might make everything as easy as possible for it, and that with fear and trembling he might watch out that no one, so far as lay in his power, should suffer harm by a direct relationship to his extraordinarity. In case he now let the serviceable reflection follow its own counsel alone, the ultimate consequence would be that he completely annihilated himself, annihilated the impression of himself, humanly understood, made himself as lowly, as insignificant as possible, almost odious, because in reflection, where every definition is dialectic, he rightly understood that the extraordinary, except at the point where it is and is in truth the extraordinary, is and may be the cause of the most frightful corruption. In the ultimate consequence of reflection he would then transform the fact of revelation into his life's deepest secret, which in the silence of the grave remained the law of his existence, but which he never communicated directly.—But, behold, just this would be to fail entirely to accomplish his task, it would be indeed disobedience to God.

For he who is called by a revelation is called precisely to appeal to his revelation, he must precisely exert authority in the strength of the fact that he was called by a revelation. In a revival it is not assumed that the man awakened in an extraordinary way should go out and proclaim this to men; on the contrary, this may remain precisely the secret of the awakened man with God, it may precisely be humble to keep silence about this in a womanly way. But he who is called by a revelation and to communicate a revelation, or the fact that he had a revelation (for the principal thing is precisely that he has had a revelation, not always so much its contents—as with regard to a letter from heaven, if you will imagine such a thing, precisely the most important point is the fact that it has fallen from heaven, not always so much what is in it), he should proclaim this, appeal to it, exert authority.

So it is to be seen that when the fact of having had a revelation is transposed completely into reflection, this fact of having had a revelation must in one way or another come to be altogether impenetrable, or else work itself into a contradiction. For if the idea of the serviceable reflection conquers, a man will keep the very fact of revelation isolated and hidden, watching out with fear and trembling for the ruinous consequences which the direct communication might have, and shuddering at the responsibility. But therewith at the same time he gives up *authority*; he makes himself presumptuously into a genius, whereas God had called him to be an apostle. That is to say: in the idea of reflection a genius is the highest, an apostle is an impossibility; for the idea of an apostle is precisely the divine authority.

So reflection is brought to a standstill before the problem whether it is possible that human reflection is capable of understanding a call by revelation, whether one revelation does not imply continuous revelation. But on the other hand, since our age is the age of reflection and the human race may be assumed to be more and more developing in reflection, it seems after all self-evident that, if in such an age a man is called by a revelation, he must have in him an element of reflection more than the man thus called in an earlier age, who belonged to an earlier formation. In earlier times the reflection required of a man that was called signified only reflection within himself, understanding himself in the experience of the extraordinary thing that had happened to him; now it must signify reflection upon his whole relation to the environment, so that at the moment of undertaking his calling he must be able consciously to take account of his responsibility and also to take account of what would befall him as it befell the elect of an earlier time. He who in our age is called by a revelation must unite in his own person the fact of being the greatest maieutic of his age and the fact of being called, the fact of being called and the fact of being devoted (in the Latin sense of the word); in addition to the divine authority granted to him (which is the qualitatively decisive point) he must have an eminent wisdom to survey the circumstances of his life.

Farther human dialectic cannot go than up to the admission that it cannot think this thing, but also up to the admission that from this there follows nothing more than that it cannot be thought. But human dialectic, if it will understand itself and so be humble, never forgets that man's thoughts are not God's thoughts, that all the talk about genius and culture and reflection has nothing to do with the case, but that the divine authority is the decisive thing, that the man God has called, be he fisherman or shoemaker, is an apostle— for nowadays it is perhaps all too easy to understand that Peter was an apostle, but in those days people found it far easier to understand that he was a fisherman.

The divine authority is *the category*, and here quite rightly the sign of it is: *the possibility of offense.* For a genius may very well at one time or another in the course of 50 or 100 years cause *aesthetically* a shock, but never *ethically* can he cause an offense, for the offense is that a man possesses divine authority.

But with respect to this determining factor of being called by a revelation, as indeed with respect to everything Christian, indolence and custom and dullness and thoughtlessness have taken the liberty of loosening the "springs" [i.e. the primal forces]. Now it was an hysterical woman who got a revelation, now it was a sedentary professionist, now it was a professor who became so profound that he almost could say that he had had a revelation, now it was a squinting genius who squinted so deeply that he almost was near to having, and so good as had had, a revelation. This afterwards became pretty much what one understood by being called by a revelation, and so in a sense Paul too had a revelation, only that in addition he had an unusually good head.

No, the divine authority is the category. Here there is little or nothing at all for a *privat-docent* or a licentiate or a paragraph-swallower to do—as little as a young girl needs the barber to remove her beard, and as little as a bald man needs the *friseur* to "accommodate" his hair, just so little is the assistance of these gentlemen needed. The question is quite simple: Will you obey? or will you not obey? Will you bow in faith before his divine authority? Or will you be offended? Or will you perhaps take no side? Beware! this also is offense.

But, as has been said, people have loosened the springs, or have weakened their tension in and through the parenthetical. Exegesis was the first parenthesis. Exegesis was busy about determining how this revelation was to be conceived, whether it was an inward factor, perhaps a sort of *Dichtung und Wahrheit*, etc., etc. Strangely enough, Paul, whom this question concerned most closely, seems not to have spent a single instant in wanting to conceive in this sense; but we others—well, we are not Paul, and so we must do something, for to obey him is not doing anything. Now, as a matter of course, from generation to generation, in every university, in every semester, there is a course about *how*, etc., etc. Yea, that is an excellent means of diversion. In that way we are diverted farther and farther from the task of obeying Paul.

Philosophy, and with that the theology which caricatures philosophy, was the second parenthesis. It said, as becomes a noble, high-born human science, "In no way shall I enter pettily into the question, with which I shall not allow myself to be disturbed, who was the author of a particular book of Scripture, whether he was only a fisherman or a lowly person of some sort. No, away with all pettiness! The content of the doctrine is the main thing, I inquire only about that. As little as an aesthetic critic inquires who was the author of a play but only *how* it is, just as indifferent is it to me who the author was"—just as indifferent also whether it was "the Apostle," a man with divine authority, which precisely is the knot. In this way one can easily be done with Paul without even beginning with him, or beginning with the fact that he possessed divine authority. People treat the Scriptures so scientifically that they might quite as well be anonymous writings.

Behold, from the moment the parenthetical got going there naturally was plenty to do for *privat-docents* and licentiates and paragraph-swallowers and squinters; afterwards, as more and more work was done in this direction, things went more and more backward for the category of being called by a revelation; it became an insignificance, a matter of indifference, with which finally every man could compete; and then it went so entirely out of fashion that in the last resort it became a great rarity to see anybody in the "equipage."

So Magister Adler proclaimed that he had had a revelation, and thus came into collision with the State-Church. Since our age is an age of movement which would bring something new to birth, it must often experience this collision between the universal and the individual, a collision which may always have difficulty enough in itself but sometimes has a difficulty which does not lie in the collision itself but in the colliding parties. In case, for example, the individual in the peculiar sense loves the universal, thinks lowly of himself in comparison with the universal, shudders with fear and trembling at the thought of being in error, then he will make everything as good and easy as possible for the universal. And this conduct is a sign that it might be possible after all that he was a real *extraordinarius*. But in case the individual does not love the universal, does not honor the established order (as one may well do in spite of the fact that he has something new to contribute), in case he is not perhaps in his inward man agreed within himself as to what he is, but only dabbles at being the extraordinary, is only experimenting to see whether it pays well to be that—then will he, partly knowingly (chicanery), make everything as difficult as possible for the established order; partly he does it, without being quite conscious of what he does, because at bottom he cannot do without the established order, and therefore clings to it, seeks to shift the burden of responsibility from himself upon the established order, seeks like a clever advocate to get the public to do what he himself ought to do. When an individual gets the idea that he must separate himself from another man with whom he is living in the closest relationship, in case he himself is certainly and decisively resolved, in this case the painful operation of separation becomes easier. But in case he is uncertain, unresolved, so that he wishes it indeed but has not quite the courage to venture it, in case he is a cunning chap who wishes to shift the responsibility from himself but to steal the reward of the extraordinary—then the separation becomes a tiresome story, and for a long time remains a painful, grievous, vexatious relationship.

Let us suppose that a theological candidate in our time had adopted the notion that the oath of office is unjustifiable. Well then, he can say this freely and openly, if he thinks it expedient. "But by this he will close the road to advancement, and perhaps not accomplish anything, not even arouse a sensation, for a candidate is far too small an entity, and moreover he has no monopoly on the State-Church, since he has no official position." So (now I will think of a selfish man who not only does not love the Establishment but at bottom is an enemy of it) what can he do? He keeps silent for the time being; then he seeks a position as teacher in the State-Church; he gets it; he takes the oath. So now he is an office-bearer in the State-Church. Thereupon he publishes a book wherein he sets forth a revolutionary view. The whole situation is now changed. It would have been easy for the State-Church to bounce a theological candidate, easy to say to him, Very well then, having these views, you cannot become an office-bearer—and the State-Church would not have had to take any action at all with regard to this case, at the very most it would have to take a preventive measure against him quite particularly by not promoting him. But the theological candidate was shrewd and shrewdly understood how to make himself far more important. The responsibility which he as a candidate would have to assume for his peculiar view and would have bought dearly by sacrificing his future in the service of a higher call, while seeking to make the affair as easy as possible for the Establishment—this responsibility is now devolved upon the State-Church, which is required to take positive action to *deprive* of his office a man who by having become an office-bearer has at the same time made an attempt to interest the whole body of office-bearers in his fate. In this way such a revolutionary who is an enemy of the established order (which one need not be to be a reformer, and which a true reformer never is) seeks in cowardly fashion to give the universal as much trouble as he can.

For however conscious the State or the State-Church may be that it is in the truth and has the right on its side, and also that it is sound enough in health to excise such an individual without fearing that many might be harmed by it, yet it never can be expedient for the State-Church to have its first principles too frequently made the subject of discussion. Every living being, every existence, has its hidden life in the root from which the life-force proceeds and produces growth. It is well enough known to physiologists that nothing is more injurious to digestion than constant reflection upon digestion.

And so it is also with relation to the spiritual life the most injurious thing when reflection, as it too often does, goes amiss and instead of being used to advantage brings the concealed labor of the hidden life out into the open and attacks the fundamental principles themselves. In case a marriage were to reflect upon the reality of marriage, it would become *eo ipso* a pretty poor marriage; for the powers that ought to be employed for the realization of the tasks of married life are employed by reflection to eat away the foundation. In case a man who has chosen a definite position in life were to reflect constantly whether this position were the right one, he would become *eo ipso* a sorry partner in business. Therefore, even though the State or the State-Church is sound enough in health to separate from it the revolutionary member, it is nevertheless deleterious that this gives rise to reflection. To everything hidden and concealed applies the saying of the ballad: "Merely one word thou hast uttered." It is easy enough to utter such a fateful word, but it is incalculable what harm may be occasioned by it, and a giant will be needed to stop the injurious effect of one word such as Peer Ruus let out in his sleep. And if the State or the State-Church must often suspend many such individuals, then at last an appearance is conjured up as though the State itself is *in suspenso*. The appearance of being in suspense always results when one does not rest upon the foundation but the foundation itself is made dialectical.

Such a situation may easily become dangerous for the State, principally because this sort of discussion is especially tempting to all insignificant pates, to all gossipy persons, to all empty blown-up bladders, and so more especially to the public. For the more concrete a subject is about which one is to think and express an opinion, the quicker and the more clearly will it be shown whether the speaker has the qualifications to take part in the discussion or not. But the prodigious problems—that really is something . . . for the most insignificant twaddlers! *[4] It is perhaps not beside the point to remind people of this, for our age, the age of movement, tends to bring fundamental assumptions under discussion, so that the consequence is that a marvelous number of men in the mass get on their feet and open their mouths all at once in the game of discussion, along with the public which understands absolutely nothing about it, whereas the prodigious size of the problem advantageously hides the ignorance of the discussers and the speakers respectively. In case a teacher wants to favor a know-nothing of a pupil, he can do it in various ways, but among others he can do it by assigning to him such a prodigious problem that the examiners can infer nothing whatever from the triviality of his reply, because the immense magnitude of the subject deprives them of any standard of judgment. Perhaps I can illuminate this by an example from the world of learning. A learned twaddler who at bottom knows nothing can seldom be got to deal with anything concrete; he does not talk of a particular dialogue of Plato, that is too little for him—also it might become apparent that he had not read it. No, he talks about Plato as a whole, or even perhaps of Greek philosophy as a whole, but especially about the wisdom of the Indians and the Chinese. This Greek philosophy as a whole, the profundity of Oriental philosophy as a whole, is the prodigiously great, the boundless, which advantageously hides his ignorance. So also it is much easier to talk about an alteration in the form of government than to discuss a very little concrete problem like sewing a pair of shoes;[5] and the injustice towards the few capable men lies in the fact that by reason of the prodigious greatness of the

* The prodigious problems from which the most eminent thinkers will shrink beckon to all insignificant pates as the task for them, and so foolish men make use of such opportunity to come forward and take part in the discussion. There even comes about a certain equality, for he who perhaps is eminently equipped by nature and has spent the best years of his life thinking over such matters admits that he dare not decide anything, and the most insignificant chatterer "expresses himself" in about the same way—so both are equally knowing.

problem they are apparently on a par with every Peer, who "also speaks out." So it is much easier for a dunce[6] to criticize our Lord than to judge the handiwork of an apprentice in a shop, yea, than to judge a sulphur match. For if only the problem is concrete, he will, it is to be hoped, soon betray how stupid he is. But our Lord and his governance of the world is something so prodigiously great that in a certain giddy abstract sense the most foolish man takes part in gossiping about it as well as the wisest man,[7] because no one understands it.

Perhaps the sophistical is all too characteristic of our age, for the fact that we bring into discussion the greatest problems in order to encourage men who are the most insignificant and devoid of any thought to take part in the discussion. Let us not forget that noble reformer, that simple wise man of Greece, who had in fact to deal with Sophists, let us not forget that his strength lay in chasing the Sophists out of their roguish game with the abstract and the all-embracing, that his strength lay in making conversation so concrete that everyone who talked with him and who wanted to talk about some prodigious subject (the government of the State in general, about educational theory in general, etc.) before he knew how to put in a word was led to talk about himself—revealing whether he knew something, or didn't know anything.[8]

But, back again to the theological candidate. Perhaps one might say, "But it is hard on a man to require him to shut the door upon his future prospects, so that he has no hope left, which he yet might have had if after he had been inducted he had been deposed—the hope of getting his pension." Yes, certainly it is hard, but it also will be hard to be an *extraordinarius*. Yes, it will be so hard that no one, if he understands it, could wish to be such a one; although he who is that in truth will surely in his relationship with God find comfort and satisfaction and blessedness. For the true *extraordinarius* will not be comforted nor seek relief nor find relief in the public, but only in God; and therein consists the dialectical, which is anguish and crisis but at the same time blessedness.

On the other hand, when an age becomes characterless it is possible that one or another individual may show symptoms of wishing to be an extraordinary; but he has no natural disposition for it, and therefore he wants the public to help him to it, he wants the public, the established order, to join forces with him to let him become an *extraordinarius*. How preposterous! It is precisely the extraordinary who is to introduce the new point of departure, in relation to the established order he is as one whose feet stand outside and will carry the old away—and then it is the established order itself that should be helpful to him! No, the universal precisely must hold him up tight; and if the established order does not do this, then there is developed here again something sophistical like that of the discussion of prodigious problems, so that it becomes the easiest thing in the world to become an *extraordinarius*, something every botcher aspires to, something for all those who otherwise are not capable of anything. There are epigrams enough in our age which the age itself produces without understanding them or heeding them. Let us not forget that nowadays a martyr, a reformer, is a man who smells of perfume, a man who sits at table with garlands in his hair, and perhaps with guests, a man who has all his goods in gilt-edged securities, a man who really never risks anything and yet wins all, even the title of reformer, his glorious title.[9] But when the established order does not hold the reins tight, then finally every man who will not obey becomes a reformer. When the father becomes weak, when the family life is stirred by a rebellious reflection, then the naughty children easily confuse themselves with a sort of reformer. When the schoolmaster loses the reins, then it is very easy for a pert pupil to regard himself as a kind of reformer. In our age therefore it has indeed gone so far that it really requires no courage to defy the King, to vex and disturb the government of the State; but indeed it requires no little courage to say a word to the opposition, even down to the triumphators of the mob, courage . . . to talk *against the reformers.*[10]

So he was a clergyman—and then for the first time occurred the event which might put him in the position of the special individual *extra ordinem.* There is the collision. For it is easy to see that Adler was so situated; and only for the sake of greater clarity shall I indicate very briefly the dialectical relationship between (a) the *universal,* (b) the *individual,* and (c) the *special individual,* that is, the extraordinary. When the individual merely reproduces in his life the established order (of course with variations in accordance with the powers and faculties he possesses and his capacity), then he stands related to the established order as the normal individual, as the regular individual; he displays the life of the universal in his existence; the established order is for him the basis which educationally permeates and develops his faculties in likeness with itself; he is related as the individual whose life is inflected in accordance with the established order as its paradigm. However, let us not forget (for discontented and evil-minded men are ready to spread false rumors) that his life is not for this cause spiritless and insipid. He is not just one of the patter of words in the glossary which follow the paradigm. No, he is free and essentially independent, and to be such a regular individual is as a rule the highest, but also the qualitatively significant, task which therefore is assigned to every man. On the other hand, so soon as the individual lets his reflection grasp so deep that he wants to reflect upon the fundamental presuppositions of the established order—then he is by way of intending to want to be a special individual, and so long as he thus reflects he refuses to follow the *impressa vestigia* of the established order, he is *extra ordinem,* on his own responsibility and at his own risk. And when the individual continues in such a path and goes so far that he no longer is the regular individual *reproductively renewing* in himself *the life of the established order* though willing, under eternal responsibility, to take his place therein, but wills to renew *the life of the established order* by *introducing a new point of departure* for it, *a point of departure which is new in comparison with the fundamental presuppositions of the established order*, then by classifying himself immediately under God he must relate himself to the established order as refashioning it—then he is the *extraordinarius*, that is to say, this place is to be assigned to him whether he has a right to it or no. Here he must conquer and face his judgment—but the universal must decisively exclude him.

It is important here especially, as indeed everywhere it is, that the qualitative dialectic be respected with ethical seriousness. For in an age which lacks character the sophistical situation may arise where one who intends to be an extraordinary wants this intention to be profitable to him in the service of the universal, so that because of this he may become an uncommon figure among ordinary men. Unhappy confusion which has its ground in the thoughtless and frivolous tendency to judge quantitatively! A man must either wish to serve the universal, the established order, expressing this in his life, and in this case his merit will be measured by the faithfulness and punctuality with which he knows how to subordinate himself to the universal, knows how to make his life a beautiful and rich and faithful reproduction of the established order by forming himself to be a type of it—or else he must be seriously the extraordinary, and so, as *extra ordinem*, he must get out of the files, the ranks, where he does not belong. But in our age everything is confused. A discontented office-bearer, for example, wants to be something extraordinary—and at the same time discontented. A sorry, immoral confusion! If he is discontented, if he has something new from God to bring us—then, out of the ranks! "with a halter about his neck";[11] and then let him speak out, for then the situation is such as a true *extraordinarius* needs and must demand in order to be able to gesticulate and start up the music. But if he hasn't anything new from God to bring us, it shall by no means be to his advantage that he is discontented—and at the same time an office-bearer. But the characterlessness and pert indolence of this age comes at last to regard it as a kind of disgraceful narrow-mindedness to be anything out and out: either an office-bearer faithful in body and soul; or a reformer with the sword hanging over his head, in mortal danger, in self-denial.[12]

What makes this difference between the ordinary individual and the special individual is *the starting point*. Apart from this it may well be that an ordinary individual is, humanly speaking, greater than a real *extraordinarius*. The final measure according to which men are ranked is the ethical, in relation to which the differences[13] are infinitesimal; but conversely the worldly mind lets the differences determine the rank. Let us take an example of what here is called the *ordinary individual*, and let us be right glad that we have an example to which we can point, let us mention *honoris causa*, but also to illuminate this situation, the much admired Bishop of Zeeland—and here everyone may well express admiration, for to admire him who expresses the universal is a glad privilege, for from him one can learn. Bishop Mynster does not possess in the very least the marks which characterize what one might call in the strictest sense the special individual. On the contrary, with lofty calm, reposing gladly in his convictions as the abundant content of an abundant life, with the admonishing emphasis, with the sober discretion of seriousness, though not without a noble little turn of expressions directed against confused pates, this man has always acknowledged that it was nothing new he had to bring, that on the contrary it was the old and well known; he never has shaken the pillars of the established order, on the contrary he has himself stood unshaken as a foundation pillar. And when he looks over the first edition of his earliest sermons he "finds nothing essential to change" (as though perhaps since that time he had been so fortunate as to run across one or another freshly arrived systematic novelty); and when the time comes that on his deathbed he reviews all his sermons, not for a new edition but as a testimony, he presumably will find "nothing essential to change." No, it was all the old and well known—which in him nevertheless found a spring so fresh and so refreshing, an expression so noble, so beautiful and so rich that during a long life he profoundly moved many[14] and after his death he will continue to move many. Yea, verily, in case a doctrine once at its very beginning may wish for an apostle who in the strictest, in a paradoxical sense is an *extraordinarius*, standing outside the ranks—ah, but then will the same doctrine in a later time wish for such householders who will have nothing new to bring out of their treasures, who on the contrary seriously find pleasure only in themselves expressing the universal and find pleasure in marching together in the ranks and teaching the rest of us to mark time.[15] But is it not insulting to the right reverend man to sit and write anything like this? In case what has been said here is true, Bishop Mynster is indeed no great man, he has never indeed followed with the times, he does not know indeed what the age requires, still less was he able to invent it. No, he has invented nothing. Whether perhaps he might have been able to do it (he who nevertheless as a sharpsighted psychologist knows human folly thoroughly, and also is in possession of the key to the great storehouse where the requirements of the age are piled up) I shall not venture to decide, but certain it is that he has invented nothing.*

* The translator remarks that S.K. gave no sign that he might wish to suppress this eloquent panegyric or to alter it in any important respect. Evidently he was glad to seize the opportunity of uttering it, and doubtless at the end of his life he was glad he had done so, he "found nothing essential to change." His youthful enthusiasm for his Bishop had long since grown cold, but here he says all he could truthfully say in his praise. But he emphatically excludes the notion that Mynster was what he called a "special individual," and still more that he was, as Martensen called him, "a witness to the truth," which in S.K.'s vocabulary meant a martyr, one who suffered or was ready to suffer for the truth. *That* Bishop Mynster certainly was not. This utterance of Martensen's in his funeral oration ignited the conflagration, that is, prompted S.K. to launch out upon his violent attack upon Mynster and the "established" Christianity which he represented. In the midst of that he died without regretting what he had said in praise of the deceased Bishop.

So the new starting point was the difference between the true ordinary and the true extraordinary individual. They both have in common the essential human measuring rod, the ethical. When, then, the individual is the true *extraordinarius* and really has a new starting point, when he understands his life's pressing difficulty in the *discrimen* between the universal and the individually *extra ordinem*, he must be unconditionally recognized for the fact that he is willing to make *sacrifices*.[16] And for this he must be willing *for his own sake* and *for the sake of the universal*.

Precisely because the *extraordinarius*, if he is that in truth, must by his God-relationship be aware *summa summarum* that κατα δύναμιν he is stronger than the established order, he has nothing at all to do with the concern whether he will now barely be victorious. No, from this concern he is entirely exempted; but on the other hand he has the terrible responsibility of the special individual for every step he takes, whether he now is following his order accurately in the smallest details, whether definitely, alone, and obediently he has heard God's voice—the dreadful responsibility in case he heard or had heard amiss. Precisely for this reason must he wish for himself all possible opposition from without, wish that the established order might have power to make his life a *tentamen rigorosum*, for this trial and its pain is yet nothing compared with the terror of responsibility, if he were or had been in error! In case, for example, a son should feel called to introduce a new view of the domestic life (and as a son is bound by filial piety, so shall or ought every individual be bound by piety towards the universal)—would he not then, if there was truth in him, wish precisely that the father might be the strong one who could encounter him with the full power of parental authority? For the son would not so much fear to get the worst of it, if he was in the wrong, so that humbled but saved he must return to the old ways, as he would shudder at the horror of being victorious if he were in the wrong.

Thus it is with the true *extraordinarius*: he is the most carefree man in comparison with the worldly man's temporal anxiety as to whether what he has to proclaim will be triumphant in the world; on the other hand he is as much in anguish as a poor sinner with a contrite heart whenever he thinks of his responsibility, whether in any way he might be mistaken; yea, for him it is as though his breathing were obstructed, so heavily weighs the weight of his responsibility upon him. Precisely for this reason does he wish for opposition—he the weak man—he the strong one who though a lone man is in his weakness κατα δύναμιν stronger than all the united powers of the established order, which of course has power to scourge him and put him to death as nothing. When the berserker rage came over our northern forebears they let themselves be pressed between shields: so also does the true *extraordinarius* wish that the power of the established order would put up a suitable resistance. In this case Magister Adler, if in truth he were the *extraordinarius*, might honestly be very glad of the fact that as the highest clerical authority in the Danish Church there stands such a man as Bishop Mynster, a man who, without being cruel or narrow-minded, by his own obedience has sternly disciplined himself with the strong emphasis or gravity of seriousness to dare to require of others the universal, a man of whom it may be said with the seriousness of a Cato that he *ad majorum disciplinam institutus non ad huius seculi levitatem*;[17] a man who very well can join in the game if only a true *extraordinarius* is there. In this case too Magister Adler did not need (as in other cases might be necessary) to lend the established order a bit of his power in order that it might be able to put up a suitable opposition to him. But in any event[18] the cause of the *extraordinarius* owes much to the firmness of such a man. A weaker man in that official position, a man who himself had some symptoms of wanting to be something of an *extraordinarius*—then perhaps Adler might not have been deposed, the situation not consistently and efficiently regulated,[19] thus the whole affair would have become a meaningless and "remarkable something." A confused *extraordinarius* introducing the new, and a weak-kneed man of government, are to be sure a perfect match for one another, but only as Punch and Judy are.[20] And perhaps the time may soon come to exhibit such a relationship. For if our age lacks the true *extraordinarius*, it lacks also those serious figures, those individuals disciplined in the highest sense, who precisely by self-discipline know how to hold others in check, and hence to educate genuine extraordinary figures; for it is not loose concepts, and it is not indefinite and shifting relationships which create the true *extraordinarius*, they only coddle and spoil him. And possibly our age does not really need the true *extraordinarius*, but on the contrary those upright men who with God-fearing resignation conceive it as their task not to invent something new but with life and soul to be faithful to the established truth. But whether or no our age needs extraordinary figures, one thing is sure, that the extraordinary one is recognizable by the fact that he is willing to make sacrifices.

In our age the man of movement (the spurious *extraordinarius*) understands and takes the matter in hand differently. Perhaps it is after a thoroughly reasonable finite reflection upon the situation, the aim, etc., that a man reaches the *result* that he has a new proposal to make. From now on he is through with the inward direction of the mind in self-searching and with responsibility before God—he has indeed already a result. He now takes up a position opposed to the established order, and the *telos* of his effort is that this proposal, this plan of his, must triumph. It is certain and sure that his plan is the true one. The problem and the labor is only to insure that it may be brought to victory.

One sees plainly that the situation of the true *extraordinarius* is the converse of this. He is concerned only about his instructions and his relationship to God, occupied alone with his subterranean labor in the mine to dig up the treasure, or to hear God's voice; he jokes lightheartedly about the question of being victorious in the world, for he knows well enough that, if only all is as it should be in his relationship with God, his idea will surely triumph, even though he fall. The true *extraordinarius* in this relationship with God is conscious of his heterogeneity with the temporal, and therefore in this *spatium* of heterogeneity he has room in which he can move in venturing for his cause, venturing life and blood. The man of movement has no eternal conviction, therefore in an eternal sense he can never be sure, neither is he busy alone about gaining the assurance: precisely for this reason he has no room and no time to venture anything especial. His cause is altogether *homogeneous* with the temporal, therefore not only is the *telos* of his effort that he shall triumph, but *the fact that he triumphs* shall at bottom convince the man of movement that *he was in the right*, that his proposal was true. The same men who constitute the established order he not only will need again but he *has need of them*, if only they will don a new uniform in correspondence with his plan.[21] One easily sees how the dialectic of his effort must shape itself: he would upset the established order, and does not dare to give it a shove for fear of falling himself, for this would not only be a fatal circumstance, but at the same time, according to his own conceptions, be proof that he was in the wrong. Everything depends, as has been said, upon victory, not only because his plan will then be true, but also that his plan by being victorious may become true. He has no certainty, but acquires it only when he has triumphed; whereas the true *extraordinarius* possesses the heterogeneous certainty, the certainty of eternity, whether he falls or no.

To wish to move people in that way is essentially as if one were to offer to perform a trick—"if it succeeds"—and now for the sake of completeness would have his name included on the placard. He who would move anything must himself stand firm, but the man of movement has nothing firm about him, he is firm only when he is taken into custody [*blevet fast*]—i.e. afterwards. He might therefore wish that the established order were weak and decrepit, in order that he might the more easily conquer. If such is not the case, then he must resort to every expedient to conquer, to cunning and wiliness, to handshaking, to conciliation, exclaiming as his trump card "the devil take me," or a concessive "beg your pardon," the reformer's behavior must be like his who seeks a position and runs errands all over the town, or like a huckster selling his vegetables on a busy Thursday he must stop and chaffer about the very plan itself, get it cluttered up by the help of committees, and above all there must be sent out a message to the public, with an exceedingly obliging and flattering invitation that a highly revered and cultured public will do the huckster—but what am I saying?—I mean the reformer, the honor of standing as godfather to the baby . . . and so at last this bungling triumphs.* Such a man of move-

* In these times one is busy solely and only about being victorious, one seems to live in the vain conceit that if only one can manage barely to conquer, it makes no difference about the means—as if the means were of no importance, whereas when there is any question of the situation in the world of spirit they are the determinant factor, or, more precisely expressed, the means and the victory are one and the same. Of course, in relation to money, titles, horses and carriages, torchlight processions and hurrah boys, and other such like indecencies, it is true that the means are of no account, that the means of acquisition are not the same as possession. So one can *really* come into possession of money— in many shabby ways; one can *really* get a torchlight procession in one's honor and have attained it in many shabby ways. But in relation to spirit there are no such outward, palpable, indecent realities. The profound and elegant thing in relation to spirit is the fact that the *mode of acquisition* and *the possession* are one. Hence he who is not aware of this fact in the spiritual sphere, but is blissful in the vain conceit of being victorious, in spite of the fact that the means were thoroughly paltry, does not notice with what elegance the profundity of the spirit makes sport of him for the fact that he has not really conquered but has written a satire upon himself. Let us refer to the most dread and highest example: in case Jesus Christ did not conquer by being crucified, but had conquered in the modern style by business methods and a dreadful use of his talking gear, so that none of the balloters could refuse him their vote, with a cunning that could make people believe anything—in case Christ had come in that way and was regarded as the Son of God, then he didn't come into the world

ment is unable—unable even to venture—to stand alone as an individual and thereby find room to venture life and all; on the contrary he has need of the majority to be certified if it is true, if what he wants is any good. He wishes to move others, and at bottom he wants the others to hold on to him in order that he may stand firm. But then indeed there is no movement, for he stands firm only when the case is decided and the majority has won. So long as this is not decided (and this in fact is the period in which the movement should go on) he does not stand firm.

When one has the view of existence characteristic of the man of movement it can easily be seen that the reflection must develop to the point where it is regarded as ludicrous madness or stupidity that one should *risk* himself; and it may be reasonably conceded that from this point of view it does look so. But in requital the man of movement betakes himself, comically enough, to another point of view; the man of movement who does not stand firm at the moment when he ought to (i.e. so long as the cause is in the minority) but first stands firm when he doesn't need to; the man of movement who, strangely enough, thinks that the whole thing is due to him. All movement presupposes (as anybody will be convinced who thinks the dialetic of this situation) a point, a firm point outside. And so the true *extraordinarius* is the point outside, he stands upon the Archimedean point outside the world—a firm point *extra ordinem—et terram movebit.*

---

at all, and Christ would not have been the Son of God. What would have triumphed would have been, not Christianity, but a parody of Christianity. To shrewd folks this may well seem a confounded *nota bene* that the spirit is not like money, that the scurvy fellow may shamelessly pride himself that he *really* came into possession of money ("the unrighteous mammon"), really was victorious; but for every optimate it is an indescribably blessed comfort that there is after all one place where eternal *righteousness* prevails. In relation to spirit nothing can conquer in an accidental and outward way, but only in the essential way; but the essential way is neither more nor less than the reduplication of victory, since in the spiritual world the form is the reduplication of the content.

But he also has room to move when it comes to life and death and scourging and other such like, which surely are of no help if one resolves to enter the majority, and could not conceivably happen to one who is in the majority. Whether the true *extraordinarius* prevails today or tomorrow or in a thousand years is a matter of no concern, for he *has conquered*, his relationship to God is his victory; yea, though what he has to proclaim were never to prevail in the world, to this he might reply, "All the worse for the world."

Behold, this attitude is the attitude of movement; but the "man of movement" has nothing eternal, and therefore nothing firm, so as a consequence thereof he has not the courage to become the *recognizable* individual who wills something and will take risks for it. Essentially he does not act at all, in the outcry he makes a feigned sally, his activity culminates in shouting out something. As when children are at play and one of them suddenly shouts, "Why not play this game?" the man of movement shouts, "Why not do this now?" Thereupon when they have become many, when the majority is on their side and the cause is forced through—then the man of movement is for the first time really recognizable, for he goes about with New Year's congratulations and says, "It was really I who stood at the head of the Movement and the New Direction." Sometimes it comes to pass that men behold with wonder several men going about with congratulations, each one of them saying, "It was really I who stood at the head of the Movement, etc." So it appears that there was not merely one but several men at the head. This comical confusion contains a deep truth, namely, that no one at all stood at the head, and therefore the one is as much justified as the other in going about with congratulations. A true *extraordinarius* who stood alone, forsaken, pointed out in the pillory of the special individual, a true *extraordinarius* who was recognizable by the fact that he was executed—well, it is a matter of course that after this he cannot very well go about with congratulations—but neither can he be mistaken for another.

The man of movement might perhaps better be called a stirring-stick (muddler). Indeed this is the essential distinction between moving and stirring, that movement is in a forward direction, stirring is movement up and down or round about, like the rod in the butter-churn, like the foot of him who treads the peat, like rumor and gossip, like the stick in the hand of the kitchen-maid when she stirs in the muddling pot. Hence it is only an illusion when these men of movement scoff at the capable men, the unshakable, who do in truth stand still—meaning that they themselves are not standing still; for stirring is not movement, there is no muddling in a running river, but in still standing water, and neither is there in that when it lies still and deep.[22] If what is said here is read by one or another, to some it will perhaps seem a horrible and inhuman demand upon the *extraordinarius*. Well, possibly; I can do nothing for it, that a modern age by becoming entirely earthly and worldly succeeds in forgetting what paganism understood.

In the dreadful responsibility which the true *extraordinarius* has to face (for he does not possess the result once for all, he has not become God's plenipotentiary once and for all)* is included also the concern lest his example when he assumes a position *extra ordinem* may beguile other men who are weak, light-minded, unsteadfast, inquisitive, to wish also to try their hand at something similar, so that his example may become a snare, a temptation for them. For with regard to the concern which torments busybodies and gadabouts to win several apes and several adherents who agree with him, to get a society founded which has his own seal—this concern the true *extraordinarius* does not know, in this respect he is

---

* This is also nonsense. A king may well nominate a highly trusted minister once for all, in consideration of the fact that the minister is perhaps a considerably shrewder pate than the king, but God does not find himself in such a position.

entirely lighthearted and jocose.[23] But the dreadful thought that he might damage another man, that he might occasion any other man to try his hand light-mindedly at what involves the heaviest responsibility of the individual—this dreadful danger he conceives profoundly. In an age of movement like ours, where symptoms of wishing to be a bit extraordinary are an epidemic disease, one must especially, with fear and trembling, be mindful of his dreadful responsibility. He will therefore here again make his position as deterrent as possible for others, as little alluring and tempting as possible. If only the light-minded see that a dose of seriousness is included in holding out for something, they soon fall away, yea, they even transform themselves into opposition to the *extraordinarius*. Light-mindedness would fain accept the *extraordinarius* as a playmate; when it observes that this is not feasible it unites against him all its childish wrath. But every *extraordinarius* owes it unconditionally to the established order that by one or another deeply considered step he first contrive if possible to make his extraordinary call seem repugnant, so that his example may not do harm, become a snare. A true *extraordinarius* in our age (since reflection and intelligence are so prodigiously developed) must be thoroughly acquainted with all possible known forms of dangers and difficulties. That a man in our age might receive a revelation cannot be absolutely denied, but the whole phenomenal demeanor of such an elect individual will be essentially different from that of all earlier examples who never encountered anything of the sort.

The true *extraordinarius* must have the presuppositions of his age constantly at his service, in a highly eminent degree he must have at his disposition that which is the conspicuous mark of our age: reflection and intelligence. The essential phenomenal difference between a man in our age to whom a revelation has been imparted, and a man in a previous age, is that the former undertakes this extraordinary task with a discretion developed to a high degree. Ours is a reflective age— it is unthinkable that the divine governance has not itself

taken note of this fact.[24] Now though a revelation is a paradoxical immediacy, yet if it should happen to anyone in our
age, it must also be recognizable in him by the serviceable
reflection with which he accepts it. His reflection must not over-
whelm the extraordinary man, but he must have reflection to
introduce it into the age.

Now it is indeed true that the affair of Adler had a highly
unfortunate outcome, so that his example was thoroughly
deterrent; but this is no credit to him, for in this respect he has
done nothing to help the universal, and presumably he had
not expected that the outcome would be so unfortunate, having even made arrangements to have the second edition come
out promptly. Supposing now that he had come off brilliantly
with getting himself a revelation, suppose this had been what
the age demands, suppose it had been a success; and then
suppose that owing to Magister Adler's example the universal
was encumbered with a small voluntary battalion of hysterical
women, of students and virtuosi who wouldn't take their
professional examinations, *item* of certain droll crotcheteers
who sit and spin out whimsical notions in a parsonage[25]—who
all had sought to renew their credit by getting themselves a
revelation.

Now, purely dialectically with the help of imagination, I
shall essay a little sketch which may show if possible what
Magister Adler might have done, or I shall lift him altogether
into the sphere of reflection. If he had been the true *extraordinarius*, then what he would have found it necessary to do
was of course far more profound than a lowly serviceable
critic can imagine. It would have been something more profound, and properly speaking profundity is the deep *existential* realization of an idea which corresponds directly with
God. Nowadays it is thought splendid when anyone is so
fortunate as to get a fancy, to make a profound remark, to put
together in writing *horis sucecivis* something profound which
every other hour he disavows existentially. No, just as per-
severance (in contrast with the flashy deception of the mo-

ment) is the true virtue, so profundity also is not exhibited in an utterance, a statement, but in a mode of existence. Profundity is the pictorial and metaphorical expression which indicates how many feet a man existentially draws, in the same sense in which this is said of a ship. But a ship is said to draw so and so many feet of water, not in the sense in which feet are measured by the lead which is cast anywhere for a moment, but it is the decisive description of the ship's whole and daily existence, that it draws so and so much depth of water. Or to describe this in another way: the greater extent the telescope can be extended, the better it is, and so also, the greater extension a man has when he reaches the secrecy of his inmost life, just so many more feet does he draw in depth.[26] Depth of mind is therefore the opposite of external-ity. A man who lives only externally has naturally a tendency to anticipate his future with great words, vows, etc.: the pro-found man is precisely the opposite, concealing the principal machinery by which he moves. He looks perhaps in daily use as if he were moving with one horsepower, and really the machinery is working at the highest power.*

In order to illustrate the whole situation, allow me to give an example, purely imaginary, and constructed with poetic license. For this I choose a genius raised to the power of reflection. But at the same time I shall make the situation as difficult as possible. He is a genius, but he did not know this from the beginning. Such a thing can very well be thought, and moreover it marks the difference between an immediate genius and a genius in reflection, for the latter needs a shock in order to become what was latent in him. So he has lived on without understanding himself, he has trained himself for the service of the state, he a clergyman.

Only now comes about the event which gives him the shock. At that very moment he understands himself as ex-traordinary, which, however, he views at the same time as his

* The following 5 paragraphs are taken from *Papirer* VIII B 12, pp. 55f., omitting 4 footnotes (VII B 252, 2-4, 9).

misery because henceforth he cannot take refuge in the universal. But, above all, with his eminent reflection he surveys the whole responsibility of his position.

Here then is his *discrimen*: either to take in vain his extraordinariness, regarding it as a glittering distinction, and so occasion irreparable confusion; or else, first and foremost, before he thinks of communicating the new view which has come into his mind, he sacrifices himself, and thus reconciles himself with the universal.

That he himself is willing to resign his office is the least part of this sacrifice, such an act of honesty will not satisfy him nor relieve his ethical anxiety.

Let us now begin. So it is assumed that something has happened to him which was extraordinary or by which he became extraordinary. From this moment his life has been sequestrated by a higher power. The question now is about the inwardness of the reflection with which he undertakes his task. Reflection is the mediator, the help of which he must use first and foremost to render himself harmless.

Dialectically he will at once perceive that the extraordinary has the dangerous *discrimen* that what he is in truth may for the others become the greatest ruin. He will therefore at the same moment shut himself up in impenetrable silence, shut himself up against every other, lest any undiatetic imprudence should corrupt the whole thing into gossip, but that the extraordinary may have time to settle on the leas in the pause of silence. "One does not sew a new piece of cloth in an old garment, nor put new wine into old wine-skins, lest the rent become worse and the wine-skins burst"—and so it will come about when the absolutely new point of departure is by over-hasty bustle bunglingly joined with the old, so that it only does harm. At the same moment reflection will also teach him silence,[27] the silence in which he dedicates himself, as a mother consecrates herself to exist only for the sake of the child, the silence which prevents any communication with any other, in order not to communicate anything wrong or in a wrong way.

But, after all, this extraordinary thing must be communicated. Silence must not mean the abortion of truth. But no impatience! There is a neurasthenic trembling which because of shaking cannot hold anything nor pass anything on. Let us not be deceived by it. Everyone who knows what it is to be truly resolute, knows very well that one can hold out and hold fast to a resolution. A man may be so situated in life that he quietly said to himself before God, "The path I am following must lead me to the stake," and in spite of that he goes forward step by step. But impatience says, "The sooner the better"; and the neurasthenic impatience says, almost at the border of despair, "If only it does not pass away again, if only the impulse in me does not disappear, so that to me might be applied the dreadful words, 'The children are come to birth, and there is not strength to bring forth'" (Isaiah 37:3). But after all it is dreadful to be in travail and bring forth wind.[28] In case one with a sacred resolution has resolved to sacrifice his life, and with neurasthenic impatience goes ahead and throws his life away and is executed "the sooner the better," has he gained anything, or has he really kept his resolution? The thing is that reflection and time be not allowed to shake his resolution. But on the other hand there is a remedy different from the foolish one of letting it occur at once, today; and this remedy is faith, humility, daily consecration.[29]*

So the extraordinary must be communicated, it must be introduced into the context of the established order; and the

---

* The necessary slowness is also a cross which the elect man has to bear with faith and humility. Let us mention the highest instance, from which we believers ought to learn. When the angel had announced to Mary that by the Spirit she should give birth to a child—no, this whole thing was a miracle, why then did this child need nine months like other children? O what a test for faith and humility! That this is the divine will, to need the slowness of time! Behold, this was the cross. But Mary was the humble believer; by faith and humility she came to herself, although everything was miraculous. She remained the same quiet, humble woman—she believed.

elect, the special individual, must receive the shock, the dreadful shock, by becoming the special individual, and therewith must pass the shock on. Dialectically we have here a duplex situation: that the shock be really a shock in the qualitatively dialectical sense; and on the other hand that the established order be spared as far as possible. As God is not a God of confusion, the elect is not called to make a confusion—and then run away from it. He must love the established order and therefore be willing to sacrifice himself. As one with the utmost caution deals with nitrate of silver [hellstone was the abhorrent name for it] (not in order to make no use of it but to use it rightly), as one wraps it up in something so that no one may come in direct contact with it, so must he take care to consecrate himself as a special individual in order that no one by a direct relationship to him may be harmed. The man who is called is at the same time the man who is "devoted." For what in him, the true *extraordinarius*, is eternal truth, a divine gift of grace, in every other man, who stands only in a direct relation to the *extraordinarius*, it is coquetry, untruth, perdition.

When we go farther along this path there must lie here at this point the profound task which has been spoken of, that the man who is called must first make himself almost repulsive. For the extraordinary character of the gift of grace is in one respect like hellstone, in spite of the fact that in another respect it is the blessing of heaven. The special individual is not in a direct sense the *extraordinarius*, he becomes such only when there intervenes the thought that he is paradoxical; and this dialectical situation may be expressed by the fact that the special individual first makes himself repulsive, so that no one could wish to be like him or to be as he is. In this pain consists, among other things, the sacrifice of himself and the atonement he makes with the established order out of love towards it.[30] The fact that inquisitive men and fools and windbags prefer something different in order to have something to run after and to imitate, that confused extraordinary men who abhor discipline and constraint would rather break loose with others as *fratres et sorores liberi spiritus*—the fact that they disdain restraint has nothing whatever to do with the case. A truly competent spokesman for the established order will judge differently. He will not deny the possibility that there may be something new to contribute, but neither will he deny that the aforementioned precaution is pretty nearly the greatest possible.*

But, now, how make oneself repulsive? Let us first recapitulate. The elect man has had a revelation, that stands fast; he has shut himself up within himself with this fact; not one word has betrayed anything, not a gesture, and neither is his silence obvious, for then he would betray something; no, he is entirely like other men, talks like other men about what is happening—hence no one can see that he keeps silent. For one may keep silent in two ways: one may keep absolutely silent, but this silence is suspicious; or he may talk of every possible subject, thus it can occur to no one that he is keeping silent. And yet the extraordinary has come to pass, and there lives a man who with a life consecrated by a holy resolution is laboring in perfect silence. If God has graciously granted him his confidence (though he knows very well how hard it must be for God to have dealings with a lowly man, even though this lowly man is exerting himself with might and main), he will at least not insult God by treating his confidence as an idle tale and as town gossip, as something that must be bawled out. For these must be no impatience! But there is a neurasthenic cry, "Confess, confess!" The neurasthenic impatience may have its ground in the fact that the individual lacks the power to bear, that he is like a broken jar,

---

* The translator remarks that anyone who knows S.K. must recognize that this long passage about the right behavior for the true *extraordinarius* represents the author's profound reflection upon the role he was preparing to play as "the special individual" (without revelations and "without authority") in opposition to "the established order." He did not need to "step out of the ranks," for in many entries in the Journal he congratulated himself that he had not become a priest.

or that the individual has been frightened by a despairing dread, or has a sort of compulsion to penitence which would make up for lost time by instant confession and would in self-mortification expose himself to all possible ridicule. For there are religiously awakened individuals so confused in their heads that they maltreat other men by getting them to ridicule them, which is in intention just as tyrannous as when a tyrant maltreats men as slaves.

So how then is he to make himself repulsive?[31] The *extra-ordinarius*, if he is the true one, must of course know in an eminent degree what I who am a lowly serviceable critic am not so badly informed of, namely, how thoroughly under-mined our age is in a religious respect, while busy men hold general conventions about unimportant matters, and while the thunder of cannon call people together for amusement.* Since this is so, it must not be difficult to find in the demonic sphere the disreputable garment which might make him repulsive. And let us remember well the foregoing postulate: there is as yet in the whole world no man who knows any more what happened to the *extraordinarius* than does the pen I hold in my hand or the inkstand into which I dip it but without drawing my thoughts from it.

Adler might perfectly well have resigned his office, have said that the whole thing of being a priest was a fleeting fancy, something he wanted to try out, and he might have seen to it that this was accepted as the authentic interpretation.[32] All this while the compass by which he steers must of course be unalterable, not varying a line with respect to his inward direction, but by holy consecration he must be renewed day by day in the same resolution.[33] Of course when one suffers from neurasthenic impotence it is easier to let it out the sooner the better.

Thereupon Adler (for his absolute silence up to this moment gave him up to this moment absolute control of the

---

*S.K. dwelt at this time near the great amusement park called Tivoli and could not but hear the goings-on—especially the cannon.

situation) might perhaps have furnished a poetical account wherein he would have described a demon who knew the lack of religiousness and of Christianity in our age, who was sent by the devil to show what Christianity was and to scorn it, he who in his heart was not merely a pagan but a Mephistopheles.[34] He became a priest and attained the triumph of scorn over men. Thereupon he resigned his office. All the better sort in the established order would be disgusted with such a repulsive thing, and it is precisely the better sort that should be protected against harm. Were it some bandit who found this situation glorious—well, a bandit is lost anyhow.

Naturally this method is slow. It is easier to bawl it out at once.* On the other hand, it is so dreadful to work thus silently, and in a certain sense to work against oneself. Suppose one were to die in the meantime, and there was no one who knew a word about it. It is harrowing when Hamlet at the moment of death is almost in despair that the hidden life he had led with prodigious exertion in the service of the idea should be understood by no one, yea, that no one would know anything of it; but if Hamlet had become softened at death, he also would have talked in his lifetime, that is, let the whole thing go. There is a remedy for neurasthenic

---

* It is true enough that in his later books Adler has gone over to the principle of silence, but without letting this quantitatively essential change make a decisive impression. Thereto add the fact that it comes rather late. God knows what he has to be silent about after having bawled out the highest thing he had, or rather more than he had, as he did from the beginning. There is something strangely feminine about Magister Adler. One can almost always count upon it that a girl when she is led into a great decision and at the decisive moment does the mad thing, then afterwards when she has changed and come at last into the right course, she will persuade herself that she has done that from the beginning. In general Magister Adler may be regarded as a good example of loquacity in a dialectical sense, which is so common in our age. One dabbles in one thing after another, gives up one system of philosophy and, as it is said, "goes farther," but at no point comes to a serious indication why one gave up the old and why one accepted the new, it never comes to a serious accounting with regard to the responsibility for thus changing oneself.

debility: it is faith, humility. The God who every day has been invoked with holy consecration, he indeed knows—and so all is well. For the result no one is responsible.[35]

[36]So if Adler had made himself repulsive in this way and thereby assured himself that none of the better sort might be tempted by his example—yea, then could he, humbly before God, have beaten his breast and said, "Now the first thing has been done, the sacrifice has been offered to the universal[37]—now I can begin. Humanly speaking, I am weakened, I cannot become anything great in the eyes of men, now I can serve God."

Now let us recapitulate and see what Adler has done, and as a motto recall the words of Paul, "Let all things be done unto edification," whether one speaks in tongues or prophesies. These words contain an exhortation to reflection and ethical responsibility, that no one should think tumultuously that it is a man's task, not to speak of the elect, to be like the darling of the fairy queen.

Did Adler resign his office, to satisfy in that way the established order? No, he remained in office and made out as if nothing had happened, until the State-Church took several steps—and then he tried to remain in office, though no one can blame him for all the chicanery which is usual in such circumstances. Has he done anything to hinder, if possible to remedy, all the unfortunate consequences his example has had for the established order? No, nothing whatsoever. Without having understood himself, without, as it seems, having given the least thought to the difficult problems he set in motion by his assertion of a revelation, he incontinently burst in upon the established order with his alarming fact. It is the business of the special individual to know everything down to the minutest details that stand related to his difficult position; instead he has left it to the established order to interpret all these difficulties. Perhaps he was like that toll-clerk who wrote so that nobody could read, and considered it his business to write and the business of the tariff commission to read—so he thought it was his business to cast a firebrand into the established order, and its business to take care of the consequences. In a vacillating age when unfortunately the growing generation almost from childhood is initiated into all sorts of doubts, in a vacillating age when the few competent men find it hard enough to hold out and to defend the pathos of the holy and the venerable—in such an age to break out impetuously with an immaturity which stands in the closest and most fatal relation to the highest interests . . . is, to put it in the mildest terms, the height of irresponsibility. That fortunately one can say of Adler that up to date he has done no special harm, is certainly no merit of his; it is due to the fact that he has been entirely ignored. And yet for all this he has done harm, for religiousness in our age is by no means so great and serious a thing that it is desirable for ridicule and lightmindedness to get hold of such a prize as Adler.

The so-called fact of revelation itself as a phenomenon coordinated with the whole modern development.

THE very thing which seems to give to Christendom and to its learned or eloquent defenders such extraordinary success, this very thing it is which in many ways holds back and hinders individuals from making a qualitative and essential decision, this very thing it is which in the end must play into the hands of the free-thinkers, this very thing is the so-much-talked-about eighteen hundred years, whether by them the question is removed to such a prodigious distance that the impression of decision or the decisive impression vanishes in the twilight of imagination, or whether we have the paralogistic argument of the eighteen hundred years to the truth of Christianity, by which glittering and triumphant proof the trust of Christianity is unfortunately undermined, since in that case it is true only as an hypothesis, is by this triumphant argumentation transformed from eternal truth into an hypothesis. How could it ever occur to an eternal truth to sink to the point of proving its truth by the fact that it has endured for so and so many years, sink to a paltry comradeship with lies and deceits—which also have endured for many centuries and do still endure; an eternal truth which from first to last is equally true, in its last instant not more true than in its first, so that it did not come into the world shamefaced and embarrassed because it had not yet the centuries to which it could appeal, then was not foolishly puffed up for having endured for so long a time. True, an hypothesis which was embarrassed at the beginning becomes pompous with the years, but in requital it may any instant be discarded.[1] This paradoxical fact (the offence of the understanding, the object of faith) does not become more true after eighteen hundred years than it was the day it happened. The fact that the eternal once came into existence in time is not a something which has to be tested in time, not something which *men are to test*, but is the paradox by which *men are to be tested*; and the eternal proudly despises every pert and impudent argumentation from the many years. And the paradox itself did not last throughout many years: it existed when Christ lived, and since then it has existed only whenever someone was offended and someone did in truth believe. If the paradoxical had existed for a thousand years or only for half an hour makes no difference; it becomes not more probable because it existed a thousand years, nor less probable because it only lasted half an hour.

If the thing of being or becoming a Christian is to have its decisive qualitative realty, it is necessary above all to get rid of the whole delusion of after-history, so that he who in the year 1846 becomes a Christian becomes that by being contemporaneous with the coming of Christianity into the world, in the same sense as those who were contemporaneous before the eighteen hundred years.* To this end it is important above all that there be fixed an unshakable qualitative difference between *the historical element in Christianity* (the paradox that the eternal came into existence once in time) and *the history of Christianity*, the history of its followers, etc. The fact that God came into existence in human form under the Emperor Augustus: that is the historical element in

* About all the dialectical problems which belong here (the paradox, the instant, the dialectic of contemporaneousness, etc.) I must refer to a pseudonym, Johannes Climacus, and his two works: *Philosophical Fragments* [pp. 78-93] and *The Concluding Postscript to the Philosophical Fragments* [pp. 45-47]. With regard to what is so dialectically composed one cannot in a few lines give a résumé; a reference, if it is to be reliable, must be just as elaborate and just as difficult as the original production, for if there be left out one single little subordinate definition, the whole dialectical construction suffers. Whether such is the case, as it is said to be, in the organic realm, that when one member suffers the whole suffers, I do not know; but in the dialectical construction the case is precisely this.

Christianity, the historical in a paradoxical composition. It is with this paradox that everyone, in whatever country he may be living, must become contemporary, if he is to become a believing Christian. With the history of Christianity he has in this respect nothing whatever to do. But the baleful fact in our age is, among others, that it is almost impossible to find a man who has time and patience and seriousness and the passion of thought to be well brought up to respect the qualitative dialectic.

When the requirement of becoming contemporary with the coming of Christianity into the world in the same sense in which the contemporaries were is rightly understood, then it is *a truly religious requirement* and *precisely in the interest of Christianity*. However, the same requirement may be made by *the enemies*, by persons *offended* at Christianity, with the intent of *doing harm*. It is strange that, so far as I know, this has not been done, since after all in our times attacks upon Christianity have ventured the utmost with renewed power and not without talent.

But instead of insisting upon this concept of contemporaneousness, orthodoxy has taken another path—by the help of the eighteen hundred years. If one were to describe the whole orthodox apologetic effort in one single sentence, but also with categorical precision, one might say that it has the intent to make *Christianity plausible*. To this one might add that, if this were to succeed, then would this effort have the ironical fate that precisely upon the day of its triumph it would have lost everything and entirely quashed Christianity. It is well therefore that the apologists who know not what they do, troubled as they are with bustling, have not quite succeeded, it is well that they see a book written against them which shall etc. To make Christianity plausible is the same as to misinterpret it. And after all, what is it the free-thinkers want? Why, they want to make Christianity plausible. For they know very well that if they can get Christianity's qualitative over-intensity fooled into the bustling busyness of plausibility—it's all over with Christianity. But the orthodox-apologetic effort also wants to make Christianity plausible, so it works hand in hand with heterodoxy. And yet it has worked thus in all simplicity, and its whole tactic, along with the relationship between orthodoxy and heterodoxy, may be regarded as an amazing example of what lack of character and lack of a qualitative dialectic may lead to: that one attacks what the other defends, that orthodoxy and heterodoxy continue to be enemies who would extirpate one another, in spite of the fact that they want one and the same thing—to make Christianity plausible.

Every defense of Christianity which understands what it would accomplish must behave exactly conversely, maintaining with might and main by qualitative dialectic that Christianity is *implausible*.[2] For I should like to ask where a trace can be found of the qualitatively altered method. Under various names, right down to the last name, Speculation, people have labored to make Christianity plausible, conceivable, to get it out of the God-given language of paradox and translated into the Platdeutch of Speculation or Enlightenment. And yet, in order to have something to despair of, they have despaired whether it would succeed (what irony!) or they have rejoiced that it has succeeded and let Christianity receive congratulations on this occasion (what irony!). The man who journeyed from Jerusalem to Jericho and fell among thieves was not so badly off as Christianity; for the orthodox apologetic which had compassion upon it and took care of it treated it quite as badly as the thieves.

The Christian fact has no history, for it is the paradox that God once came into existence in time. This is the offense, but also it is the point of departure; and whether this was eighteen hundred years ago or yesterday, one can just as well be contemporary with it. Like the polar star this paradox never changes its position and therefore has no history, so this paradox stands immovable and unchanged; and though Christianity were to last for another ten thousand years, one would get no farther from this paradox than the contemporaries were. For the distance is not to be measured by the quantitative scale of time and space, for it is qualitatively decisive by the fact that it is a paradox.[3]

On the other hand, so soon as one confuses Christianity with the Christian fact, so soon as one begins to count the years, one begins to change the implausible into the plausible. And one says, Now that Christianity has lasted (the Christian fact indeed occurred eighteen hundred years ago) for three hundred, now for seven hundred, now for eighteen hundred years—so it certainly must be true. By such a procedure one accomplishes the feat of confusing everything. The decision (that of becoming a Christian) easily becomes for the individual a mere trifle, already it seems to him easy enough to follow the use and wont of the town in which he lives, because the majority do so, it might well seem to him a matter of course to join in being a Christian—when Christianity has lasted eighteen hundred years! On the other hand the Christian fact is weakened, made a mere trifle by the help of the distance, by the help of the eighteen hundred years. That which if it happened contemporaneously either would be an offense to him which he would hate and persecute and try if possible to eradicate, or would appropriate by faith; that now one regards as something one can accept in a way and believe (i.e. regard it with indifference) since it was eighteen hundred years ago.[4]

So now throughout a long course of years a disoriented orthodoxy which knew not what it did, and a revolutionary heterodoxy which knows demoniacally what it does, and only to that extent does not know what it does, have united with the help of the eighteen hundred years to confuse everything, to be guilty of delusions each one madder than the other, of paralogisms each one worse than the other, of μετάβασις εἰς ἄλλο γένος each time more confusing than the other—so that the principal concern now is to be able to clear the ground, get rid of the eighteen hundred years, so that the

Christian fact takes place now, as if it happened today. That which has blown up the attack upon Christianity and the defense of it to the size of folios are the eighteen hundred years. That which has stupefied the defenders and helped the attackers are the sixteen, the seventeen, and the eighteen hundred years. That which has held the lives of countless multitudes in a vain conceit are the eighteen hundred years. By the help of the eighteen hundred years the defenders, going backwards, have made Christianity into an hypothesis, and the attackers have made it into nothing.

What Johannes Climacus, by no means the least busy person, has done to scent out every delusion, to detect every paralogism, to apprehend every deceitful turn of phrase, cannot be repeated here.[5] It has been so done by him that every man of culture, if he has a certain amount of learning and will seriously spend a little time to initiate himself into dialectics, will easily understand it. Otherwise, indeed, it was not done, nor could it have been done in any other wise. Such a thing cannot be propounded in a newspaper and read by a man who "is having his beard taken off."[6] Climacus' presentation is fatiguing, as the case required. His merit is to have "drawn" (as it said of a telescope) the unshakable Christian fact so near to the eye that the reader is prevented from looking askant at the eighteen hundred years. His merit is by the help of dialectic to have created a view, a perspective. To direct one's eye towards a star is not so difficult, because the air is like an empty space, and hence there is nothing in the way to stop or divert the glance. It is different, on the other hand, when the direction the eye must follow is straight ahead, as along a path, and at the same time there is a crowding and thronging and tumult and noise and bustle through which the eye must pierce to get the view, whereas every sidelong glance, yea, every blinking of the eye, produces absolutely a qualitative disturbance; and it becomes even more difficult when at the same time one has to stand in an environment which labors *pro virili* to prevent one from getting the view.—And to be contemporary with the decisive Christian fact is the decisive thing. This contemporaneousness, however, is to be understood as having the same significance that it had for people who lived at the same time that Christ was living.

What is needed first of all is to have the prodigious libraries and writings of every sort and the eighteen hundred years thrust to one side in order to get the view. And this is by no means the impudent suggestion of an ambitious dialectician, it is the modest and genuine religious requirement which every man may make, not for the sake of learning or for the public but for his own sake, quite personally for his own sake, if he is serious about becoming a Christian, and this is what Christianity itself must demand. For Christianity wishes precisely to stand immovable like the polar star, and hence would get rid of all the twaddle which takes the life out of it.[7]

However, the contemporaneousness here in question is not the *contemporaneousness of an apostle*, but is *merely the contemporaneousness which everyone who lived in Christ's time had*, the possibility in *the tension of contemporaneousness* of *being offended*, or of *grasping faith*. And to this end precisely it is necessary to let in air so that it may be possible, as once it was, for a man seriously to be offended, or to appropriate Christianity, so that with the Christian faith it may not become as in a law case which has gone on so long that one does not know his way in nor out by reason of so much knowledge. The situation of contemporaneousness is that of tension which gives the categories qualitative elasticity; and one must be a great dunce not to know what an infinite difference it makes when one for his own sake in the situation of contemporaneousness reflects about something, and when one thinks in a way about something in the vain conceit that it was eighteen hundred years ago—in the conceit, yes, in the conceit, for since the Christian fact is the qualitative paradox it is a conceit that eighteen hundred years is longer ago than yesterday.

Since then the situation in Christendom is such that it is

precisely necessary to put an end to the tough-lived indolence which appeals to the eighteen hundred years, it cannot be denied that a desirable incitement might be given if suddenly there were to appear a man who appealed to a revelation, for then there would be created an analogous situation of contemporaneousness. Yes, I am sure, all the profound and speculative and learned and sweaty praters who can well understand that eighteen hundred years ago someone received a revelation—they would fall into embarrassment. He who understands in general that a man might receive a revelation, must after all understand it quite as well whether it happened six thousand years ago, or will happen six thousand years hence, or has happened today. But perhaps the prater has been living off the eighteen hundred years, has prated himself into the belief that he could understand it—because it was eighteen hundred years ago. If the case were not so serious, I could not deny that it is the most precious comedy that ever could have been written in the world: to let modern exegesis and dogmatics go through their curriculum in the situation of contemporaneousness. All these deceitful psychological inventions, all this about "up to a certain point," all this *bravura profunda*, and above all the eloquent meditation which explains —since this was eighteen hundred years ago, as has been explained. All this would make a splendid effect in contemporaneousness with the matter which was explained. It is quite certain that far better than all learned attacks, one single comedy in the style of Aristophanes would clear up the confusion of modern learning.

Hence when I, without having seen the *Sermons* or the preface to them, heard that Adler had stepped forward and had appealed to a revelation, I cannot deny that I was astonished.[8] When I heard this I thought: Either, thought I, this is the man we need, the elect who in divine originality possesses the spring for refreshing the parched ground of Christendom; or he is a man offended at Christianity, but an accomplished knave who to demolish everything, even the dignity of an apostle, to topple everything over, brings such a Christendom as we now have to the painful and laborious test of having to go through its course of dogmatics in the situation of contemporaneousness.

On the latter supposition it would indeed have surprised me that an offended man had really been so shrewd. For though it cannot be denied that the "offended" have talents and demoniacal inspiration, yet for the most part they are generally rather stupid in a total sense, that is to say, they do not quite know how to take hold of a thing in order to do harm, they attack Christianity, but they take a position outside of it, and precisely for this reason they do no harm. No, the offended man must try to get a different hold on Christianity, try to work his way up like a mole into the midst of Christianity. Suppose Feuerbach, instead of attacking Christianity, had gone to work more slyly, suppose that with demoniac silence he had laid his plan, and thereupon had stepped forward and announced that he had had a revelation, and suppose now that, just as a criminal is able to maintain a lie, he had unshakably maintained this claim, while at the same time he had been shrewdly watching out for all the weaker sides of orthodoxy, which however he was far from attacking, but only in a simple-hearted sort of way knew how to hold up before the light; suppose now that he had done this so well that no one was able to discover his stratagem—he would have put orthodoxy in the greatest embarrassment. Orthodoxy fights in the interest of the established order, to preserve the appearance that we are all Christians of a sort, that the land is a Christian land, and that the congregations are Christian.[9] Now when one attacks Christianity and takes a position outside it, orthodoxy defends it with the help of the eighteen hundred years; it talks in lofty tones of God's great works performed in his time, i.e eighteen hundred years ago. And now it may be said of the extraordinary and of God's extraordinary works that they go easier into people the farther they are away. So then the offended man attacks

Christianity and the orthodox defend it by the help of the distance, and the congregation thinks thus: Since it was eighteen hundred years ago one may well understand that something extraordinary happened—and so again the offended man accomplished nothing. On the other hand, it would have been different if he himself had slyly come forward with a revelation,[10] and thereupon read nothing but orthodox works and then transferred all this to himself, and then forced orthodoxy in the situation of contemporaneousness to speak out.

It is often said that in case Christ were now to come forward in Christendom, if in a stricter sense than in time gone by "he came unto his own," he would again be crucified[11] —and especially by the orthodox. That is quite true, for contemporaneousness gives the necessary qualitative pressure; on the other hand, it helps both to make something nothing, and to make something extraordinary, almost in the same sense as nothing. Why was it that most everyone was offended in Christ while he lived, unless it was that the extraordinary occurred before their eyes, so that he who would talk about it might say,[12] the miracle occurred yesterday. But when a miracle happened eighteen hundred years ago—well, yes, one can surely understand that it happened and that it was a miracle. Among the many precious and priceless syllogisms of thoughtless clerical eloquence this must be regarded as the most precious, that what one cannot understand if it were to happen today, one can understand when it happened eighteen hundred years ago—when this, be it noted, is the miraculous, which at every time of day, at 4 o'clock or at 5, surpasses man's understanding. For if one were only to say that such and such a man eighteen hundred years ago believed it was a miracle, then he may declare bluntly that he himself does not believe it. However, one prefers to help himself out with deceitful phrases, as with this which appears so believing yet precisely denies the miracle, as when one says of such and such a man that he believed it, i.e. he thought so,[13] i.e. after all there was no miracle.

As has been said, in trying to interpret the extraordinary event that a man appeals to a fact of revelation I proposed to myself a dilemma: that he either was the elect; or an offended man demoniacally shrewd.[14] And this dilemma was what, according to my view, a revelation in our time in the situation of contemporaneousness might help us to. And (even if this should not come to pass, what Christianity absolutely needs, if it is not to perish and be brought to naught) is a little air, an either/or with respect to becoming and being a Christian. Adler's appearance has, however, convinced me that there must be a third term, for he is neither of the two. That he is not the elect, that the whole thing about his revelation is a misunderstanding, I shall later show and prove directly,[15] not by the force of any view or theory of mine, no, but from Adler's later attitude and from his later works it can be sufficiently made out that he himself essentially does not believe it, though he has not found himself moved by this to revoke penitently his first claim. Still less, if possible, is he the offended man of demoniacal shrewdness. Of that there is not the least trace or symptom. But he is not for this reason without significance, and I know of no other man in my time who in a stricter sense may be called a phenomenon. The powers of existence have got hold of him, and as a phenomenon he is an anticipation of the dialectic which is fermenting in our age. But the phenomenon itself knows nothing about the explanation, i.e. one must oneself be a teacher to learn anything from Adler.[16] At the same time he tumbles into the old heresies, and all this pell-mell. Thus Adler is quite properly a sign. He is a very serious proof that Christianity is a power which is not to be jested with. But, on the other hand, rather than being an elect, he is a soul whirled about, flung aloft as a warning of dread, like the terrified bird which with anxious beating of its wings rushes out ahead of the storm which is about to follow, though as yet one hears only the hissing of it; and his thoughts are like the confused flocks of birds which flee helter-skelter before the storm. That for this reason one might be justified in giving him up or of thinking meanly of his possibilities is by no means my opinion.[17] Undoubtedly as a theological candidate he lived on in the vain conceit that the meager theological knowledge required of a candidate in the official examination is Christianity. So when the Christian experience came over him he fell into the strange situation of knowing all about it in a certain sense, but by the aid of an (unfamiliar) nomenclature. In his haste he grasped at the strongest expression to indicate what he had experienced—and so we have his fact of revelation.

CHAPTER III

Alteration of Adler's essential standpoint, or
documentation of the fact that he did
not himself believe he had experienced
a revelation. This is elucidated by his
four latest books and a brochure containing the documents having to do with
his deposition.[1]

1

DOCUMENTS CONCERNING HIS DEPOSITION[2]

THIS BROCHURE, apart from a lot of correspondence regarding a dispute about a chaplain's wages, contains chiefly the
questions put to Adler by the clerical authority requiring an
explanation about himself and about his teaching, along with
Adler's answers and his subsequent answers.

In order that all this may be precise and vivid to the reader,
it will be best to recall that preface to his *Sermons*. Here
Magister Adler reports how he was at work on a book which
would have been called "Popular Lectures on Subjective
Logic," a work in which "with a superficial knowledge of
the Bible he had assumed to explain creation and Christianity."
Thereupon he continues, "One evening I had just developed
the origin of evil, when I saw, illuminated as by a flash of
lightning, that everything depends, not upon the thought, but
upon the Spirit. That night a hateful sound went through our
chamber. The *Saviour* bade me stand up and go in and write
down the words." Thereupon follow the words,* which in
stereotype form recur again and again in verse and prose.

* The words are as follows: "The first men might have had an

[69]

We shall not deal directly, either pro or contra, with the factual question involved in this quotation, nor with the remarkable fact that Christ talks almost like a privat-docent; we argue only *e consessis;* but this at least is perfectly clear, that he declares in the most solemn way that he has had a revelation in which the Saviour imparted to him a doctrine. It may indeed seem striking that already, even before he had received the revelation, he was on the point of discovering the same thought which was imparted to him by the revelation; for it was in the evening "he saw as in a flash of lightning that everything depended, not upon the thought, but upon the Spirit." But again we shall not dwell directly upon this either, but only remark that the expression, "as by a flash of lightning," should not be regarded after all as more or less than a metaphorical expression for the suddenness of the insight, or for the suddenness of the transition from not having perceived to having perceived. Moreover, the content of the doctrine communicated by the revelation is concentrated in the statement that "man's thought is absorbed in itself." But this also seems to have been fathomed before the revelation was imparted to him; for in the preface he says about his work ("Popular Lectures on Subjective Logic"): "It was my thought which was absorbed in itself." Hence there is not much left over which was imparted to him by a revelation; but all the more definitely the accent falls precisely upon the fact that this was imparted to him *by a revelation*, that "the *Saviour* at night bade him stand

---

eternal life; for when the thought unites God's Spirit with body, then the life is eternal; when man unites God's Spirit with the body, then man is God's child; so Adam would have been God's son. But they sinned. The thought is absorbed in itself. It separated the soul from the body, the Spirit from the world, then must man die, and the world and the body become evil. And what does the spirit become? The spirit goes out of the body. But God does not take it back. And it becomes his enemy. And where does it go? Back into the world. Why? It is angry with the world which gave it up. It is the evil spirit. And this world itself created the evil spirit."

up and go in and write down the following words." Insofar as Adler, unshakable, holds to this fact, I have no yea and no nay: I am engaged merely in arguing *e concessis*. But, on the other hand, if he does not hold it fast, he must put up with it if out of his own mouth one concludes that he does not himself believe he has had a revelation, or in any case that he is in such confusion regarding the categories that he does not himself know what he says, because he associates no sharp thought with the words.

In the preface it is further related, "Thereupon Jesus bade me burn my own [works] and for the future hold to the Bible. Of the Sermons and addresses from No. vi to the end I know that they were written with Jesus' cooperative grace, so that I have been only an instrument." In case Adler did not know this of the other addresses, or in case he knew of the other addresses that they were not that, it is certainly strange that he published them, especially in one volume, which like Noah's Ark seems to contain species qualitatively very various. This, however, is Adler's business. The principal point for me is that he said in the most solemn way that he knew the discourses from No. vi to the end were written with Jesus' cooperative grace, so that he was only an instrument.* So we have here with Adler's call by a revelation the

* The solemnity of this assertion suffers, however, from a little defect due to a couple of notes in the same book, of which I, were the matter not so serious, might be tempted to say that they surely were written with the cooperative assistance of distraction. From the preface one learns indeed that the discourses from No. vi to the end were written with the cooperation of Jesus' grace; but on page 20 (in a note to sermon No. iv, Maundy Thursday, April 13, 1843) one reads: "Here for the first time Jesus' cooperative grace came to my aid." Good Friday, as everyone knows, comes after Maundy Thursday, sermon No. v after sermon No. iv, and yet one learns in the note to No. v that Jesus' cooperative grace came then for the *first* time to Adler's aid—after one has read the note to No. iv, and after one has read in the preface that he *knows* of sermons No. vi to the end that they were written with Jesus' cooperative grace, this seems to indicate that he was doubtful about the notes to iv and v, unless in distraction he had written the notes, and again in distraction had forgotten that he had written them.

analogy with the call of an apostle; in his writing with the
cooperation of Jesus' grace we have the analogy with the
situation of a man who was inspired.[3] Adler had both a
doctrine which was communicated to him by a revelation,
and a development of this doctrine which was inspired. So
reliably is hardly the New Testament guaranteed. If only he
had left out the first five sermons, this book would have been
instar omnium.

Now we pass on to the questions which the clerical authority
found itself obliged to put to him.

THE QUESTION OF THE ECCLESIASTICAL AUTHORITY

*(1) Whether you (Mag. Adler) recognize that you were
in an exalted and confused state of mind when you wrote
and published your printed "Sermons" and so-called
"Studies"?* *

The letter of the authority was dated April 29, 1845.
Magister Adler's reply under date of May 11, 1845 is as
follows:

"Since I can point out meaning and connection in what
I have written in my *Sermons* and *Studies*, I do not recognize
that I was in an exalted and confused state of mind when
I wrote them."

Strictly considered, this is not an answer to the question.

* The question itself has moreover a curious difficulty with respect to
the answer which might be expected. When one challenges a person for
an explanation whether in a previous moment of time he was in a
confused state of mind, it seems to be implied that if he is willing to
explain this, willing to admit it, then all is well again, and the person is
no longer in a confused state of mind. However, it is possible to think
that the person precisely by his willingness to make further admissions
proves that he is in a confused state of mind. Suppose he answered, Well,
if nothing more is required, then I shall not make them wait for me, but
with the greatest pleasure will explain, etc. In such a case the questioner
is brought again into the same embarrassment. In general it is very
difficult to check the dialectic which develops when one begins to assume
that a man has been in a confused state of mind, and especially difficult
to check it by an explanation made by the man himself.

By "meaning and connection" one may think rather only of the grammatical consistency one may require of a speech. But, supposing that there was such meaning and connection in what was written, the author might very well have been in an exalted and confused state of mind. Moreover the act of publishing what was written is something for itself, and one might, e.g., write something quite calmly, but betray an exalted state of mind by publishing it. Hence Adler's reply is in no sense an answer to the question; neither is it veracious, for not only is there one but there are many passages in the *Sermons* which are plainly wanting in meaning and connection. So the answer may be regarded as evasive, and also one cannot yet say that by this answer he has altered in the least what he originally said about himself. In this he is still consistent. This I reckon to his credit, for I argue only *e concessis*.

But some time later there followed a further answer. We shall suppress nothing which might seem to speak in Adler's favor, and therefore we recall that in speaking of his last reply he himself says, "In order to reach a point of agreement with the authorities, I made, after a conversation with Bishop Mynster, as great a step towards approach as was possible by sending on July 5th the following confession:[4]

"I recognize that the unusual, the strange, the objectionable, aprioristic and abrupt form may with reason have aroused the suspicion of the authority."

Now it is coming. It is true that A. does not say that the authority was right in concluding that he was in an exalted and confused state of mind, but he says it is right in affirming that the ideas in many places in his *Sermons* and *Studies* are presented in an unusual, strange, offensive, aprioristic and abrupt form; he says moreover that the authority has reason to be suspicious. So A. admits the premises but lets the conclusions remain doubtful. In his first answer he had denied the premises, in his second letter he admits the premises and says nothing to oppose the conclusion. Precisely because A. admits the premises (unless he would give support to the assumption of the authority, and in that case he might say it straightforwardly) he must defend himself with all his might against the conclusion, he must say in perfectly definite words: But in spite of this (and precisely because I have admitted the premises I have to hold to this all the more firmly), in spite of all this I can by no means admit that I have been in an exalted and confused state of mind. It is a well-known method of advocates to admit the premises in this way, and then by drawing no conclusion make it seem as if the conclusion was something quite different, something that comes from an entirely different hemisphere, something over which the person in question arbitrarily disposes whether he will admit it or not, something which by a qualitative definition is separated from the premises. But when a premise pregnant with the conclusion inclines threateningly over a man; when he himself knows that by admitting the justice of the premises he makes the angle of inclination all the greater; then he must with the utmost definiteness defend himself against the conclusion, or it falls upon him, and he has himself admitted it. Of course, even if he had defended himself against the conclusion with a definite statement, he might not have parried the conclusion, for sometimes the conclusion may be a pure formality which makes no difference one way or the other, but he may be regarded as having lost this point. The cunning or the thoughtlessness which further proves his confusion is the fact that he lets this answer serve as an explanation, that he does not understand the simple consistency which requires him to revoke officially his first position, his first answer, acknowledging that the *Sermons* along with the *Studies* were written in an exalted and confused state of mind.

In the last letter there remains a third point which, regarded as an answer, may well be referred to question No. 1 of the authority, to which we here hold fast. No. 3 in the last letter reads as follows:

"That with a longer time to labor and quietly develop the ideas for the future* I will find myself able to let the Christian content unfold itself in a form more appropriate and more consonant with the express words of Holy Scripture."

In connection with Adler's hope for the future one is tempted involuntarily to raise the question: But was there need of such haste in getting said (in an inappropriate and less Biblical way) that which with a longer time to labor and to develop the ideas will be able to unfold itself in a form more appropriate and more consonant with the express words of Holy Scripture? Is there any, or can there have been any reasonable ground for haste in doing in an inappropriate form that which with the employment of a longer time may be done in a more appropriate form? And when did Magister Adler begin with the longer time which is needed for quiet work? He has already written four books since then, but it does not seem as if he had got any nearer to the appropriate!

And in case it is so (as will be shown in the following where Adler's answer to No. 2 of the authority will be dealt with) that Adler himself authentically explains (i.e. alters his first statement to this effect) that he has nothing new to contribute†—in case this is so, then precisely it is important that

---

* This hope . . . has not been exactly fulfilled, but it is talked about again in one of Adler's four last books.[5] So since that hopeful word in the letter of July 5, 1845, Adler has written four new books, but the hope still finds its place as a repeated hope in the preface of one of them. In this way Adler may be able to remain for a long time a hopeful and promising author; yea, in all probability this hope will become a standing article in his prefaces—a sort of fixed idea, which sometimes is found in authors who never give it up, not even with death. So it is said that we have an example in an author who in the preface to each little book he published regularly wrote that in the future he meant to collect himself for a great work which he soon meant to publish—even in the last preface to a fragment of a little book this hope still found its customary place.

† That again in the preface to one of his last four books he fantasticates on the theme that "he who has something new to contribute must not permit any amalgamation with the old" may be regarded as a new

one take care that the form be as appropriate as possible, that one uses time and patience for the work to make it as appropriate as possible, since there is no reason at all for haste. Even if a man contributes something new, it is yet unpardonable to do it in a tumultuous way, but when one admits that he has nothing new to contribute it is doubly unpardonable.

That now Adler himself authentically admits (as an *explanation* of the assertion that he had a revelation by which a new doctrine was imparted to him by the Saviour) that he has nothing new to contribute, we go on to show by illuminating Adler's answer to question No. 2 by the authority. This No. 2 contains the principal point, for here the question is asked whether he has actually had a revelation, whether he himself thought so, etc. Question No. 1 is of far less significance, and actually I have dwelt upon Adler's answer to No. 1 only to give a foretaste of his confusions.

THE QUESTION OF THE AUTHORITY

Whether you perceive that it is fanatical and wrong to expect and to follow such supposed revelations as, for example, that which you have described in the preface to your "Sermons"?

Adler's two answers, though they pretend to be explanations, are not explanations but alterations, which alter his first assertion, without requiring him to revoke it decisively. Yet between his two answers there is a difference. In the first the fact of having had a revelation by which a new doctrine was imparted to him is transformed into an awakening by which he is rescued. In the last answer the fact of having had a revelation by which a new doctrine was imparted to him is

---

confusion Adler has to contribute. One is justified in assuming that in this preface Adler is referring to himself, and so one may conclude further that he still regards that first declaration (which in the most solemn way gave itself out to be a revelation, and thereafter was authentically explained as not being anything new)—that he nevertheless regards it as something new.

transformed into the beginning of an enthusiasm, into an expression as vague and indefinite as enthusiasm. Instead of one called by a revelation to whom a new doctrine was entrusted, we get in the first case a religiously awakened man in the ordinary sense; in the second case, an enthusiast. Educated as Adler is with some Hegelian dialectic, it is not strange if he himself lives in the notion that these three determinants (an apostle, an awakened man, and an enthusiast) signify pretty much the same thing, or that the one term can be used to explain the others. But in case there exists something called qualitative dialectic, one of these terms annuls the other, and the dilemma must constantly be posed: if Adler acquiesces in the explanation, then he must revoke the first claim; for the explanation is not a further predicate of the first claim but is a new position. So one may be very willing to concede to Adler that he is a sort of enthusiast so called, but cannot truly be willing to regard this notion as an explanation of what in the preface to his *Sermons* he gives himself out to be.

His first answer of May 10, 1845, is as follows:

"By having written in the preface to my *Sermons* that Jesus bade me in the future to hold to the Bible, by having preached him, by having quoted the words of Scripture as proof-texts, it must be evident to what Gospel and to what revelations* I hold and have taught others to hold. But that one may be rescued in a miraculous way is—as I have described it in the preface—a fact which I cannot deny. Even if one regards my *Sermons* and *Studies* as a babe's first babbling, tender, imperfect voice, I believe nevertheless that an occurrence took place by which I was seized by faith."

Now the volatilization is in full course, and I would beg for the reader's patience so that I may set to work quite

---

* There is moreover something rather confused in the plural which Adler here uses in a different connection than the authority does, for the authority spoke in the plural of the fanatical revelations, Adler speaks in the plural of the Christian revelation.

slowly to show in every line the uncertainty and confusion—
it serves to illuminate very well a part of modern philosophy
and dogmatics. According to my conception it is not uninterest-
ing to go to work for once with exactitude, and in our times
of dialectical confusion there might be someone who would
find profit in reading it, even if he had no interest at all in
the case.

So then: "By having written in the preface to my *Sermons*
that Jesus bade me in the future to hold to the Bible, by
having preached him, by having quoted words of the
Scripture as proof-texts, it must be evident to what Gospel
and to what revelations I hold and have taught others to
hold." But this is by no means evident. Even if one will make
the greatest possible concessions to Adler, there remains the
decisive consideration, the very point, which he leaves out,
while by his answer he seeks to *identify himself with every
Christian in general*. For even though Adler holds to the
Christian revelation and the Christian Gospels, there still
remains the difficulty about which the question was asked,
that he *by a revelation* was directed to hold to the revelation.
A believing Christian in general holds to the Christian revelation, but Adler is directed by a revelation to hold to it.
Therefore it is not by any means evident to which revelation
he holds, for he holds first and foremost to the revelation
which has fallen especially to his lot, by which he has been
directed to hold to the Christian revelation. Besides, he says
himself that Jesus bade him in the future; but the question
is not what Jesus bade him do and bade him do in the future, but
about the assertion that *Jesus appeared to him and bade him do
something*. Even though Adler in the future remained like
every believing Christian in general, there still remains always
the decisive qualitative difference about which the question was
asked, that through a revelation by Jesus himself he was
directed to be like the others.* To this may be added, and

* The fact should not be overlooked that Adler involves himself in
a new difficulty. For dialectically a new contradiction is contained in the

it is really the principal point, that Adler in his answer has left out what was chiefly emphasized in the preface. For according to this Jesus did not call him at night to bid him in the future to hold to the Bible; no, the Saviour bade him "stand up and go in and write down these words," i.e. the whole passage which contains the new doctrine. When this was done, then "Jesus bade him thereupon to burn his own [works] and in the future to hold to the Bible."[6]

When moreover A. in the first sentence of this answer appeals to the fact that "he had preached Jesus," in order thereby to make it "evident to which Gospel and to which revelations he holds and has taught others to hold"—this again is not evident from what he says. He again leaves out the decisive thing (about which the question was asked) and, volatilizing the whole thing, seeks in his answer *to identify himself with every believing priest in general*. The believing Christian priest preaches Christ and thereby shows to which revelations he holds, but the believing priest in general is *not called by any revelation* to preach Jesus. Inasmuch then as Adler preaches Jesus, it is by no means evident to which revelations he holds. It would only be evident in case that preface to his *Sermons* did not exist; but that preface and the revelation described in it is precisely what the authority asked about. The authority did not ask Adler whether he like every believing priest preached Jesus; no, it asked whether he recognized that it is fanatical to hold to such revelations as are described in the preface to his *Sermons*. Adler answers: I preach Jesus. But thus he does not answer the question— or else the answer implied the concession: I have never had

---

notion that by a paradoxically extraordinary measure (a new revelation) one should be called to be like all others. By the paradoxically extraordinary call a man can be called only to be the paradoxically extraordinary man. By a revelation with which one is entrusted with a doctrine a man cannot be called to become what all others are or could be, nor to become a faithful adherent of this doctrine, but he is called to become the extraordinary, to become the apostle of it.

a special revelation, and such being the case the whole preface to the *Sermons* must be officially revoked.

Moreover, in his answer he again leaves out something, and something very important, which stood in the preface. For in the preface there stood: "About the Sermons and Addresses from No. vi to the end I know that they were written by Jesus' cooperative grace, so that I have been only an instrument." But no believing priest in general preaches in this way.[7] For example, I assume that had another preached literally the same sermon as Adler, there would yet have been between the two a decisive qualitative difference, for the fact that Adler's was in the capacity of "being only an instrument."

The first sentence in his first answer to authority's No. 2 thus shows itself to be sophistical and thoughtless. If there is to be any seriousness in calling this an explanation, he must repentently revoke the preface to his *Sermons*[8] for the answer is no more an explanation of what was said in the preface to the *Sermons* than it was enlightening information a messenger once brought back that he had found what he was sent to seek but it was not a widow but a bricklayer.

The next sentence in his first answer to authority's No. 2 is as follows: "But that one may be rescued in a miraculous way—as I have described in the preface to the *Sermons*—is for me a fact which I cannot deny." It is not required of him at all that he should deny a fact; I for my humble part am as far as possible from requiring that, I require only that he shall either stand firm decisively by what he himself has said he was, or else solemnly revoke that which by him in the most solemn way was affirmed. He does not hold fast his first decisive declaration, he alters it, and yet he would give that alteration the appearance of being an explanation. That he does not stand fast by what he said of himself in the preface to the *Sermons* (the point of the authority's question) it is not difficult to see; for after all there is a decisive qualitative difference between *receiving from the Saviour by a revelation a doctrine entrusted to him,* and *being rescued in a miraculous way.* In case A. when he wrote the preface and later the answer had been in possession of the necessary Christian knowledge, he naturally would have known this; but one who has no other presuppositions with which to make Christianity secure except some Hegelian dialectic can readily go astray.

Let us now define a little more precisely the difference between the two statements. When a man is said to be rescued in a miraculous way it is assumed that what he has been rescued into or to is in existence, perhaps has long been in existence, but he, alas, has frittered away his years in light-mindedness and dissipations, or wasted them in confused studies, or turned his back upon the well known, or reaped the sorry consequences of a weak and spoiled bringing up, etc. He is now rescued in a miraculous way, it may be in various ways which, and according to the psychological knowledge one has of such stories of religious awakening, it may be told in a longer or shorter form. It is assumed that Christianity is that into which one is rescued, but he is rescued in a miraculous way. Suppose, for example, it happened this year, and with that Christianity has been in existence eighteen hundred years, in it there certainly comes about no alteration for the sake of the rescued man; ah, no, but the wayward one is rescued in a miraculous way into that which has been in existence unchanged for eighteen hundred years and in which all others are assumed to have their life. On the other hand, it is something quite other and qualitatively different when one by a revelation is entrusted with a doctrine. This doctrine indeed was not in existence before, there has therefore come about an alteration in that in which rescue is to be found. The man thus called may not, humanly speaking, have been in the way of perdition. No, there comes about an alteration of an objective sort, and this it is which the man called must communicate as it was communicated to him. He who is called by a revelation and entrusted with a doctrine may be called to be a teacher; he is called indeed for his own sake, but principally for the sake of others (the teleological), that he may preach the new doctrine. On the other hand, he who is rescued in a miraculous way is entrusted with no new doctrine, he is not appointed to be a teacher in an extraordinary sense or to communicate something new; he has to be quiet and subordinate himself humbly to the old order; the consciousness of being *rescued* in a miraculous way cannot tempt him to regard himself as something extraordinary, since this consciousness rather reminds him constantly, to his humiliation, that he was so far out on the way of perdition that a miraculous way was needed to rescue him.

Thus I think I have defined the difference. Let us now look at Adler. In the preface to the *Sermons* there is no hint that he was saved, "rescued"; no, in the preface Adler was the one called by a revelation, to whom a new doctrine was entrusted. For the first time in the answer (which, be it noted, is in reply to the question about the meaning of the preface to the *Sermons*) this explanation comes out. Naturally, it is no explanation of the preface, it is an entirely new view, a new character in which Adler appears upon the stage, as though he were just now beginning, as though he had no antecedent history—he who precisely had antecedents about which the question was asked. In case one had given himself out to be king, and then the authority put to him the question what he meant by saying such a thing about himself, and he then explained that thereby he had meant that he was a councilor of chancery—this answer is no explanation, it is a new assertion: first he gives himself out to be king, then councilor of chancery. The dialectical cunning or thoughtlessness consists in not revoking the first claim but treating the last claim as though it were an explanation of the first.

The last sentence in Adler's first answer to authority's No. 2 is as follows: "Even though one may regard my *Sermons* and *Studies* as a babe's first babbling, tender, imperfect voice, I believe nevertheless that the words witness to the fact that

an event has taken place whereby I was grasped by faith."
Now this last is a very vague determinant: that an event
has taken place whereby I was grasped by faith. The event
moreover is exactly described in the preface to the *Sermons*:
"that there was heard a hateful sound which went through
the chamber, and then the Saviour bade him stand up and
write down the words." The authority indeed had not
asked A. whether an event had taken place, but about the event
described in detail in the preface to the *Sermons*. This statement of Adler about himself, that an event had taken place
by which he was grasped by faith, is something entirely different from what is related in the preface. Thus there have been
many examples of men who have been grasped by faith by
falling into mortal danger.[9] It is well known, and it made
an extraordinarily deep impression and had a decisive influence upon Pascal's life, that at one time the horses ran away
with him. But this again is something quite other and qualitatively different from having by a revelation received a
doctrine.

As for the *first* statement in the last sentence of the answer,[10]
it might seem indeed a praiseworthy modesty on the part
of an author, a compliment to others, to refer thus in relation to his first effort to "a babe's first babbling, tender, imperfect voice" and "a highly educated and cultured public"
who, lacking any categories, has a fond predilection for
complimentary twaddle, would surely like it—if there was
nothing to hinder.[11] But here there is no call for modesty,
there up and here down, but for a categorical definition in a
highly serious case. When a man begins an effort in a confused
and exalted state it may be quite right for him to hope for
perfectibility, that he will succeed later when he has attained
calmness and reflection in doing it better. But a man who
begins with a revelation and with the Saviour's dictation has
only in an unessential sense to hope for perfectibility—so this is
blasphemy. It is true that Adler does not say expressly that
he thus regards these words in the preface and in the *Sermons*,

but how does he dare (in case what stands in the preface is truly true) to engage in any such accommodation by saying, "even though one might regard my *Sermons* and *Studies* as a babe's first tender, imperfect voice," and engage in it in such a way that he "believes nevertheless that the words witness to the fact that an event has taken place."[12] So then, when his solemn assertion that Jesus bade him write down the words does not avail to make his voice heard, he hopes then that an insignificance will do it. Just think how almost detestable it is merely to be obliged to write such a thing; imagine that Paul as an explanation of the words: "I have received of the Lord that which also I deliver unto you, that our Lord Jesus Christ, etc.," were to have added: even though some were to regard this as a babe's first babbling, tender, imperfect voice, etc.! Where in all the world did Adler come upon this about a babe's tender, imperfect voice! So may a man speak in relation to a production which in a perfectly common human sense is his own—but in the preface to the *Sermons* it is indeed not Adler's voice, it is in fact Jesus who dictates it and so through Adler speaks to us . . . and his voice surely is not that of a tender babe, and surely it has not occurred to any one, or occurred to the authority, to raise the dilemma, but surely it meant to ask Adler what he means by thus making Jesus dictate something to his pen. On the other hand, in case this whole preface is poetry and vanity and confusion of mind—then it is quite right, and yet, no, it is not right to talk about a babe's tender voice . . . for then the whole thing must be penitently revoked.

But then what was it the authority had asked him about? Whether he had been in an exalted and confused state of mind when he wrote the preface and the *Sermons*. And when one has begun in an exalted condition it may be quite right to hope for a certain perfectibility,* to hope that, as Adler

---

* The whole affair about Adler's perfectibility is one of those unblessed reminiscences of the theological seminary. If only Adler had been a layman! For his misfortune among other things is that his inward-

himself said, "with a longer time to labor and quietly develop the ideas I will find myself able to let the Christian content unfold itself in a more appropriate form and more consonant with the express words of the Holy Scripture." Yes, when one has begun in an exalted and confused state—but it is precisely not right when one has begun with the plainest and clearest of all, with the fact that Jesus himself dictates to one what he shall write down. Even with regard to a purely human effort it is true for all competent men that the first is the best; the first of enthusiasm, of resolution, of love is the best, as is the dialectical first judgment of a situation. It is true only of confused men that the first comes stumbling into the door like a drunken man—and so it may sometimes be true enough that afterwards, when reflection enters little by little, something quite good may come out of it. But then is the first not something one may leave as it was, but, on the contrary, something one must revoke.

So it has been shown that Adler's first answer to authority's No. 2, either sophistically or thoughtlessly, contains an alteration of his whole first standpoint: instead of being called by a revelation and entrusted with a new doctrine he substitutes the statement that he was rescued in a miraculous way. According to his own authentic view (from which we are of course justified in drawing an argument, since we protested against it only when it pretended to be an explanation of the first, as it is not an explanation but an essential alteration, and as an essential alteration demands its recognizable expression in a decisive form, which can only be the revocation of the first). He holds to the Bible, preaches Jesus, appeals to Scriptural words as proof-texts, in short, he is quite like every other Christian, only he was rescued in a miraculous way. *But ergo, he has in*

---

ness stands in no proportion to his wretched theological learning. Christianity is a revelation—seventeen hundred years later men began indeed to develop it so that it might be perfectible. Now that is something to be said for the many centuries. But in one's own lifetime to go through this exegetical curriculum with regard to what he himself has experienced, is really comical.

conformity with his own authentic view nothing new, no new doctrine to communicate, nor ever has had. The confusion then consists merely in the fact that he allows the first to stand. If there is to be the least ethical meaning and seriousness in Adler's whole effort, he must revoke[13] his first claim, saying: "Neither did Jesus appear to me, nor did he have me write down those words—but I was in a confused and over-strained condition. For me, however, that moment has had a decisive significance, so that I may say of myself that I was rescued in a miraculous way." Yes, then the case is different. Honor to him who humbly but frankly acknowledges of himself that he had to be rescued in a miraculous way. But in Adler's first and decisive statement (in the preface to the *Sermons*) there was not a word said about being saved or rescued—there he was the one called by a revelation to whom a new doctrine was entrusted. Now, to let the first stand, and to give the answer the appearance of being an explanation, is a total confusion. The answer is no explanation but a qualitatively new statement, the explanation does not explain the first, it explains the first to be something different. In case one were to explain a circle and explain that it was a square, that is no explanation, it is a new assertion. When I explain something I make of course no alteration in the nature of what I explain; what is to be explained must remain unaltered, but by the explanation it becomes plain what it is. When one says that by a revelation there was communicated to him a doctrine according to Jesus' own dictation, and one asks him what he means by this and requires an explanation, and he then explains that by this he means that he was rescued in a miraculous way, with this he does not explain the question asked but produces a new story.

This was the first alteration, but it did not stop with that. With the first alteration we still remain after all in the religious sphere, though there is a decisive qualitative difference between being rescued in a miraculous way, and being entrusted by a revelation with a new doctrine.

We pass on to Adler's last letter and the answer it contains to that question No. 2 of the authority. In order to do everything that can be done in favor of Adler we will again call attention to the fact that he himself regards this letter "as the greatest possible step towards approachment."

His second answer is as follows:

"I do not insist upon regarding my *Sermons* (or *Studies*) as revelations alongside of or over against Christianity, but I regard the words written down in the preface to the *Sermons* and my frequently recurring dogmatic categories as points of reference which were necessary to me at the beginning of the enthusiasm to hold fast the Christian matter in a form."

Now the game is in full swing. Ah, what was the use of burning those Hegelian manuscripts when one remains so much of a Hegelian that he is able to accomplish so much by mediation! First Adler says that he cannot insist* that these are revelations—that is; he says both yes and no; that is, he freshens up the old claim: A is surely B; but on the other hand it is after all not B. They are revelations; but he does not insist upon it, for after all to a certain degree they are not revelations. Ah, what was the use of burning the Hegelian manuscripts? *Naturam forca pellas*, but it comes back again at once.

To go further—he says, "I do not insist in regarding my *Sermons* (or *Studies*) as revelations."[14] Here Adler in his answer goes beyond the question of the authority, for the authority had asked him only about the revelation in the preface to the *Sermons*. How could it occur to the authority to ask Adler whether he regarded the whole collection of sermons

---

* The reader will perhaps remark how droll it is that in his first answer he had said less than this, for then he altered the claim that he had had a revelation by which a new doctrine was entrusted to him, into the statement that he had been rescued in a miraculous way; but in the last answer, in which he yet makes the greatest possible step towards approach, he begins again about having had after all to a certain degree a revelation.

and studies as revelations, since he had not said that they were?

Now comes the principal point: he regards the words written down in the preface to the *Sermons* and his frequently recurring dogmatic categories as points of reference which were necessary to him at the beginning of the enthusiasm to hold fast the Christian matter in a form. So these words he regards as points of reference. But the authority had not asked him *how* he regarded these words, but how he regarded the statement that *Jesus bade him write down these words.*[15] So the principal thing is altogether omitted.—Adler speaks of "those words *written down* in the preface ˙ . .": by this careless phrase he beguiles everyone into believing that the question is about words which Adler himself had written down, in the same sense as I am now writing these words down. But according to the preface it was in fact when the *Saviour* at night bade him stand up and he (Adler) wrote down these words as they were dictated. This is surely the qualitative decisive point.—Adler "regards those words written down *and* his frequently recurring dogmatic categories as points of reference." So for Adler himself there is no essential difference between those words and his dogmatic categories, both of them stand as authorities on the same plane—and yet those words in the preface were dictated by the Saviour, whereas the dogmatic categories are Adler's invention, so that he may quite rightly use the possessive pronoun and say "*my* dogmatic categories." If then the dogmatic categories and the words in the preface are in Adler's view qualitatively on the same plane with one another, it follows quite simply that he may say, *my* words written down in the preface. And yet those words were dictated to Adler by the Saviour himself.—Adler regards those words in the preface and the dogmatic categories (both of them alike) as "points of reference." A point of reference, according to linguistic usage, indicates the provisional. It may well happen that a point of reference does not turn out later to be altogether true; but in danger, in a moment of haste, one grasps it to have something to hold on to.* When two men are arguing with one another and confusion begins to set in, one grasps something as a point of reference which one establishes provisionally in order to have something to hold on to. When one has not had time to make his thoughts thoroughly clear and yet would communicate them, one grasps a particular definition and fixes it provisionally as a point of reference. Afterwards when one gets more time one investigates whether the particular definition which had served as a point of reference is quite right or no. As for Adler's categories, it may be permissible then and justifiable to call them points of reference, though later they may have to be subjected to a sharp test, for there is nothing to prevent one from hoping for this perfectibility—their perfection at least is not a hindrance. But as for those words in the preface which were written down by Adler at the Saviour's dictation, it is blasphemous to call *them* points of reference which for him (Adler) "were necessary in the beginning of the enthusiasm."[16] So Adler has been in a state of enthusiasm. Yes, that is something different. In case Adler in the preface to his *Sermons*, instead of what stands there now, had written: "In a moment of enthusiasm at night a light appeared to me, whereupon I stood up and lit a lamp and wrote down the following words"—then perhaps it hardly would have occurred to the authority to call him to account with questions. Then Adler's hope for perfectibility would have been fitting, for those words give indeed the impression (assuming that they are Adler's own words—for ordinarily I argue only *e concessis*) of not being so perfect that they could not be made more perfect. On the other hand, it seems either inconceivably thoughtless and confused or else impudent to present to the authority such an answer, as though the question were about a determinant so infinitely vague as enthusiasm, and in what degree Adler was enthusias-

* The Danish word is *Holdningspunkt* (point of holding)—in German *Verhaltnispunkt*, in French *point d'apui*.

tic, since the question after all is about the fact that he said that he had had a revelation and had had a doctrine dictated to him by the Saviour.—Adler himself regards those words in the preface as something imperfect. He says indeed that the points of reference were "necessary *for him* (the purely subjective determinant) *in the beginning of the enthusiasm* (that is, when he was still a little confused) in order to be able to hold fast the Christian matter *in a form* (this careless expression, "in a form" points clearly to the hope for a more appropriate and more perfect form, in comparison with which the Saviour's form was inappropriate). Who in all the world, merely reading Adler's answer, would think that he was talking about words which, according to his own declaration, were written down at the Saviour's own dictation? If then the words in the preface, as indeed Adler has said, are the words of the Saviour, his answer is nonsense; but if they are Adler's own words, then the preface must be most solemnly revoked. That Adler himself could not perceive this is precisely the best proof that he is confused.

When then these words in the preface, according to Adler's authentic view (against which I protest only when it pretends to be an explanation of his first claim), are to him only what his dogmatic categories are, when to him these words are points of reference, when to him, Adler (the subjective determinant), these points of reference were necessary only at the beginning of the enthusiasm, and then only necessary in order to hold fast another thing, and this other thing is and was the Christian matter, *then in Adler's own authentic explanation it is implied that he has had nothing new, no new doctrine* to contribute,*[17] *that he has had no revelation.*

---

* Already I have in a note referred to the fact—and will do so here again to give the reader at the proper place an impression of contemporaneousness—that Adler, as was indeed to be expected, begins all over again like Jeppe.[18] In the preface to one of his four last books he dwells especially upon the fact that "he who has something new to contribute must prevent any amalgamation with the old." Ah, if Adler has not been amalgamated with the old,[19] he has chiefly Bishop Mynster

The other points[20] in the letter of the authority are less important—but now we come to the end of the story. Adler's deprivation followed on September 13, 1845. It might seem strange and uncalled for, coming immediately after concessions so compliant and so important on the part of Adler. So it might appear, but if one will give himself due time, one will see more properly that it was called for by the concessions, for the importance of the concessions is that when they do not contain a formal and solemn revocation of his first claim they make his deprivation inevitable. The fact that he, in spite of such concessions, still fancies that he holds fast his first claim makes it perfectly evident that he is confused, that he knows neither the in nor the out of what he says about himself. Had Adler laconically, without budging a hair's breadth, maintained stubbornly his fact of revelation, the case would have been far more difficult for the State-Church, which would have come fairly near to judging how far a man in our age may be justified in asserting that he has had a revelation. But herein precisely consists the profundity of Bishop Mynster's conduct of this case, that he has helped Adler by some concessions to prove further that he is confused, and thereby to necessitate his deprivation, when, as Hegel says, the concept veers and the concessions precisely prove that he is confused.

For the State-Church the total result of the case of Adler[21] is null. No believers will thereby be thrown into an intense state of anxiety at the thought that a teacher has been declared to be in a confused state of mind and has been deprived of his living because he said he had a revelation. No, because he said this he was suspended in order that the case might be looked into more thoroughly, but by the help of conces-

---

to thank for it that by the help of his most compliant concessions he did not remain in his office. So, after all, Adler has something new to contribute. However, he has, as it seems, in the last books chosen the least embarrassing of all categories, namely, that he is something of a genius or such like.

sions he slew himself. In case one does not think that profundity consists in profound and clever sayings, in case one
assumes, as I do, that profundity stands in an essential relation to action, one cannot deny that Bishop Mynster, precisely
by his profundity, has conducted excellently a difficult case.
It was important above all that the blow fell at the right
place (precisely after the concessions) and that the thing
had no disastrous consequences, which now it cannot possibly
have. For something might well have resulted from Adler's
assertion that he had had a revelation, his deprivation being
connected with that; but from his concessions nothing results
for other men. Of course, the State would be right in depriving a man who quietly and coolly appealed to a revelation,
for the *extraordinarius* must leave the ranks. It is true that
Christianity is built upon a revelation, but also it is limited
by the definite revelation it has received. It must not be built
upon the revelations which John Doe and James Roe may get
—and in any case John Doe and James Roe must venture out
into the same danger which those men faced who once built
the Church upon a revelation. But I am thinking only of the
impression such a necessary step might have made upon the
weaker brethren, and I rejoice therefore that this was not
the case with Adler. Moreover I am convinced that the true
extraordinarius would of his own accord resign his official
post.[22]

2

ADLER'S FOUR LAST BOOKS.*

*Adler seems now to wish to be promoted to the position of
a genius, or to be content with that; that nevertheless he treats
this difference as nothing and thinks he is in identity with his
first claim (according to which he was a man called by a
revelation and entrusted with a doctrine). — The qualitative*

* *Studies and Examples; An Attempt at a Brief Systematic presentation of Christianity in its Logic; Theological Studies; Several Poems.*

difference between an apostle and a genius. — Even if A. Adler had not from the first wished it, regarded as the author of the four last works he must be characterized as a confused genius, a judgment which is suggested already by the form of the books.

[23]The last words of a man at the moment of departure [the same word as deprivation] have always a special value, are always impressed more strongly upon the memory. A.'s last words (the last in his last publication of July 5, 1845) contain, as the reader will remember, a hope, a beautiful hope, or anyway a hope confidently expressed, that he "with a longer time to labor over and quietly develop the ideas will be able for the future, etc."—a hope which does not seem to have made much impression upon the ecclesiastical authority, for there followed what does not seem to imply any hope for the future, his deposition with grace and with a pension, depriving him for the future of his parish. And from this what does one learn for the future? In a little land where not much is done to encourage arts and learning, where an author or an artist only after the accomplishments of considerable importance, and then after many laborious and miserable journeys of supplication from Herod to Pilate, after having been obliged to make his bow before the Head of the State (which is and ought to be a delight to any subject), not only before the high officials of the government (which itself is a satisfaction), but almost before each of the clerks in the bureau, between whom he is sent to and fro and fro and to—he obtains a little pinch of public support. In this land one may also take another way. One may undergo an official examination, or an examination which qualifies one for an official position. So one seeks it—it turns out that he is not competent for it, and the State thanks God it can get rid of him. One need not go to a single man, one may sit quite quietly in one's room—it comes to one: deprivation and pension. One has only to give utterance to slightly revolutionary principles—then by deprivation and

grace one is relieved of the tiresome official duties which really prevent one from becoming an author, which one would like to be, one gets a pension—and now has leisure and sometimes a considerable pension from the State, in order without disturbance and with favor to write against the State. Alas, a faithful subject who cannot make himself interesting by attacking the government will with great difficulty obtain some support for an undertaking which is both permissible and distinguished.

Favored by leisure and a pension, Adler kept still for one year, yet presumably, as we read of Ulysses, βυσσοδομεῦον [bruding]—for in the early summer of 1846 he came forward quite unexpectedly with four books at once. Four books at once! If this custom is more generally introduced, the standard for being an author will thereby be raised to an extraordinarily high pitch. When in the future there is talk of somebody being an author, one must ask at once if of one book or four— thus pashas are classified according as they wear one horsetail or three, and barbers as having one or three basins. To publish three or four books at once is something so striking that an essential author, even if he had them ready, would surely wish to avoid what easily might draw a wrong sort of attention to him, and what, regarded as a whim, would at the most have a little charm the first time it was done, not the first time for the individual, but the first time in the little world to which as an author he belongs; and anyhow, every real author must have a special reason for doing such a thing. Subjectively he must be conscious of a youthful force which will permit him to realize in due measure a task which will challenge in so high a degree the envy of the critics; perhaps his impetus is strengthened by an accidental circumstance, by the sad consciousness that the externally favorable conditions will permit him only for a short time to labor on a scale almost too great for him.[24] But principally the four books must have objectively a deeper aim—for example, as I think of it, to compass, if possible maieutically, a certain field from various sides at once. It must be important for the author of the four books, a half-poetical artistic task for him, that each book, which *in itself* is essentially different from the others, may be *characteristically* kept apart from the others; the author must know how to express poetically the illusion which is essentially confirmed by the special point of departure of each book, he may himself try in the notice of the books to separate them, so that the impression of the four books at once is really the product of the reader's self-activity, so that no one is obliged to know that they are four books at once, so that the literary specialist, if he happened to learn that there is one author, may feel a certain pleasure in entertaining the illusion that they are not four books by one author but by four authors, and that the one and the same does not appear even in the newspaper advertisements as presenting himself and offering his wares as an author of four books at once. In such an artistic way the thing was done not long ago in Danish literature.* I at least had not expected to find the memory of this so quickly refreshed—and so much by way of parody. Four books at once, one dedicated to his father, all bearing Adler's full name, all essentially in the same form, dealing essentially, sometimes word for word, with the same subject, in short, four yards in one piece, but each yard for itself bearing Adler's full name! There seems to be no trace of any reasonable ground for making four books. If any such a writing, such a merry-go-round, is to be published, it may just as well be run together in one volume; and if in the publication it is divided, it may just as well be twelve books as four. Neither is there any reasonable ground

* Here S.K. obviously refers to his own pseudonymous works. In 1843 (only three years before Adler's four books) S.K. had published on the same day, October 16, *Fear and Trembling* and *Repetition*, each ascribed to a different pseudonym, and *Three Edifying Discourses* in his own name and, like one of Adler's books, dedicated to his father. But his method illustrates what he says here in criticism of Adler, and shows how Adler's four books might have been produced maieutically, poetically, and artistically, dealing with the same subject, but characteristically separated.

for the one and only variation A. has attempted on the title-page of a book by calling it "An attempt at a *short* presentation," for essentially all his books are equally long and short, inasmuch as they all come under the rubric of *fortuitous length*. In case A., to make the variation quite obvious, on the title-page of the voluminous *Studies and Examples* had modestly added, "An Attempt at a Long Book," in spite of the modesty and the unmistakable effort to write a long book (which we leave to other critics to encourage by their praise), one would be justified in saying that, in spite of its length regarded as a book, it is essentially short. What gives itself out to be a book cannot without more ado, like stuff sold by the yard, be comprised under the categories of the long and the short, it must first prove itself to be a book. With regard to a book we must judge as with the grammatical concept of a period. Two lines of premises without a conclusion is not a short period, and a whole page of premises without a conclusion is not a long period: regarded as a period, both the one and the other have only fortuitous length, and are therefore equally long and equally short. In order that something may be called "a short presentation" it must have essentially the character of completeness and precisely prove its shortness by the fact that within so small a space it reproduces nevertheless the whole matter on a shortened and diminished scale. On the other hand, three pages may very well be a long twaddle, and thirty pages may quite rightly be called a short book. With regard to the first production the author in question may say[25] with Lessing that, "it was so long because he had not time to write it shorter"; and with regard to the last the author in question could say that "it was such a short brochure because he had not a longer time to write, as he had to publish."[26] And Adler's books are a singular sort of production. Had he had a longer time, the book might have become . . . well, here we are at a standstill, not knowing whether it would have become longer or have become shorter. And now Adler! His hope indeed is "with a longer time to labor and quietly develop the ideas for the future, etc." But, whatever the future (to which Adler can always hold) may bring forth, he who critically holds to the completed whole which lies before him must admit that A.'s books are a singular sort of production, an almost anguishing sort of production. When a clergyman has luckily reached the third point of his sermon and already is so far along in it that one who knows the proportions of clerical elocution ventures with a good deal of security to assume that he is about to hum and say Amen—then it may be anguishing when he, instead of pronouncing the significant Amen, becomes gossipy and adds one period after another, while the knowing hearer may say that essentially the sermon is over and essentially the Amen has been said. This is an example of fortuitous length, recognizable by the fact that it begins where, essentially viewed, the Amen should have been said. One knows instances of people who, embarrassed and embarrassing, may remain sitting in one's home a whole hour merely because they are embarrassed to leave: so perhaps it is the case with such a clergyman, that he, after having been embarrassed to mount up to the solemn place, is now embarrassed to say Amen and go down again. But in any case, the sermon which really begins where the Amen should be said, like the visit which begins when the moment has come when it properly should end, are both examples of fortuitous length, the sign of which is the negative category, *beginning when one should stop*. But essentially the same negative category is expressed by *beginning before the beginning*, that is, before the tug of the ideal resolution has indicated: Now thou canst begin. In case a man in this way, before he had gained enough clarity and ripeness to write a book (which he could not yet write) began to write the preface to the book, then would the preface come under the rubric fortuitous length. And this is precisely Adler's case as an author, that he began before the beginning. That "longer time," so often and for so long a time talked about, by the right use of which Adler "in the future" hopes (this is the present tense in the historical style) "in order to let the ideas unfold themselves in a more appropriate form, etc.," must either not yet have come about, or not have been long enough, or not have been rightly used. A. has begun before the beginning, and therefore his productions come under the rubric fortuitous length. All three of the new books (for the fourth contains verse) are an aggregate of tumultuous aphorisms, the beginning of them fortuitous, the factual range without *telos*, and the possible prolongation endless.

To indicate the content of the books is clearly impossible, but one may characterize them by referring to a verse of Horace interpreted in a special way:[27] *Dum meum canto Lalage et ultra terminum vagos curis expeditis.** For often indeed it is outside the ploughed land, on the further side (*ultra terminum*) that A., free from all cares of authorship (*curis expeditis*), carelessly dawdles about (*vagatur*), humming about his Lalage, in whose honor he strews epigrams along his path and sprinkles it with fancies.[28] As one who in a rural spot, left entirely to himself, now in love with one impression, now with another, now making a spring for gladness, now a long leap for sheer pleasure, now again stands still and ponders, now is really profound, and then again is rather insipid and without flavor—thus does Adler dawdle as a reader of the Bible. When a Biblical text attracts him he writes something about it, and then he goes along another street; sometimes he makes a note of something for the sake of using it another time, but this too will be given up.[29] If Adler as a private reader lives in this way, I have no objection to make; but he lives thus as an author. For all this he does not forget his Lalage. By Lalage many different things may be understood, according to who interprets the ode. I remember from my school days that the Rector under-

* A line from the well-known ode which begins with *Integer vitae*: While I sing of my Lalage and wander freely beyond the border [in the Sabine forest] free of care.

stood thereby life's innocent pleasures. Adler's Lalage may be understood to be that doctrine communicated to him by a revelation, which now he interprets, now cites; for he does not seem *to have quite forgotten that the doctrine was communicated to him by a revelation*, neither has he forgotten the doctrine, the words, which rather have fixed themselves fast in his head. — In case being called by a revelation must make a man serious in the highest and deepest sense — then it is certainly strange to see such a one who in distraction must have forgotten the revelation, just as one may forget his hat, and as people very much *distrait* may forget their heads— to see him now carrying on like an adventurer in the religious style, a mystical knight errant, an itinerant, or like one who without aim or object makes motions in the Bible for the sake of motion, one essentially without occupation who seeks and finds and seeks and gossips—and that man was called by a revelation! In case being called by a revelation must in the highest and deepest sense make a man a zealous and active servant who takes part actively in life as one called in an eminent sense to be a laborer—then it is certainly strange to see a man thus called (who acts as if it were nothing and as if it were all right with the identities) transformed into an *otiosus*, who now has some womanish work to putter over, now with a humorous swing of the hat à la one or another of the Pseudonyms reflects upon this and that or upon himself, and upon the staggering sight of the pale countenance of fearful Jonah,* and then again lets himself be heard melodiously on the erotic pipe of reeds.

Now what is of special importance for an understanding of Adler is that in these last books *absolutely nothing more is said about that fact of revelation, or of continuous revelation, or that this thing and the other was written by direct inspiration.* But even if we assume that this last is as it should be, inasmuch as Adler had no later revelation and later found no occasion to distinguish what is of the Spirit and what is his own, yet

* Alluding to a passage in Adler's *Studies and Examples.*

surely that fact of revelation in the preface to his *Sermons* cannot be laid to one side as a girl lays aside her decorations for the ball. He indeed often returns to the doctrine communicated to him, but nothing at all is said about its being communicated to him by a revelation, from it he draws no inference to his divine authority, he does not appeal to this as a proof of the truth of the doctrine, on the strength of it he does not defend himself as one who has divine authority. And yet, as was shown in the introduction, the fact that a doctrine was imparted to him by a revelation is the decisive point, that which categorically transposes the whole matter and the whole relationship into an entirely different sphere from that in which Adler with all his learning belongs. But then it is wonderful that the very thing which one who has a revealed doctrine to communicate reminds people of again and again, namely, the fact that it was revealed—that this very thing with respect to his revealed doctrine Adler himself seems to have forgotten, and I must constantly remind him that it was indeed, according to his own statement, a revealed doctrine.

Perhaps, however, Adler (the Hegelian, later the Apostle) finds himself along with his revealed doctrine in a new stadium, and now from the "immediate" (which in Hegel's veiled language means revelation) has entered the stadium of "reflection" and now understands the revelation, and then too, in the Hegelian way, he "goes farther" and does not stop with the revelation—with the revelation he himself has had. At the time Christianity came into the world it proclaimed itself to be a revelation and has persisted in that claim. But then time went on, by degrees we all became Christians as by accident, and then many centuries after that there lives a generation (in geographical Christendom) which likes to think that one can understand and comprehend the revelation. The same revealed doctrine is then dealt with in many different ways by a generation which is separated by many centuries from the first. But the one and identical man who has announced that he has had a revelation must surely know precisely what is what with regard to the revelation imparted to him: he must either stand fast by the fact that it was a revelation, and in that case he must speak and act and write in accordance with it; or he must say that now he has understood and comprehended it. But here a little caution. What may it be after all that he has understood? Has he understood that there was no revelation? Then he must revoke the first claim. Or has he understood, what surely he must have understood originally, since he said it, that it was indeed a revelation? Then he must stand by it, argue from it, act in accordance with it, transform his whole existence in relation to it.[30] One cannot deny that there is some excuse for the confusion of Christian truth in modern speculation at the distance of eighteen hundred years from its beginning; but that one and the same man in the course of a few years should strike up this music before us is, if the thing were not so serious, exceedingly comic, and is surely a good proof that he is confused. But above all, one who is supposed to be called by a revelation must with the utmost conscientiousness strive to act honestly. He must not cast a revelation from him as a thief casts away stolen goods when the police are after him—for then he is an intentional deceiver, which Adler certainly is not—but neither must he let the revelation go unexplained while he, treating it as nothing, takes another path . . . for then he is confused.

In the four last books, while again and again there is talk about the doctrine, *absolutely nothing more is said about that fact of revelation whereby it was imparted, or about the fact that the doctrine was imparted by a revelation;* on the other hand, almost to one's disgust, there is talk about *genius—genius here and genius there, that genius is something inexplicable, that genius is something nobody can understand, that "the autodidactical foal"** etc.

* Adler's quaint characterization of that "coalt the foal of an ass" upon which Jesus rode into Jerusalem.

We will stop here and look carefully before us, for it seems clear enough that the upshot of Adler's whole story is that he is a genius. *Quel bruit pour une omelette*! All honor to genius. In case Adler is a genius, in God's name! I certainly shall not envy him for that. But he began by having had a revelation—though *summa summarum* by this we are to understand that he is a genius. This surely is confusion doubly confounded. The first claim may perhaps be a sort of hasty expression for being a genius. This is a hitherto unheard-of confusion! After all, the category of genius is surely something other and qualitatively different from that of having by a revelation from the Saviour received a new doctrine! To have, if you will, by virtue of being a genius a new doctrine to contribute is surely after all (since it lies within the sphere of immanence, so that newness can only indicate the originality of the reproduction)—it surely is something other and qualitatively different from having by a revelation from the Saviour received a new doctrine! We speak of the primitivity of genius, its originality; but these categories, or this category, surely is not identical with having had a revelation by which the Saviour communicated to the elect man a new doctrine!

An erring exegesis and dogmatic has certainly played on Christianity the trick of going on and *understanding* the revelation, or going on and *comprehending* it, pretty much in these terms: a revelation, that is, immediateness, that is, the quality of genius, something in the way of genius, the new, newness, originality, primitivity, etc. A. does about the same, but then he does a little more, whereby, ironically enough, he wins the credit of making indirectly evident how this behavior hostile to Christianity proceeds. A. begins by saying that he himself has had a revelation, and thereupon exegeticizes in the modern style upon the concept of revelation, that is to say, he exegeticizes in *action* by letting go his first claim and then becoming a genius, pretending that there was good sense in this connection, or sense in the fact that there was no connection. — What is it the erring exegesis and speculation have done to confuse Christian truth? And how has it been done? Quite briefly and with categorical precision they have done as follows: they have thrust back the sphere of paradox into the aesthetic sphere and thereby have gained the result that every Christian term, which remaining in its own sphere is a qualitative category, now, in reduced circumstances, can do service as a clever expression which may signify pretty much everything. But the erring exegete and dogmatician have not said at the same time of themselves that they have had a revelation; this is reserved for Adler. He can . . . well, that is how the nursery rhyme goes: "Who can do it best? Surely our priest."

All the many explanations of Adler about genius are quite right aesthetically, and some of it would be quite right, if he had not had the first: being called by a revelation. In his explanations of the genius there is not to be found a trace, categorically understood, that he has any sort of conception of the qualitative and specific peculiarity of Christianity, and that in spite of the fact that he uses Christ's name perpetually, yea, in spite of the fact that he claims to have had a revelation from the Saviour. When* the sphere of paradoxical

* Here begins the passage about "The Difference between a Genius and an Apostle" which S.K. salvaged from his "big book on Adler" and published in 1849 as one of the *Two Minor Ethico-Religious Treatises*. He felt free to publish it because it makes no mention of Adler. It reproduces almost exactly the text of the first draught of 1846, without taking into account any of the alterations he had proposed, and making only a few which occurred to him when he was transcribing it. At the time when he began the second systematic revision of *The Book on Adler*, about the middle of 1848, he wrote (*Papirer* IX A 498): "My health daily deteriorates, soon I shall be decrepit; but I do not fear death, I have learned like the Roman soldiers that there is something worse." He lived in fact five years longer and during that time wrote some of his most striking works; but in his decrepitude such a task of revision as I have undertaken here was likely too much for him. As a translator I must (or at least may) follow the text which S.K. thought

religion is abolished or explained back into the ethical, then an apostle becomes nothing more nor less than a genius—and then good-night Christianity. *Esprit* and spirit, revelation and originality, a calling from God and ingeniousness, an apostle and a genius, all coalesce in one and the same thing.

Thus can an erring* *Wissenschaft* confuse Christianity, and from the sphere of *Wissenschaft* the confusion has sneaked into religious eloquence, so that one not infrequently hears clergymen, bona fide, in all learned simplicity, prostitute Christianity. They talk in lofty tones of the cleverness and profundity of St. Paul, of his beautiful similes, etc.—sheer aesthetics. If Paul is to be regarded as a genius, it looks very bad for him. Only to clerical ignorance could it occur to praise Paul aesthetically, because clerical ignorance has no standard but thinks in this wise: If only one says something good about Paul, it's all to the good. Such good-humored and well-intentioned thoughtlessness is to be referred to the fact that the person in question has not been disciplined by qualitative dialectics, which would have taught him that an apostle is not served by saying something good about him when it is crazy, so that he is recognized and admired for being what in an apostle is a matter of indifference and what essentially he is not, while with that what he is is forgotten. It might just as well occur to such thoughtless eloquence to laud Paul as a stylist and for his artistic use of language, or still better, since it is well known that Paul practiced a manual trade, to maintain that his work as an upholsterer must have been so

fit to publish, without introducing any of the changes he had previously proposed.

This "minor treatise" was translated by Alexander Dru and was published in a volume entitled *The Present Age* which Charles Williams put together and to which I contributed the other "minor treatise." Though I of course kept Alic Dru's translation before me and relished his style, I was not tempted to imitate his translations—if only for fear of incurring the charge of plagiarism.

* The errors moreover are not merely those of heterodoxy but also those of hyper-orthodoxy and, principally, those of thoughtlessness.

perfect that no upholsterer either before or since has been able to equal it—for, if only one says something good about Paul, then all is well. As a genius Paul can sustain no comparison with Plato or with Shakespeare, as an author of beautiful similes he ranks rather low, as stylist his is an obscure name, and as an upholsterer—well, I may admit that in this respect I don't know where to place him. One always does well to transform stupid seriousness into a jest— and then comes the really serious thing, the serious fact that Paul was an apostle, and as an apostle has no affinity either with Plato or Shakespeare or a stylist or an upholsterer, who are all of them (Plato as well as the upholsterer Hansen) beneath any comparison with him.

*A *genius* and an *apostle* are qualitatively distinct, they are categories which belong each of them to their own qualitative spheres: that of *immanence* and that of *transcendence*. (1) The genius may well have something new to contribute, but this newness vanishes again in its gradual assimilation by the race, just as the distinction "genius" vanishes when one thinks of eternity. The apostle has paradoxically something new to contribute, the newness of which, precisely because it is paradoxical and not an anticipation of what may eventually be developed in the race, remains constant, just as an apostle remains an apostle to all eternity, and no immanence of eternity puts him essentially on the same plane with other men, since essentially he is paradoxically different. (2) The genius is what he is by reason of himself, i.e. by what he is in himself: an apostle is what he is by reason of his divine authority. (3) The genius has only immanent teleology: the apostle's position is that of absolute paradoxical teleology.

1. All thinking breathes in immanence, whereas the paradox and faith constitute a qualitative sphere of their own.

---

* S.K. here copies the first draught, but the correction of this paragraph made a year later (VII B 261, 8) omits the tiresome insistence of 15 lines of italics (spaced type), and here I have preferred that simplification.

Immanent (in the relationship between man and man *qua* man) means that every difference is, for essential and eternal thinking, a vanishing point, a moment which has indeed momentarily its importance but essentially vanishes in the essential indifference of eternity. Genius is again, as the word itself says (*ingenium*, what is inborn, original from *origo*, primitivity and pristine from *primus* etc.) immediateness, a natural characteristic—the genius is *born*. Already long before there can be any question to what extent the genius will devote his unusual gifts to God, or will not do it, he is a genius, he is a genius even though he doesn't do it. In the case of the genius there may come about the change that he develops himself to be what κατὰ δύναμιν he is, that he attains conscious possession of himself. Insofar as one uses the expression "paradox" to indicate the new which a genius may have to contribute, it is used only in an unessential sense of the transitory paradox of anticipation which is compressed into something paradoxical and in turn disappears. A genius in his first effort at communication may be paradoxical, but the more he comes to himself the more the paradox disappears. A genius may perhaps be a century ahead of his age and hence stands there as a paradox, but in the end the race will assimilate what was once a paradox, so that it is no longer paradoxical.

Quite otherwise with the apostle. The word itself indicates the difference. An apostle is not born, an apostle is a man called and sent by God, sent by him upon a mission. An apostle does not develop in such wise that he successively becomes what κατὰ δύναμιν he is. For previously to becoming an apostle he possessed no potential possibility. Every man is equally near to being an apostle. An apostle can never in such wise come to himself that he becomes conscious of his apostolic calling as a stage in his life's development. The apostolic call is a paradoxical fact which in the first as well as the last moment of his life stands paradoxically outside his personal identity with himself as the definite person he is.

A man has long before perhaps reached mental maturity and the age of discretion—then he is called to be an apostle. By reason of this call he does not become a better head, acquire more imagination, greater acumen, etc. By no means. He remains himself, but with the paradoxical fact of being sent by God upon a definite mission. By this paradoxical fact the apostle is for all eternity made paradoxically different from all other men. The new which he may have to proclaim is the essential paradox. However long a time it may be preached in the world, essentially it remains equally new, equally paradoxical, no immanence can assimilate it. The apostle did not behave like a man distinguished for natural gifts who was born before his time, he was perhaps what we call a simple man, but by a paradoxical fact he was called to proclaim this new thing. Even if thought might think that it could assimilate the doctrine, yet the way in which it came into the world it cannot assimilate, for the essential paradox is precisely the protest against immanence. But the way such a doctrine came into the world is precisely the qualitatively decisive point, which only by deceit or thoughtlessness can be overlooked.

A genius is appraised on purely aesthetic grounds, according to the content and specific gravity his productions are found to have; an apostle is what he is by reason of the divine authority he has. *The divine authority is the qualitatively* decisive factor. It is not by appraising aesthetically or philosophically the doctrine that I must and can reach the conclusion that *ergo* he who has taught this doctrine was called by a revelation, *ergo* he is an apostle. The order of sequence is exactly the reverse: the man called by a revelation, to whom was entrusted a doctrine, argues from the fact that this was a revelation, from the fact that he has authority. I am not obliged to obey Paul because he is clever or exceptionally clever, but I must submit to Paul because he has divine authority; in any case it is Paul's responsibility to take care to produce this impression, whether anybody will submit to his authority or no. Paul must not appeal to his cleverness, for then he is a fool; he must not enter into a purely aesthetic or philosophic discussion about the content of his doctrine, for then he is *distrait*. No, he must appeal to his divine authority, and precisely by that, while he is willing to sacrifice life and all, he must *prevent* all aesthetic and philosophically direct objections against the content or form of the doctrine. Paul must not recommend himself and his doctrine by the help of the beautiful metaphors; conversely, he should say to the individual: "Whether the simile is beautiful or not, or whether it is tattered and threadbare, that is of no account, thou shalt reflect that what I say was entrusted to me by a revelation, so that it is God himself or our Lord Jesus Christ who speaks, and thou shalt not engage presumptuously in criticizing the form. I cannot, I dare not compel thee to obey, but by thy conscientious relationship to God I make thee eternally responsible to God for thy relationship to the doctrine for the fact that I have proclaimed it as revealed to me by a revelation and therefore proclaimed it with divine authority."

Authority is the qualitatively decisive point. Or is there not, even within the relativity of human life, though is disappears in immanence, a difference between the king's command and the word of a poet or a thinker? And what difference is there except that the king's command has authority and therefore prohibits all critical and aesthetical impertinence with regard to form and content? On the other hand, the poet or the thinker, even within this relativity, has no authority, his saying is appraised purely aesthetically and philosophically by appraising the content and form. But what is it that has fundamentally confused Christianity, unless it is that people have at first in doubt become so nearly uncertain whether there is a God that in rebellion against all authority they have forgotten what authority is and the dialectic of it? A king is sensibly present in such a way that one can sensibly convince oneself of it, and, if it should be necessary, the king can quite sensibly convince one that he exists. But God does not exist in such a sense. Doubt has taken advantage of this to put God on the same plane as all those who have no authority, geniuses, poets, thinkers, whose utterances are appraised precisely by aesthetic and philosophical criteria; and in case a thing is well said, then the man is a genius, and in case a thing is unusually and especially well said, then it is God who has said it!!!

By that trick God is really conjured away. What is he to do? If God stops a man on the street, calls him by a revelation and sends him out to the other men armed with divine authority—then they say to him, "From whom art thou?" He answers, "From God." But, lo, God cannot help his ambassador as a king can who gives him an accompaniment of soldiers or policemen, or his ring, or a letter in his handwriting which everybody recognizes—in short, God cannot be at men's service by providing them with a sensible certitude of the fact that an apostle is an apostle—this too would be nonsense. Even the miracle, if the apostle has this gift, gives no sensible certitude, for the miracle is an object of faith. And moreover it is nonsense to get *sensible* certitude that an apostle is an apostle (the paradoxical determinant of a spiritual connection), just as it is nonsense to get *sensible* certitude of the fact that God exists, since God indeed is spirit. So then the apostle says he is from God. The others answer, "Well then, let us see whether the content of the doctrine is divine, for in that case we will accept it along with the claim that it was revealed to thee." In that way both God and the apostle are mocked. The divine authority of the man thus called should be the surest defense which secures the doctrine and keeps from it at the majestic distance of the divine all impertinences; instead of which the content and form of the doctrine must allow itself to be criticized and sniffed at—before one is able in this way to reach the conclusion that it was a revelation or no. And meanwhile the apostle and God must presumably wait at the door or in the porter's lodge until the case has been decided by the wise men in the *bel étage*. The elect man should according to God's ordinance assert his divine authority to chase away all impertinent people who will not obey him but argue. And instead of obeying, men transform an apostle into an examinee who comes as it were to the market place with a new doctrine.

What then is authority? Is authority the profundity of the doctrine, its superiority, its cleverness? Not at all. If authority thus predicated is merely profundity, raised to a higher power, or reduplicated, then precisely there is no authority; for if a pupil by his understanding of it appropriated the doctrine totally and fully, there would in fact be no difference left between the teacher and the pupil. Authority, on the contrary, is something which remains unchanged, which one cannot acquire by having understood the doctrine in the fullest sense. *Authority is a specific quality which comes from another place and makes itself felt precisely when the content of the saying or of the action is assumed to be indifferent.* Let us take an example, as simple as possible, where nevertheless the situation is plain. When the man who has the authority to say it says, "Go!" and when he who has not authority says, "Go!"—then indeed the saying "Go" along with its content is identical; appraised aesthetically, if you will, they are both equally well said, but the authority makes the difference. In case authority is not "the other" (το ἕτερον), in case it might in any way indicate a higher power within the identity, then precisely there is no authority. In case a teacher is thus enthusiastically conscious that he himself in his existence is expressing and has expressed by the sacrifice of everything the doctrine he preaches, this consciousness may well give him a sure and firm spirit, but it does not give him authority. His life as a proof of the rightness of the doctrine is not "the other" (το ἕτερον) but a simple reduplication of the doctrine. The fact that he lives in accordance with the doctrine does not prove that it is right; but because he is convinced of the rightness of the doctrine he lives in accordance with it. On the other hand, whether a policeman be a rogue or an honest man, being on duty, he has authority.

In order to illuminate more clearly this concept which is so important for the paradox-religious sphere, I shall pursue the dialectic of authority. *In the sphere of immanence authority cannot be thought, or it can be thought only as vanishing.** Insofar as there may be question of authority or of the exercise of authority in political, social, civic, household, or disciplinary relationships, authority is only a transient, vanishing factor, which either vanishes later in temporal existence, or vanishes for the fact that earthly life itself is a transitory factor which vanishes with all its differences. At the bottom of all relationships between man and man *qua* man it is only possible to *think* that the differences lie within the identity of immanence, that is, within the essential equality. The one man cannot be *thought* to be different from all others by reason of a specific quality—otherwise all thinking ceases, as it quite consistently does in the paradox-religious sphere or the sphere of faith. All human differences between man and man *qua* man vanish for thought as factors in the totality and quality of identity. In the moment I must be so good as to respect and take pleasure in the differences, but I am permitted to edify myself religiously with the certitude that the differences vanish in all eternity, both those which distinguish me and those which depress me. As a subject I must honor and obey the King with an undivided soul, but I am permitted to edify myself with the thought that essentially I am a citizen of

* Perhaps with one or another it may be as with me who recall with reference to the subject of "authority" Magister Kierkegaard's *Edifying Discourses* where it is so strongly accented and emphasized by the fact that every time the words are repeated in the preface: "These are not sermons because the author has not the authority to preach." Authority is either an apostolic call, or the specific quality of ordination. To preach is precisely to exercise authority, and that this is what preaching means is altogether forgotten in our age.

heaven, and that, if once I should encounter there his deceased majesty, I shall not be bound to him by the obedience required of a subject.

Such is the relationship between man and man *qua* man. *But between God and man there is an eternal, essential, qualitative difference,* which no one without presumptuous thinking can allow to vanish in the blasphemous assertion that God and man are indeed differentiated in the transitory moment of temporal existence, so that man within this life ought to obey and worship God, but in eternity the difference must vanish in the essential equality, so that God and man would become equals, just like the king and his valet.

Thus between God and man there is and remains an eternal, essential, qualitative difference. *The paradox-religious situation* (which quite rightly cannot be thought but only believed) *comes to evidence when God appoints a particular man to have divine authority—nota bene* in relation to what was entrusted to him. The man thus called does not relate himself to [one must use here the literal translation of a phrase which idiomatically means "behave"] the relationship between man and man *qua* man, nor is he related to other men by a quantitative difference (like a genius, a man of distinguished gifts, etc.). No, he behaves paradoxically by reason of having a specific quality which no immanence can recall into the equality of eternity; for it is essentially paradoxical and after thinking (not before, in advance of thinking)—against thinking. If such an elect man has a doctrine to communicate according to a divine order, and another man (let us imagine it) has found out for himself the same doctrine, then are these two nevertheless not equal; for the first is by reason of his paradoxical specific quality (the divine authority) different from every other man and from the qualification of essential likeness and equality which immanently lies at the basis of all human differences. The qualification "an apostle" belongs in the sphere of transcendence, which, quite consistently, has a qualitatively different expression for the relation of other men to an apostle: they relate themselves to him [behave] believingly, whereas all thinking is and remains and breathes in immanence. But faith is not a transitory qualification, no more than the apostle's paradoxical qualification was transitory.

In the relationship between man and man *qua* man we found that no *established* and *lasting* differentium of authority was *thinkable*, that it was a vanishing factor. Meanwhile let us dwell for a moment upon some examples of such so-called relationships of authority between man and man *qua* man (which are true relationships under the conditions of temporal existence) in order to observe in them how authority is essentially to be regarded. A king is indeed assumed to have authority. Why is it then that one is almost offended at learning that a king is clever, is an artist, etc.? Surely it is because in his case one essentially accentuates the royal authority, and in comparison with this the commoner qualification of human difference is a vanishing factor, is unessential, a disturbing accident. A government board is assumed to have authority in a determinate sphere. Why is it then that one would be offended if such a board in its decrees, etc., were really clever, witty, profound? Because one quite rightly accentuates its authority. To ask whether the king is a genius, with the implication that in such case he is to be obeyed, is really *lèse majesté*, for the question contains a doubt concerning subjection to authority. To be willing to obey a board in case it is able to say witty things is at bottom to make a fool of the board. To honor one's father because he is a distinguished pate is impiety. However, as has been said, between man and man *qua* man authority, if there be any, is a vanishing factor, and eternity does away with all earthly authority. But now for the sphere of transcendence? Let us take an example as simple as possible but for that reason as obvious as possible. When Christ says, "There is an eternal life," and when Theological Candidate Petersen says, "There is an eternal life"—they both say the same thing; in the first statement there is contained no more deduction, development, profundity, thoughtfulness, than in the latter; both statements, aesthetically appraised, are equally good. And yet there is an eternal qualitative difference! Christ as the God-Man is in possession of the specific quality of authority which no eternity can mediate and put Christ on the same plane with the essential human equality. Christ therefore taught with authority. To ask whether Christ is profound is blasphemy and is an attempt (whether consciously or unconsciously) to annihilate him; for in the question is contained a doubt about his authority and an attempt is made with impertinent simplicity to appraise and judge him as though he were up for examination and should be catechized—whereas instead of that he is the one to whom is given all power in heaven and in earth.

Yet seldom nowadays, very seldom, do we hear a religious address which is perfectly correct. The better sort are fain to dabble a bit in what one might call unconscious and well-intentioned rioting, defending and upholding Christianity with might and main—in erroneous categories. Let us take an example, any one that comes to hand. I take it from a German. With that I know that nobody—not the stupidest and not the most ill-natured—will suppose that I write this concerning a matter which to my thinking is infinitely important in order to aim at some clergyman or another. Bishop Sailer of Regensburg, in a homily for the Fifth Sunday in Lent, preaches on John 7:47-51 as his text. He selects the verse: "He that is of God heareth God's word," and "If a man keepeth my saying he shall never see death." Then he says: "In these words of the Lord are solved three great riddles over which men in one way or another have racked their brains since the beginning of time." There we have it. The word "riddle," and especially "three great riddles," and then the next clause, "over which men . . . have *racked their brains*," at once lead one's thought to the profound in the intellectual sense, to meditation, pondering, speculation.

But after all how can a simple apodeictic statement be profound?—an apodeictic statement which is what it is only by the fact that this or that man said it, a statement which does not at all demand to be understood or fathomed but only to be believed. In the case of a simple statement, an assertion, how can it occur to a man that an enigma had to be solved by way of profound pondering and fathoming?* The question simply is, Is there an eternal life? The answer is, There is an eternal life. Where then in all the world is profundity to be found in this? In case Christ is not the one who said it, and in case Christ is not what he said he was, then, if the statement itself is profound, the profundity indeed has yet to be discovered. Let us take Mr. Petersen the theological candidate, who indeed also says, "There is an eternal life." Who in all the world would think of accusing him of profundity because of a plain statement? Thus the decisive point does not lie in the statement but in the fact that it is Christ who uttered it; but the confusing thing is that one, as though to entice men to believe, talks a lot about the profound and the profound. A Christian priest, if he would speak correctly, must say quite simply, "We have Christ's word for it that there is an eternal life—therewith the matter is decided. Here there is no question either about racking one's brains or about speculation, but about the fact that it is Christ who said it, not in the capacity of a profound thinker, but with his divine

* In 1847 (*Papirer* VII B 261, 13) S.K. proposed the following substitution for the remainder of this paragraph which has at least the advantage of being a notable abbreviation; but perhaps, according to an adage which S.K. adopted, "First thoughts are better than second thoughts." In this big book abbreviations are always welcome; yet perhaps I ought to have included S.K.'s first thoughts along with his second thoughts—if only it could be done without making this book look pedantic.

Instead of all this clerical twaddle about enigmas and racking the brain, Sailer ought to say: "We have Christ's word for it, and when he has said it the thing is decided. Here there is no question either of racking the brain or of enigmas, but of the one who has said that to him is given all power in heaven and in earth."

authority." Let us go further, let us assume that one believes that there is an eternal life because Christ has said it, so believingly he circumvents all the profundity and pondering and fathoming wherewith people rack their brains. On the other hand, let us take one who wants to rack his brains profoundly with the question about immortality—I wonder if he will have a right to deny that the simple assertion is a profound answer to the question? What Plato says about immortality is really profound, won by deep pondering—but poor Plato had no authority whatsoever.

Meanwhile this is the situation: Doubt and superstition, which make faith vain, have, among other things, made men embarrassed about obeying, about bowing to authority. This rebelliousness sneaks into the thinking even of the better sort of men, perhaps without their being conscious of it, and then begins all this extravagance, which at bottom is treachery, about the profound and the profound and the wondrously beauteous features which one can dimly descry, etc. If one were to describe with one single predicate the Christian-religious eloquence which one now hears and reads, one would have to say that it is *affected*. Ordinarily when one talks about the affectation of a clergyman one thinks perhaps about how he dresses and gets himself up, talks in a sweet and languishing voice, rolls his R's like a Norwegian, wrinkles his brow, strains himself with forceful gestures and with leaps of religious enthusiasm, etc. All such things, however, are of minor importance, though it is always desirable that they should not be. But the pernicious thing is when the whole train of thought in his priestly eloquence is affected, when its orthodoxy is won by laying the accent entirely on the wrong place, when basically he requires people to believe in Christ and preaches faith in him on grounds which cannot possibly be the object of faith. In case a son were to say, "I obey my father, not because he is my father, but because he is a genius or because his commands are always profound and clever"—then this filial obedience is affected. The son accentuates something which is entirely beside the point, he accentuates the cleverness and profundity in a *command*, whereas a command is precisely indifferent with regard to this qualification. The son is willing to obey by virtue of his father's profundity and cleverness, and by virtue of this it is precisely not possible to obey, for his critical attitude with regard to the decision whether the command is profound and clever undermines obedience. And this too is affectation when there is so much about accepting Christianity and believing in Christ on account of the profundity and profundity of the doctrine. One accepts orthodoxy by accentuating something which is entirely beside the point. The whole of modern Speculation is therefore "affected" by reason of having done away with *obedience* on the one hand and *authority* on the other, and by then wanting to be orthodox. A clergyman who is entirely correct in his eloquence must speak thus in introducing a word of Christ: "This word was spoken by him to whom, according to his own statement all power hath been given in heaven and in earth. Now, thou, my hearer, must consider by thyself whether thou wilt bow to this authority or no, receive it and believe it or no. But if thou wilt not do so, then for heaven's sake do not go off and accept the word because it is clever and profound or wondrously beautiful, for this is blasphemy, it is wanting to treat God like an aesthetic critic. For so soon as the dominant note of authority, of the specific paradoxical authority, is heard, then this sort of appropriation, which otherwise is permissible and desirable, is a crime and a presumption."

But now how can an apostle prove that he has authority? Could he prove it physically, he would be no apostle. He has no other proof but his own assertion. And thus precisely it ought to be, for otherwise the believer would come into a direct relation to him, not into a paradoxical relationship. In the transitory situation of authority between man and man *qua* man the authority will ordinarily be recognized physically by means of force. An apostle has no other proof but his own assertion, and at the most by his willingness to suffer every-thing for the sake of the doctrine. With regard to that his speech will be brief: "I am called by God; do with me now as you will, scourge me, persecute me; but my last word is my first: I am called by God, and I make you eternally responsible for what you do to me." In case it were true in real life (let us imagine it) that an apostle had power in a worldly sense, had great influence and powerful connections by the force of which he is victorious over the opinions and judgments of men—in case he employed this power he would *eo ipso* have lost his cause. For by employing force he would have defined his effort as essentially identical with that of other men, and yet an apostle is what he is only by reason of his paradoxical heterogeneity, by reason of having divine authority, which he can have, absolutely unaltered, even if by men he is regarded, according to Paul's saying, as worth no more than the filth on which they tread.*

[3. *The genius has only immanent teleology; the apostle is put paradoxically in an absolutely paradoxically teleological position.*

If any man can be said to be put in an absolutely paradoxi-cally teleological position it is an apostle. The doctrine im-parted to him is not given to him as a problem to ponder over, it is not given to him for his own sake; on the contrary he is on a mission and has to proclaim the doctrine and exercise authority. Just as one who is sent to town with a letter has nothing to do with the contents of the letter but only with the delivery of it; just as an ambassador who is sent to a foreign court has no responsibility for the content of the message but only for conveying it properly; so an apostle has principally the single duty of being faithful in his service, which is the performance of his mission. In this

* Here ends the passage which S.K. salvaged from *The Book on Adler* and published as a dissertation on "The Difference between a Genius and an Apostle"; but in the published work he added the four para-graphs which for the sake of completeness are here added between brackets.

essentially consists the sacrificial character of the apostle's life, even if he were never to be persecuted, namely, in the fact that "as himself poor he makes many rich," that he never can give himself time or repose or freedom from care, in *otium*, in the enjoyment of "good days," to be enriched by that with which his preaching enriches others. Spiritually understood, he is like a busy housewife who herself hardly gets time to eat, so busy is she in preparing food for the many mouths. And though he at the beginning might venture to hope for a long life, yet his life until the last will remain unchanged, for there will always be new and newer people to whom the doctrine must be proclaimed. Although a revelation is the paradoxical fact which surpasses men's understanding, one can nevertheless understand this much, which has everywhere been manifested, that a man is called by a revelation to go forth into the world to proclaim the word, to act and to suffer, called to a life of ceaseless activity as the Lord's messenger.

It is very different with genius. Genius has only immanent teleology, and as it develops itself it projects this self-development as its work in the world. That acquires importance, perhaps great importance, but it is not itself related teleologically to the world or to other men, and without taking his gifts in vain the genius can live only humoristically, self-satisfied, in a place withdrawn from the world, where without concern whether or not others profit by it, he develops himself with seriousness and diligence. The genius is for this reason by no means inactive, he works within himself perhaps more than ten businessmen, accomplishes perhaps a great deal, but nothing that he accomplishes has any *telos* outside itself. This is at once the high humanity and the pride of genius: the humanity consists in the fact that it does not define itself teleologically in relation to any other man, as though there might be someone in need of it; the pride consists in the fact that it immanently relates itself to itself. It is modest of the nightingale that it does not require anyone to listen to it; it is proud of the nightingale that it doesn't care whether anybody listens to it or no. The dialectic of the genius will be especially offensive in our age when the multitude, the masses, the public, and other such abstractions, are bent in turning everything upside down. The "highly honored public" and the domineering multitude want the genius to express the fact that he exists for them and for their sake; the "highly honored public" and the domineering multitude are only one side of the dialectic of the genius, they are offended by his pride and do not notice that this same thing is also modesty and humility. The "highly honored public" and the domineering multitude would also take the existence of the apostle in vain. For it is true indeed that he exists absolutely for the sake of others, is sent forth for the sake of others, but it is not the multitude and not the masses and not the "highly honored public" and not even the "highly honored cultivated public" that are his lord or his lords—it is God, and the apostle is he who has *authority* to *command* both the multitude and the public.

The humoristic self-satisfaction of the genius is the unity of modest resignation in the world and proud elevation above the world, of being an unnecessary superfluity and a precious ointment. If the genius is an artist, then he produces his work of art, but neither he nor his work has any *telos* outside itself. Or he is an author who abolishes every teleological relationship with the world about him and defines himself as a lyric poet. Lyric art has quite rightly no *telos* outside itself; whether one writes a page of lyric or folios of lyric, that makes no difference with regard to determining the direction of his activity. The lyrical author is concerned only about his production, enjoys the delight of producing, perhaps through pain and effort, but he has nothing to do with others, does not write *in order to*, in order to enlighten men, in order to help them along in the right way, in order to put something over—in short he does not write *in order to*. And so it is with every genius. No genius has an "in order to." The apostle has absolutely paradoxically an "in order to."]

Now we return again to Adler and to his transmogrification already referred to, whereby from being one called by a revelation he became a genius, still thinking that he is identical with himself. For he who is called by a revelation must *eo ipso* assume a teleological attitude, being precisely God's instrument which is to be used to produce an effect. It is different with a genius, who may live humoristically withdrawn from the world in self-satisfaction.[31] This is pretty much the attitude Adler assumes in his last works—but Adler began by being called by a revelation, and Adler now thinks that he is in identity with himself, that is to say, he fails to notice that there is a qualitative decisive difference between his first position and his last. Although a revelation is the paradoxical fact which surpasses men's understanding, yet one can understand this much, which is everywhere in evidence, that a man is called by a revelation to go out into the world to proclaim the word, to labor and to suffer, to lead an unremittingly active life as God's messenger. That on the contrary a man might be called to sit at ease in his own ample mansion employed in an active literary *far niente* in a quiet place, to be clever from time to time, and thereupon to be publisher as well as collector of the dubious proofs of his cleverness—is a thought almost blasphemous. Here again Adler's later attitude contains a proof against the reality and truth of his first claim, while the fact that he does not revoke his first is a proof that he is confused. At the beginning of his activity as an author he was also on another path when he shouted before all the people, "Confess! Confess!"[32] Now in his last books he has adopted the principle of silence. "Silence is genius," says he. He does not develop this thesis more in detail, as in general he seems to have abandoned himself to the habit of touching tangentially upon the most various subjects and publishing his observations in a book— but, no, in four books at once. The significance of silence, moreover, is quite simple. For us simple men silence is a way for the expression of inwardness, and is the way by which originality is acquired, an originality which is more than a surrogate for the originality of the genius. (A revelation lies in an entirely different sphere, and therefore nothing is said about it here.) By holding fast a definite expression of one's life, a definite single thought, in absolutely silent inwardness, by not wishing to open the least communication with any other man (by which relative and comparative standards, the standards of mediocrity, are made accessible) every man will, if in the meantime he does not lose his reason (for this danger is inescapable), *acquire originality*. The converse and opposite of this situation of freedom, this slow acquisition, is the direct, immediate characteristic of genius (and hence again what lies within the paradoxical religious sphere, the fact of being called by a revelation). The idea of silence, the whole conception of silence as the way of inwardness, which for every man leads to the highest attainment, whether originally he was a genius or no, this conception has found an adequate expression in the writings of the Pseudonyms, to which therefore, so far as this subject is concerned, I refer everyone—only not Adler, who in his thesis, "Silence is genius," annihilates this idea of the Pseudonyms— which is comical enough and becomes still more so when one reflects that his four last books also annihilate his first position. Even though it be conceded that Adler is a genius, he wants, however, to be an immediate genius, and by the aid of silence it is impossible to become anything immediate, since after all it is nonsense to think of a method in relation to immediacy, which precisely is anterior to a method.*

* At this point S.K. proposed to suppress six pages of the first draft of this book and to substitute about two pages of a very different character. (VII B 256, 14-20) I have followed his proposal in the text, but the discarded pages contain something we ought to know about Adler and suggest a shrewd diagnosis of his derangement, so I have translated them in this footnote:

In the four last books A. is merely a genius, a pure and genuine genius—and yet, in this opinion, presumably he is in identity with his first position. He has forgotten that those words in the preface to his *Sermons* were imparted to him by a revelation dictated by the Saviour;

he has forgotten that the *Sermons*, to which A. often refers, were written under the influence of Jesus' cooperative grace; A. as a genius has, so it seems, undertaken the whole management of affairs, presumably in distraction—in distraction, for, if it were done consciously, he must solemnly revoke his first claim. How far A. can go in distraction one can further ascertain by reading his four last books; for there one has an opportunity to observe with what levity (which only distraction can excuse) he deals with God and Christ, represents them as chatting with one another, and he chats with them. In the last books he is poetically inventive, he represents God and Christ as talking with one another— and this surely is an invention! Thus Adler's *Attempt at a Short Exposition of Christianity* begins as follows: "Before God created the world he said to Jesus, 'I can do everything as perfectly as possible,' " etc. God and Jesus are introduced as speaking and conversing. But this surely was not communicated by a revelation! But what is it then? Well, it is a little poetical effort to enliven the presentation. But, lo, Adler later quotes the same conversation, he founds an argument upon it. He says in many passages, "as Jesus promised to let himself be born"; that is, he talks of that conversation between God and Christ as something which actually occurred and to which one can make appeal as though these were the *ipsissima verba* of Jesus. Indeed in one place Adler even says: "For finally we must remember what Jesus said to God," etc., and thereupon he quotes several of the invented words. So first one ventures with frivolous inventions out into the sphere where one should rather leave inventions alone, and thereupon fixes his own invention so tightly in his head that he thinks it is reality. In that way a lightminded person can easily get a revelation. He needs only to fumble for some time as a crocheteer with the fantastic notion of a revelation until this notion that he has had a revelation at last fixes itself so fast in him that he poetically conceives he has had a revelation, and then this invention fixes itself fast as an actuality—until something new sets itself fast.

But, whereas Adler treats his own inventions as though they were realities, he treats the New Testament in an equally frivolous way, as though it were not a reality—he who undoubtedly has many a pretty word to say about the Bible, and precisely in view of this his behavior indicates that he is in a confused state of mind. With an arbitrariness which is perfectly fantastic he lays claim to words of the Bible as his own without using quotation marks. As between one author and another that would be called plagiarism; to plagiarize from God is blasphemy. Indeed there are passages where in his frivolity he actually reaches the point of identifying himself with Christ. A saying begins with the words of Christ in the first person: I say unto you. These words are not quoted, there is no indication that they are Bible words, which is important especially because they are in the first person. Immediately after these words in the first person comes the next sentence which

Instead of a man who was called by a revelation we get a genius, and one may say of Adler that by becoming a genius he is somewhat deranged, which in turn is precisely proved by the fact that he has not found himself obliged in the least degree to explain anything about the dreadful and topsy-turvy metamorphosis he has undergone, for he seems constantly to be blissful in the vain imagination that he is in identity with himself from first to last, which in fact he is as a deranged genius.

He is a deranged genius of the instantaneous sort, and hence precisely has no conception of himself, is entirely without continuity. In the instant something grips him—then he is that. The next instant something else grips him—then he is that. His existence explains nothing, as though another might be directing his life and guiding him by a foreign will; and there is no aesthetic or religious concept he has developed in such a way that it has gained new clarity or is thought out with true originality. On the other hand, he touches upon the most diverse subjects and almost everywhere confuses them. It cannot be denied that he makes profound remarks, but he surely does not reach absolute profundity, if the explanation we gave at the very beginning of this book is right, that profundity is connection and continuity. And even in his profound remarks there is a certain uniformity, for in large part they are made on one last. Understanding a thought is something like being able to decline a paradigm: one can also decline all the words which come under that paradigm. If one has understood a thought, one can, by using it in many "examples," seem to make many profound remarks, and yet the many are really repetitions, and hence (to refer again to the simile of the last) one is not justified in saying that he

_____

likewise is in the first person but are the words of Adler. A reader generally must assume, as Adler leads everyone to assume, that it is he who utters the whole saying, that the "I" in the first sentence is the same as the "I" in the second and in the third sentence. And yet the first "I" is Christ and the other "I" is Adler.

has learned many declensions because he has learned the many words which come under the same declension. So it is too with having understood one thought: if the repetitions are not to be tedious, there must be added a poetical factor which makes the application of the examples aesthetically worthy. But for this Adler has no time—he has (according to his own authentic interpretation, cf. 1) nothing new to contribute—he who lives in a lyrical *otium*! With respect to form he is at a disadvantage. He who has not and never has had anything new to contribute by way of content must strive precisely by means of the form to accomplish something. The thought which Adler especially rides is the old Hegelian notion that the concept "veers about," only that it is used rather under the qualification of the ironical. This thought is thus expressed in my master's dissertation ("About Irony"): Irony makes the phenomenon evident; irony consists in the cunning that, while the opponent believes he is talking about another thing or even has grasped another thing, irony perceives that the individual has given himself away. Every idea consistently carried through has *eo ipso* the power to require the contrary to become manifest. How this is more particularly to be understood, how it proceeds, has often been explained and exhibited by the Pseudonyms. The ironical cunning consists in transforming oneself to nothing by nega-tive-active consistency in order to help the phenomenon to become manifest. At the first glance and for stupid men it may seem as if the ironical man were the loser. The ironical cunning consists in keeping oneself negative, thus transform-ing the attack into self-revelation. The attacker raises a storm and makes a great fuss; in the eyes of foolish men it seems as though he were the stronger, and yet he accomplishes nothing more—and there sits irony so cunning and on the lookout—he accomplishes nothing more than to reveal his own nature, his own paltriness or his own insignificance. Thus, for example, one may employ irony against a shrew, and her shrewishness becomes more and more manifest. So too it is ironically correct when a man says something extraordinary about himself, for example, that he has had a revelation, then precisely to believe him (the negative attitude, not opposing him directly as foolish men do), in order in that way to help him to make it evident to himself that he has had no revelation. When a man really has ataraxia and self-mastery he will by negative consistency be able to make any kind of a dialectically complicated phenomenon plain; thus A. seems so awfully well pleased at the profound remark that "The law put its foot in it by condemning Christ, and thereby did away with itself." This whole thing is neither more nor less than Hegel's "veering about" of the concept carried out with a little ironic coloring. Hegel, it is well known, is nothing less than he is ironical; with him it is always a serious matter when the concept veers about. That irony owes its life to a dialectic of comparison is in 1846 not much of a discovery. Hegel believes that the concept veers about by an immanent necessity; nevertheless irony notices the transition inasmuch as it notices its drollery or its ingenuity. The qualitative dialectic is in the first place really in essential understanding with the category of the leap, a category which Adler also bungles.

Among Adler's profound remarks there are sometimes reminiscences of other writers to be found, and in view of this it may be quite natural that Adler frequently recurs to the thesis and defends the thesis that stealing in the world of spirit is entirely permissible. Well, about that every man has his own opinion. I don't deny that I hold the opposite opinion. But the strange thing is again that it is Adler (one who has a revelation to which he can appeal) who adopts this thesis; for after all a revealed doctrine cannot have been borrowed from others, and there is surely no one up to date that has stolen anything from Adler. On the other hand, in case Adler thinks himself guilty of a theft, or innocent of it, inasmuch as this theft according to his opinion is permissible, there results this strange and preposterous situation that he who is placed above other men by reason of a revelation should pilfer a little from poor folks. However, perhaps Adler after all does himself an injustice in suspecting himself of stealing; for in the world of spirit theft is so far from being permissible that it is impossible. For in the world of spirit, and only in the world of spirit, the security of property rights is absolute. If one leaves a manuscript lying about, another may steal it, he may publish it, but he cannot steal its thoughts, nor can he propound the thoughts contained in the stolen manuscript, in one way or another he will alter them, so that they do not remain the same thoughts.

If one regards Adler as a deranged genius (who neither as thinker nor as artist is in control of himself, who in the rapture of production touches tangentially upon the most diverse subjects) and if one would define totally and essentially the character of his genius, one may say that it is dizziness. With this it is not denied that individual utterances and remarks may even be profound. A drunken man may well utter good sayings, but the essential character of his genius is drunkenness. I shall now illustrate this dizziness by several examples from Adler's last works, while begging the reader not to forget that the principal characteristic which further illustrates his dizziness is the fact that he propounds dizzy aesthetic views which remind one strongly of paganism and the worldly view of life, though he gives himself out to be not only a believing Christian but claims even that he has had a revelation from the Saviour. It is simple dizziness to adopt a dizzy, aesthetic view, but it is dizziness raised to a higher power to wish at the same time to be a Christian in an eminent sense and to wish to help the understanding of Christian doctrine by means of aesthetics.

In a physiological sense attention has quite rightly been called to the fact that dizziness results when the eye has no fixed point on which to rest. Hence one becomes dizzy on looking down from a tower, for the glance plunging down finds no limit, no bound. For a similar reason one becomes dizzy at sea, because everything is constantly changing and so again there is no limit or bound. A physician has explained somewhere that it was *seasickness* the French soldiers died of in Russia, produced by the fact that there was nothing before the eye in the endless breadth of the plain. When therefore one notices that one is becoming dizzy one may stop it by catching upon something with the eye. In case a man who becomes thus dizzy in driving down a steep hill will himself undertake to be coachman he will hardly become dizzy. As a coachman, the definite way he is obliged to watch the reins will prevent dizziness. So it is with physical dizziness. The dizzy is the wide, the endless, the unlimited, the boundless; and dizziness itself is the boundlessness of the senses. The indefinite is the ground of dizziness, but it is also a temptation to abandon oneself to it. For surely indefiniteness is contrary to man's nature, and it is not merely science which, according to Aristotle's saying, abhors the boundlessness of vacuity, not merely ethics which abhors ambiguity, but precisely because indefiniteness is against nature it is at the same time tempting. The dialectic of dizziness has thus in itself the contradiction of willing what one does not will, what one shudders at, whereas this shudder nevertheless frightens only . . . temptingly. The remedy for dizziness is therefore limitation; and, spiritually understood, all discipline is limitation. So then he who, physiologically, has a tendency to become dizzy does well to avoid open places for the time being and feel his way along the walls of buildings, in order that the manifold may be of help as a relative scale. So also must he who, spiritually understood, suffers from dizziness try to limit himself. The limit is not only in the Greek sense the beautiful, but in the ethical sense it is a saving power.

Spiritually understood, dizziness may have a double character. It may be occasioned by the fact that a man has so wandered astray in the infinite that nothing finite can acquire for him substantial existence, that he can get no standard of measurement. This kind of dizziness consists rather in an excess of imagination, and, inasmuch as one might conceive of dizziness metaphorically with relation to the eye, one might perhaps call it *single-sighted dizziness*. The other kind of dizziness produced by an abstract dialectic, owing to the fact that it sees absolutely everything double, sees nothing at all. This kind of dizziness one might call *double-sighted dizziness*. Salvation from all dizziness, spiritually understood, is essentially to seek the ethical, which by qualitative dialectic disciplines and limits the individual and establishes his task.

It is especially from the first kind of dizziness that Adler suffers. As a dialectitian he was first educated by Hegel, whose System has no ethic and whose dialectic, far from being an existential dialectic, is a sort of fantasy-intuition. From the dizzy height of the Hegelian metaphysic Adler plunges down headlong into the religious sphere, and now discovers, if one will, orthodoxy, but, be it noted, an orthodoxy without the ethical. When relationship to ethics is abandoned one may say that dizziness must come about by necessity.

As an example of A.'s dizziness I* will *first adduce* his teaching about *the instant*, which, it is true he nowhere lectures upon, but every instant he alludes to it. His teaching is to the following effect: Grasp the instant, everything depends upon the instant, the next instant it is too late, so you have to go through life like the Wandering Jew. Throughout Adler's last works runs a paganish despairing joy at having himself grasped the instant, and a despairing dread at the mere thought—what if he had not grasped it?! For to Adler the instant means nothing more nor less than what luck meant in paganism—only he is man enough to combine this dialectically with the Christian conception, so that he also in a lucky

* What here and in the next following I must explain briefly belongs to the problems which the Pseudonyms have explained so clearly that I can refer to them—only not for Adler, that would certainly come too late.

instant was called by a revelation from the Saviour and got a doctrine entrusted to him. The play of luck disposes not only as it did aforetime over riches, honor, power, the most beautiful maiden etc., but a revelation is also a play of luck.

Regarded as a problem, "the instant" is undeniably a very difficult one, since it must concern itself with the dialectic between the temporal and the eternal. The eternal is infinite in content, and yet it must be made commensurable with the temporal, and the contact is in the instant. Yet this instant is nothing. Thinking here comes to a stop with the most dreadful contradiction, with the most taxing of all thoughts, which, if it were to be held for long at the highest pitch of mental exertion must bring the thinker to madness. To build card-houses on the table is not difficult, but that a huge edifice might be built upon what is smaller than the edge of a card, upon a foundation which is nothing (for the instant as such does not exist, it is merely the confine between time past and time future, it *is* when it *has been*)—that certainly is a dreadful contradiction. If fantasy is allowed to run wild, then from this comes about the pagan doctrine of luck and fate, or the *un*christian doctrine of election by grace, conceived in the despairing sense. To be saved by election in the despairing sense is dialectically entirely like fate, it is the unhappiest of all happiness. The despairing election by grace posits in mankind the most dreadful discord, and in another sense it makes all mankind unhappy. For it is unhappy to be shut out, rejected; and it is unhappy to be saved in that way. To be saved, to be happy—and to know that all others are not and cannot be saved, to know that one has not and in all eternity cannot acquire conditions in common with them, that one has no fundamental fellowship with them, to be saved and to know that one has no word to cry to others, no highest and last comfort which is common to all—yea, what human heart could endure such blessedness! If that word of the Scripture, "Call upon the Lord while he is near," were to be understood as though it said "the second," as though the Lord were a fleeting traveller who the next second would be far away, in case it were to be understood so enigmatically of "the second" that no one knew or could know when the second was—who could presume to preach about it? And how meaningless that once every year (*anno redeuente*) it is preached about! It must not be understood with a nervous dread, and it cannot be the understanding in what is written about the sick man who lay beside the Pool of Bethesda, that he who came first was saved. The Gospel recounts precisely that the sick man who for many years had come too late—nevertheless was healed. This is the Gospel, the glad tidings, that the cruelty of fate is abolished, that first and foremost the salvation of the soul is promised, whether a man be bodily sound or no. Who must not despair if it were necessary also for the salvation of the soul to come first—if such were Christianity? And who must not be in a desperately dizzy state in order as a Christian to bring back paganism again?

But what then can put a stop to this dizziness which comes about when a man stands still and will not seriously consider any life task for himself and therefore is like a galvanized frog which for an instant has a spasm? What can check this dizziness? What can master that desperate supertension of the instant? The ethical can. When in every moment of one's life there is a work to be done, a task, when often enough, alas, there is a serious concern for the fact that one has not attended to his work as one should—then there is no time to be fantastic or to give oneself to fantastic speculation about the instant and about the dialectic that it is all and nothing. The ethical, and the religious which has the ethical in it, resists with all its might the bringing over us again the hopelessness of paganism. And where does paganism show itself more hopeless than its theory of luck? The ethical knows nothing and will know nothing about luck, about one becoming a genius, about one having the lamp, about one coming first, about one winning the lottery. Ethics is weary of all the anecdotical twaddle, it shudders at the horror of those times when fantasy wrought havoc with the human race and played the unhappy game of luck. Ethics would only know how to speak of the universal human tasks—and therefore precisely it has power over the luck of the instant, which is a horror. Even to the most despairing, even to him who has lost most, the ethical cries: The instant *still* is there! The ethical does not let itself be fooled, any more than God lets himself be mocked; by qualitative dialectic it knows well how to make the instant important as *decision*; but it will not alarm a man to the point of madness, nor madly make him happy with a game of hap or luck.

As an example of Adler's dizziness *may next be adduced his view of Abraham*, to whom he often returns in verse and prose. Here he warms up the old story about its being an evil spirit, the devil, who puts into Abraham's head the notion of sacrificing Isaac. Now by this explanation nothing is gained, for the difficulty recurs in another place, as was shown in *Fear and Trembling*. If such were the case, how can one explain that it could occur to the Church to make Abraham the father of faith and the friend of God? For he must himself after all have discovered at a later moment that it was a temptation he yielded to, hence he should not have been represented as the father of faith, but perhaps as the discoverer of repentance. Adler, however, is original. He assumes, as has been said, that it was the devil who suggested to Abraham the idea; but, lo and behold, God was so well pleased with this idea, "because it was brave and bold and great" (and suggested by the devil!) that, though he prevented it from being carried out, he made Abraham his friend—and in that way Abraham became the father of faith. The thing is carried so far that we men presumably might not be supposed to know exactly the difference between good and evil, that the evil may become so imposing that we mistake its greatness for its goodness, but that God himself sits like a fool while he is given a course of treatment such as one administers to a little girl of sixteen who wishes only that she might have a lover who does something great and even falls in love with a robber chieftain.[33] — That his dizziness might express itself thus is only to be expected. From Hegel he had no ethics, and when he plunged down into the land of orthodoxy hitherto unknown to him, he still was without ethics. Ethics lives and moves and has its being in the distinction between good and evil. The aesthetical, on the other hand, consists in the quantitative dizziness—the great, the astonishing—and metaphysics consists in disinterestedness.

As an example of Adler's dizziness may *finally be adduced the recklessness with which he counts that the great idea, the brave and bold idea of the individual, should be permitted to make itself heard, even though a little injustice is done thereby, even though some men thereby go to the dogs.* In defense of this view he appeals constantly to natural phenomena, to the fact that the sun remains just as glorious though it scorches several creatures, etc., quite à la Don Juan,[34] who says to Leporello: "Thou seest me walk only in nature's tracks," and precisely about the sun, to which he appeals as a pattern, he says: "All round the course of the sun lovers are dying and being born, and he heeds not the sacrifice of their corpses." Well, naturally, for all that, Don Juan remains just as bold, and the sun remains just as glorious; for gloriousness, boldness, etc. are not exactly ethical terms. Everyone who has but a meager and commonplace conception of the ethical knows very well that nature is a very poor analogy of the ethical, and that to want to live à la nature is to want to live unethically, as well as that by way of such analogies one will come at last to the Neronic burning of Rome —but that was a proud and glorious sight! Nature is precisely indifferent to the distinction between good and evil, which to ethics is all in all.

Ethical sobriety, which is the opposite to Adler's dizziness, consists essentially in the fact that man's effort reduplicates itself in the dialectic of the means, so that the means we use, so that the way one fights for his idea, so that the least means one allows oneself for the sake of realizing them, are equally important, absolutely equally important, as the object for which one fights and labors. Think, for example, of the strictly orthodox Church teachers, of Augustine's strict teaching about truth, that no one may save even one's own chastity by an untruth. And why not? Because untruthfulness is more unchaste than the physical violation unaccompanied by concupiscence. Think of the scrupulousness of Pythagoras,[35] who in ancient times was praised for his purity, who hardly dared to step upon the ground lest by his tread he might kill a living animal. But a Don Juan, a Napoleon, a Nero, in short, all headlong individuals, hail analogies from nature— and so does Adler, to whom a new doctrine was entrusted by a revelation from the Saviour. A new doctrine—but that is not the point, the important thing is that it was from the Saviour.

In his four last books then Adler is a deranged genius, and as *summa summarum* of his first and last positions it remains true that he is to be regarded as confused. So when one has made good this interpretation of him, as now has been done precisely by showing the astonishing incongruity between the first position (that of being called by a revelation and having received a new doctrine from the Saviour) and the last (that of being a genius of sorts), along with the fact that this incongruity has entirely escaped Adler's attention, then one can still further illustrate his confused condition by a glance at the external features of the books, which undoubtedly will suffice most readers for forming a judgment. It cannot be denied that it gives one a queer sensation to look into the books. In an extraordinary degree he has emancipated himself from every restraint as an author, from every requirement of order, from every regard for a reader. That this might be art, a maieutic tactic, cannot without great difficulty be assumed. Moreover, I have confirmed the denial of this notion by illuminating the total confusion in essential respects. — Not rarely A. treats the reader like a child to whom one is giving a lesson. Thus he prints the self-same Scripture passage, which is six lines long, three times as a whole on two pages. Now one cannot well deny that every word of Scripture has the admirable quality that it always merits being read—wherefore one certainly ought to possess a Bible and read it again and again. But to fill a big book by having the same Scripture passage printed so often in so brief a space is something after all rather strange. Also in another way he sometimes treats the reader altogether like a child. It is well known that as a task for composition in the mother tongue one sometimes uses single disconnected words from which the pupils must form a connected sentence. So it is that Adler throws out quite abruptly brief clauses, sometimes meaningless, perhaps to give the reader an opportunity of practicing the composition of connected sentences. In other places he seemed to behave quite as if the reader did not exist, that is to say, as though what he wrote were not meant to be printed, but as though from time to time it had been written in a notebook and got printed through a misunder-standing.

Naturally, however, about all such matters I desire to speak as briefly as possible. I am very little concerned about dealing aesthetically with his works; his revelation and his relation to that is the only thing that concerns me. Neverthe-less, I will make one remark which belongs here and which, as I believe, characterizes Adler essentially. Upon reading his last four books one gets the impression (and it is impossible to avoid it), one gets a suspicion and a notion that Adler is not really a thinker, but, on the contrary, that he must have the habit of putting himself into an exalted mood; he grasps at a solitary expression, a brief saying, detaches it without thinking, neither does he put it thinkingly together with something else, but continues to repeat it until the monotonous repetition stupefies him and puts him in a state of exaltation, so that it seems to him there must be something deep in it. But he is not much concerned about what this is, he is concerned only to reach the exalted state. One cannot help thinking of him as walking to and fro on the floor, constantly repeating the same particular phrase, supporting the particular phrase by altering his voice and gesticulating, till he has bewitched himself into a sort of intoxication so that he is aware of a wondrous and solemn buzzing in his ears—but this is not thinking. In case a person wanted to put himself into a solemn mood and therefore were to walk back and forth on the floor and say incessantly: 7—14—21; 7—14—21; 7—14—21— then would this monotonous repetition have the effect of a magical formula or of a strong drink upon a neurasthenic, it would seem to him that he had got into touch with something extraordinary. In case another to whom he imparted his wisdom were to say, "But what then is there in this 7—14—21?" he likely would reply, "It depends upon what voice you say it with, and that you continue to say it for a whole hour, and moreover that you gesticulate— then you will surely discover that there is something in it." In case one were to write on small scraps of paper such short phrases as, "He went out of the castle," "He drew the knife," "I must have dislocated my hip"—in case one were to hide all these scraps in a drawer, and then sometime later were to go and open the drawer, take out a single slip of paper and repeat uninterruptedly what was written on it, he would in the end find himself in a fantastic state of mind and it would seem to him that there was something extraordinarily deep in it. For the abrupt, by reason of its accidental character and by reason of the play of accidental combinations it suggests, has something about it which is enticing to the imagination. Who has not experienced it? When one in rummaging among old papers finds such short phrases the whole connection of which has long been forgotten, there is some amusement in giving oneself over to the play of imagination. When one has done that he burns the papers. Not so Adler—he publishes them. And it is also certain that, if he can get a reader to indulge in this game, he too will be able for a moment to amuse himself with it. But in this way one becomes an author in a very improper sense of the word. Instead of desiring and requiring the reader to keep his mind in repose in order to reflect upon the thought communicated, as an author commonly does, Adler must rather recommend to the reader that he put himself into a state of ecstasy; for the more tense one is, the more droll the effect of the abrupt will be. In view of this it would be quite consistent of Adler if, after the analogy of sorcerers and wizards, he were to recommend and prescribe certain ceremonies, that one should arise at the stroke of midnight, then walk three times around the chamber, then take the book and open it (as simple people read their fortunes in the Bible), then read a single passage, first in a low voice, then raise it to its highest pitch, and then again backwards (like Peer Degn with his sol—mi—fa) till the voice becomes quite low, then walk the length of the room seven times—and at the eighth time see if there is not something in the passage! The abrupt and fantastic effect is enhanced essentially by mimicry and pantomime; on the other hand, it is disturbed by reflection and by connection of thought. And yet in the abrupt there lies hidden as it were a deep and unfathomable profundity of riches, whereas a clear, well-thought-out discourse must be quite simply what it is. In the formulas of witches and conjurers the effect is due to the abrupt, to the enigmatical meaningless, and it is enhanced by mimic and pantomime: the witch comes riding on a broomstick, she dances around three times, etc. In case a man could make a multitude believe that he possesses a hidden wisdom, and thereupon he were to write abrupt phrases on small scraps of paper, in case he borrowed, moreover, the entire scenarium used in drawing the lottery, the big tent, the wheel of fortune, a company of soldiers, a minister of chancery before whom the soldiers would present arms, while one stepped out on the balcony, then to the accompaniment of soft festal music mingled with a swirl of notes in a higher pitch, let the wheel turn round and the boy in festal costume draw a ticket the content of which was read out—on that occasion several women at least would lose their senses.

What is said here about Adler's passion for raising himself into a state of exaltation contains absolutely no exaggeration, as I am very far from being tempted to exaggerate about Adler. It is not affirmed that his books contain such traits through and through, but there are plenty of passages which do. And inexcusable as it would be, according to my notion, were one to write something like this last and say nothing more about Adler; just as inexcusable would it be, to my thinking, if a veracious interpretation of his confusion found no place in a rather elaborate investigation of him.

As was said, his writings do not concern me directly; essentially my investigation deals only with that fact of his revelation, and with the question how he understands himself in such a thing as he has experienced, or with the suspicion that he has not understood himself in it. I use his works only with a definite aim. Had I to deal with them aesthetically and directly, it would give me pleasure to admit as officially as possible what my judgment is, that one really can learn something from them, or, to express myself quite explicitly, that I actually have learned one thing and another from them. A reviewer, it is true, is commonly accustomed to express his opinion with a superior air to the effect that, in spite of learning nothing himself, he can recommend the author's works to the public, for the public is not so loftily wise as he. But such is not the case here. People in general indubitably, nay, absolutely, can only be injured by reading A.'s works, for he confuses totally. But he who has what Adler lacks, dialectical clarity about the spheres and the totality, he and he alone, will in truth be able to learn something from the individual clever, lively, edifying, moving, sometimes profound sayings; and only he, secure against losing more than he gains, will find joy in what sometimes he succeeds in producing in a purely stylistic sense, though as a stylist he has no primitive merit. It is, strangely enough, a rather common opinion that it is easier to read epigrams than connected writings. And yet this is far from being the case, for to have any profit from epigrams one must be in full possession of a connected view in which one understands himself. This it is that Adler lacks, he does not understand himself, if the demands one makes upon him are according to a proper scale. And in this respect I cannot haggle. I do not believe that I will be taxed with clipping coins invidiously when as a reviewer I gladly pay the meed of praise to the distinguished author, but on the other hand, neither will I haggle, though I must admit with pleasure that, measured by another scale, a slipshod requirement, Adler appears to better effect, and that appraised by a reviewer who is just as good a dialectician as he (and no more), he naturally will be seen to stand like a victor with a palm branch in his hand.

SUPPLEMENT TO CHAPTER III

RECAPITULATION

The reader will remember that throughout this whole work the argument is only *e concessis*. Nowhere is it directly denied that A. has had a revelation: on the contrary, this is assumed, since he himself says so; and thus everything he says is assumed to be true, but thereby in turn the contradiction is made evident.

1. To illuminate the fact that confusion is present, Adler's reply to the ecclesiastical authority is employed. The dilemma may be expressed thus: *either* all the several answers are nonsense; *or* essentially they silently imply the revocation of his first claim (that he had a revelation and received from the Saviour a new doctrine). If we assume the latter (that revocation is implied in his answers), then the confusion is this: that he does not take seriously the matter of revocation, that he treats it as nothing, or does not himself notice anything, regards his answers as having meaning and reality, which they can only have insofar as they imply the revocation of his first claim.

Within the dilemma the argument is this: Adler so identifies himself with the first publications (the preface to the *Sermons*, the *Sermons* themselves, and the *Studies*) that in the ordinary and vulgar sense he must be regarded as the author of them; but then the doctrine was not revealed, then it was not written after Christ's dictation, he has not been merely an instrument. Adler admits authentically that he has nothing new, since like every Christian in general he holds to the Scripture, preaches Jesus, appeals to Scriptural passages as proof-texts in support of what he says—but with this he must essentially revoke all that first about the revelation etc. — Adler hopes that later he will be able to state better the doctrine (revealed and dictated by the Saviour), he hopes in the perfectibility of the doctrine. But this hope is entirely meaningless, nay, blasphemous, if that doctrine is not Adler's own; and if it is his own, then he has had no revelation through which the doctrine was communicated to him by the Saviour.

2. In the next place, in order to illuminate the confusion, attention was directed to Adler's four last works. Instead of what one might be justified in expecting, in case a person did not remain in a confused condition, we find that now, occupied as he is in a literary way with all sorts of things, he has put himself to rest and settled down as an amateur lyrical genius. That he is a genius may well be conceded here where we have nothing whatever to do with such a thing. But so soon as his last four books are put side by side with the first claim in the interest of meaning and identity, then the dilemma appears: *either* the last four books, even though the occasional content were the most excellent, *regarded as books by A.*, that is to say *regarded as a part of his total production*, are to be regarded as nonsense; *or else* there is silently implied in them the revocation of all his first claims. If the latter is assumed, the confusion consists in the fact that he treats this as nothing, or notices nothing, and does not take the revocation seriously. The metamorphosis from an apostle to a genius is so decisive, so qualitative, and besides that so topsy-turvy, that least of

all can it be ignored or treated as nothing. In civil situations, and generally in the world of finiteness, this may very well be done; there a person may more than once begin afresh and let the past be forgotten without more ado, there a person changes his situation in life, tries his fortune in a new career, and without more ado lets the past be bygone and forgotten. But in case a man thinks that also in the world of spirit this can be done, such an opinion is enough to prove that he is confused. In the world of finiteness it may be well enough to live haphazardly, it may be true, as the saying goes, *variatio delectat*; but in the world of spirit continuity is not only a joy but it is spirit itself, that is to say, continuity is spirit, not to respect continuity qualitatively is to lead one's life outside the sphere of spirit, either in worldliness or in confusion. Continuity is not monotony, in continuity too there is change, but continuity means that every change is made dialectic in relation to the foregoing. When the change is qualitative (as the change to genius from apostle) the last expression of continuity is revocation of the first position, which again, inasmuch as one has communicated his first, ought to be made officially. In the world of spirit highflown romanticism is confusion, and just as much so is the distraction which does not notice that the change is a qualitative one. And to the same degree that one has ventured out, even to the point of saying that he has had a revelation, to that same degree is romanticism or distraction the more suspicious. — The confusion in the case of Adler becomes even greater by reason of the fact that he, in his position in life as an amateur lyrical genius, continues with a clever, paraphrastic exegesis, etc. to hold fast to that doctrine of his (communicated to him, according to his first claim, by a revelation from the Saviour). All the more clearly is his distraction and confusion manifested for the fact that he has entirely forgotten that this doctrine was communicated to him by the Saviour through a revelation.[36]

He may revoke the first claim—then, as the author of the

four last books, he confesses that he is in a confused genius. He may revoke the last and seek to array himself in the character of the first. But to let both stand is a proof that he is in a confused state of mind.

Psychological interpretation of Adler as a phenomenon and as a satire upon the Hegelian philosophy and our age.[1]

1

PSYCHOLOGICAL EXPOSITION

THE AIM of this section is to pave the way for an understanding of the catastrophe, to explain several presuppositions by which the catastrophe in Adler's life might have been psychologically motivated. Undoubtedly it would be a more interesting and a more grateful labor if one might venture to operate by the aid of possibilities alone, for even the most copious reality never has the pure ideality of possibility, but constantly has along with it something fortuitous. But to poetize in this way is not allowable since it is a contemporary whose life is in question.[2]

Hence the psychological exposition is limited by reality and a respect for reality which always contains an element of the fortuitous. Even the understanding and explanation of his life which Magister Adler may possess internally will contain something fortuitous, because no actual man is pure ideality, so that any particular episode in his life will have a fortuitous *lack* or a fortuitous *redundance*. And the psychological exposition which can be furnished here is limited in another sense by reality. Thus it would be possible to think that one who knew Magister Adler thoroughly, one who was in possession of his confidence, might know of something (an impression of his life, an occurrence, an expression, etc.) which as a presupposition would in the highest degree be worthy of attention, but into which he as the knowledgeable person is in no wise justified in initiating others, let alone by publishing it in print. The investigation must therefore keep within more common terms, have a more universal character, making use at the most of single hints which Magister Adler himself may have given. The art consists in so putting together these qualifications that something results from it all the same. In this way the investigation can in no wise take too great liberties with Magister Adler, for the fact that essentially it makes use of only such general characteristics as universally explain the presuppositions of the age as a whole, whereas I completely renounce every private interpretation of Magister Adler for which I have no data at all.[3]

We may imagine then a theological candidate who has passed with credit his professional examination, he is more than commonly gifted; it may be assumed that, aesthetically understood, he has lived so much that existence will one day be able in a decisive way to point him out. On the other hand, up to this moment he may not, either as a child or as a youth or as a theological candidate, have come into any decisive relationship with Christianity, still less with the serious question whether he himself is a Christian. In this respect it may be assumed that he has lived on, as so many do, according to the current definitions in everyday language of what it is to be a Christian: to have been baptized and confirmed as a Christian, to have legitimated his standing when he matriculated in arts, etc., to have acquired a *quantum satis* of theological learning, to have become a candidate.

So now he is a theological candidate, but as one who is eminently gifted he naturally cannot conclude his studies with the ordinary examination for a pastorate. On the contrary, he now begins for the first time to study properly, and with that begins the study of the Hegelian philosophy, a philosophy which, supported by almighty opinion, is supposed to stand at the very summit of all scientific knowledge, apart from which there is no salvation but only darkness and stupidity. With enthusiasm for the hero of philosophy, following gladly the slogan, "You lack everything, study Hegel and you will have everything," likely thanking the gods in the Greek style for the privilege of being contemporary with the highest development of the human race, he sets to work on his study. He is not in possession of one single presupposition which would make him inwardly aware of the fact that this philosophy totally confuses Christianity, there is in him no deeper religious life which might restrain him from going into this philosophy; in a religious respect he is without the heavy equipment of theology or the deeper impression of religion, he is a light-armed soldier to whom it comes only too natural and too easy to understand negligently what Hegel has negligently expounded, to the effect that his philosophy was the highest development of Christianity. Yea, in a religious respect he likely is so light-armed that it would hardly occur to him to question this.—So then he studies, and what many vain persons do carelessly and only to be in the fashion, he (though he too is carried away by the spirit of the age) does with zeal and interest; he even gives lectures in the university on this philosophy and publishes a popular exposition of Hegel's objective logic,[4] but the question how the Hegelian philosophy comports with Christianity does not occur to him at all.

Magister Adler has now reached the age when one ordinarily feels an urge to conclude his student years and thereafter to teach others. This is the transition from *discere* to *docendo discere*. Also at that age, which is the critical time of maturity, there commonly develops an urge to reflect deeply upon one's own life. And again when making the transition and going farther in life one turns back to one's first recollections, to the first unforgettable impressions of one's upbringing and tests how one now stands related to that which one then understood as a child and childishly appropriated, and tests whether one is in accord with oneself, whether and to what extent one understands oneself in understanding one's first impressions, and the concern is that one's life in a deeper sense might be a personal life essentially in agreement with oneself. One and another man surely stands at this parting of the ways, asking whether he shall let the first go, cutting down the bridge, and hold to what has been learned later, or whether he shall look back to childhood and learn conversely; for as a child he indeed learned from his elders, and now, being himself an elder, he should learn from a child, learn from his childhood. If now it had been Adler's case that he, turning back to himself, were to be struck by one or another essential Christian recollection, by one or another decisive impression of Christianity—then the case would have been different and at the same time rather more serious. Adler, on the contrary,[5] may likely have found it all right as a result of his life's development to remain a Hegelian. The whole question about Christianity and Hegelian philosophy does not emerge at all.

Magister Adler seeks a place, not as professor of philosophy or of the Hegelian philosophy in particular, but as priest, as a teacher of the Christian religion, for which *also* he has fitted himself . . . by studying the Hegelian philosophy. And he was called. Relying upon having passed his examination for the priesthood creditably, relying upon his general culture, relying upon his talents, he hopes to be equal to the task; relying upon his exceptional knowledge of the Hegelian philosophy, he hopes to be an exceptionally able priest. This is by no means immodest on his part, not at all. If it is true that the Hegelian philosophy is the highest development of Christianity, then indeed it is an advantage for a priest to know this philosophy perfectly—not as generally happens, or at least sometimes, that a man, after having with the seriousness of reflection renewed himself by his childish impressions of Christianity, being in good understanding with a strict Christian upbringing, with the Bible in his hand, enters upon his work as a clergyman; no, in reliance upon his examination, with Hegel's eighteen volumes elegantly bound,[6] almost regarding ordination and all that as an unwelcome interruption of his study of Hegel and writing about him—Magister Adler becomes a priest.

He does not become a pastor in the metropolis, where it would not be unthinkable that he might succeed in skulking through, yea, in going through life proudly as a priest, as a Christian priest ... in Hegelian categories. Magister Adler becomes a priest in the country, and so is brought into contact and into responsible relation with simple and ordinary people who, lacking a knowledge of Hegel, have as perhaps men in the country still have, a serious though meager Christian instruction, so that, unacquainted with every volatilization of it, they simply believe in the Christian doctrine and have it before them as a present reality. For simple, believing men so deal with Christianity that they do not hold it historically at a distance of eighteen hundred years, still less fantastically at a mythical distance.

Magister Adler becomes a priest in the country and finds himself living in rural retirement. The conception he has of the Hegelian philosophy, perhaps also the conception this philosophy may give him about himself, makes it seem plausible that Magister Adler will hardly find among his clerical brethren or among his other acquaintances anyone with whom he can or really wishes to strike up an intimacy. So Magister A. finds himself living altogether isolated with his Hegelian philosophy, which after all is perhaps more appropriate for royal residences. So it must be if the relationships are to be tightened up to the point of a catastrophe; the individual in question must first and foremost be kept in isolation or keep himself in isolation.—On the other hand, that Magister A. might rusticate is entirely improbable, for that he is too highly gifted, and he is too much intellectually employed to become "a card-playing priest," or to reach the anti-apostolic climax, as sometimes happens—for the apostles were called from fishing to catch men: a man is appointed a priest to catch men and ends by fishing, hunting, etc.

The situation is now prepared: a man who is fully occupied

with the Hegelian philosophy becomes a country parson in rural retirement, intellectually understood, in complete isolation.[7]—The simple congregation represents quite simply the Christian position, and Magister A. as pastor and spiritual guide is *in duty bound* to deal with them. In capitals where a Hegelian has support in distinguished and cultured circles it may perhaps be possible to defend oneself against "simplicities" proudly and with aristocratic superciliousness;[8] but Magister Adler as a Hegelian is like a wild, strange bird in the country, entirely without support and, intellectually understood, as thoroughly out of proportion with his environment as was Gulliver among the little bits of men or among the giants, whereas Gulliver had the advantage and the consolation that he was only a casual traveller. A., on the contrary, in spite of his disproportion and unrelatedness is essentially in relation for the fact that he was appointed pastor, and besides that he is too good a head not to perceive that after all it would be foolish to be proud of his philosophy before the simple peasants.

One cannot deny that this is a desperate situation, and yet inwardly, in the direction of responsibility, it is still more desperate. To stand in the pulpit (and so before God's face) and preach what in consequence of his culture he presumably was through with long ago, to sit by a deathbed and comfort a dying man with what he himself was through with long ago, to sit by the deathbed and perhaps witness the fact that the dying man presses the hand of the priest and dies blessedly in the faith of that which the priest by the bedside was through with. To witness how a poor but God-fearing family prepares for the Holy Communion, with what solemnity they step up to the holy place[9] (allow them in God's name to remain stupid!)—and then the priest who is through with all this, and then the priest, the teacher, who, if only he gets into the mood, actually steals this from these simple people at seeing their emotion and agitation! To be so developed that one, if he were really serious about the

Hegelian philosophy, might rather feel himself obliged to pluck the simple people out of their errors—and then to be a priest, appointed to teach them the truth! And then the responsibility, that one is a priest! And then that one lacks any diversion, is without support and harmony with others; for in the metropolis one perhaps vaunts the Hegelian philosophy, but hardly in the country, and impossibly on the part of a priest.

It is well enough known that loneliness may drive a man to extremes; but Magister A.'s situation is worse than loneliness, for it is also contradiction and self-contradiction, and over all hovers the terror of responsibility. When then some time has gone by, when the contradiction and the terror hem him in closer and closer, the situation at last is this: that a Hegelian who has "gone farther" has now about reached the turning-point of decision, whether he will become a Christian—and this moment occurred in his life a *year after* he had been *well and happily installed as a Christian pastor*.

2

THE CATASTROPHE IN
MAGISTER ADLER'S LIFE

Then there came to pass an occurrence, and Magister A.'s life was changed. How this occurrence is more precisely to be understood, I naturally am unable to elucidate. The only thing I might do is to explore poetically the possibilities, but in that way no factual elucidation is to be won. The one person from whom we might reasonably expect a precise and definite elucidation would be Magister Adler himself.[10] But from him one seeks it in vain. After having in the first place furnished a detailed description of the occurrence, which was said to have taken place at night ("when an evil sound goes through the chamber and thereupon the Saviour bade him write down the words"—write down the words which are communicated in the preface to his *Sermons*), for this concrete statement he substitutes at the instance of the ecclesiastical authority the more vague and indefinite one that it was "an occurrence."

Every third party, including me and this investigation, when the desire for a more particular elucidation is checked by the confusion of Magister A. (the person directly concerned), may perfectly well rest satisfied with the statement that there came to pass an occurrence, and Magister A.'s life was changed, yea, even with the more meager notion that the occurrence consisted in the fact that Magister A.'s life was changed. *The principal point is* (and had not Magister A. originally undertaken to say more, all would have been well up to this point) that Magister A. *with a qualitative leap was transported from the medium of philosophy, and more particularly from the fantastic medium of the Hegelian philosophy* (pure thought and pure being), *into the sphere of religious inwardness. The principal point is that Magister A. from the objectivity of abstract thinking came to himself.* It is another question whether Magister A. within the religious definition of coming to oneself may be said to have as yet come to himself, inasmuch as, though now religiously determined, yet as a person in an exalted state he is still outside himself. But in contrast to the objectivity of abstract thought he may be said to have come to himself, inasmuch as he has reached the point of being concerned about himself. This is the new factor with which hitherto his whole life development has been unacquainted, this religious impression of himself in self-concern.—Nevertheless, as Magister A. himself says in the preface to the *Sermons* before he began to tell the story about the revelation, there arose before him a light, and it was not by thinking it arose but by the Spirit.

The catastrophe was accompanied by a symbolical action about the factual character of which there is no reason to doubt: Magister Adler burned his Hegelian manuscripts.

When one has so decisively broken away from the Hegelian philosophy there is assurance that one will never more deal with it again diffusely, that by a single step one is assured against temptation from that side and from relapse into it again. Alas, the need of giving an inward resolution a striking outward expression is often an illusion. Perhaps it has not seldom happened that a young girl in the presence of the whole family has destroyed every reminder of the unfaithful lover, burnt all his poisonous letters, and then, without being conscious of it, longed to see the faithless man. Not rarely there is a suspicious incongruity between inward decision (the strength of resolution, salvation, healing) and the outward signs of decision. One can hardly draw conclusions from the latter to the former, one can rather conclude conversely that the stronger the need of striking decision in an outward sense, the less the security. That the outward expression is not always the inward is true not only of the ironists who intentionally deceive others by a false outward expression, but it is true also of immediate natures who unconsciously deceive themselves, yea sometimes feel a need of self-deception. Thus in case a man hardly takes time to sleep and eat, merely for the sake of being able to preach and spread abroad a view which would be a blessing to mankind, is intent early and late to prove its rightness—one might indeed believe that the man must have a firm and lively conviction. Alas, and yet it is not always so, sometimes he has no firm conviction, but feels the need that many might be in agreement with him, in order that his conviction might be convincing to himself. Strangely enough, he has a view, he has something to impart, it looks as if it were the others who had need of him and of his firm conviction—alas, it is he who has need of the other men, he wants to convince himself by convincing others. In case one were to put him, intellectually understood, in a vacuum, he would have no conviction; and, on the other hand, in the degree that many listen to him, in the same degree he is aware that he has a conviction, and in the degree that they agree with him, in the same degree—he is himself convinced. Every person of some seriousness who is accustomed to treat himself with precaution is inclined rather to avoid the striking outward exhibition of decision, or is on the watch lest it come too early. A man of some seriousness would rather hide the decision and test himself in silent inwardness in order to see whether it might not deceptively be true that he the *weak* one felt the need of a *strong* outward expression of resolution. If a man can hold out in silent inwardness, endure to be totally changed without being changed outwardly in the least, then likely he can take the striking step. The converse is not true. If I were to imagine two drinkers who both have resolved to drink no more: one has solemnly thrown bottles and glasses out of the window and gone in for total abstinence; the other has a bottle and a full glass in sight—but he does not drink. Which of these two may be regarded as surely saved? One so easily confounds the physical with the moral. No, to be able to be precisely as usual, to be able to live on with the daily and continuous reminders of the old, and yet to be changed in the deepest ground of his nature—that indeed is the art. But if the change has really come about, then it is permissible, then one always may change little by little the outward expression, if one has quite seriously been on the watch lest the change might be *before others in the outward*, not *before God in the inward*. I will imagine two men: at a decisive moment there comes about an essential change in both of them, but one of them at once expresses the change, the other only in the course of seven years expresses the change by outward signs which correspond with the inward change he underwent in that decisive moment; his change therefore is not conspicuous to others, because it is distributed through seven years—of these two changes, which may be regarded as the most secure?—It would therefore perhaps have been wiser and more prudent of Magister A. if, instead of burning the manuscripts, he had allotted an hour or two every day to occupation with Hegel, in order to assure himself that he really was changed, for one can so easily confound the moral with the physical: the abandoning of Hegel with the burning of his manuscripts. If my memory does not deceive me, it was the celebrated Johann Arnold Kanne, whose life was acquainted with considerable spiritual alterations, when one time he was gripped by Christian truth, he also burnt up all his mythological manuscripts—and yet relapsed once again. Goethe also burnt his manuscripts containing his poetical works—and when he had done that he became in a full sense a poet.

As it was with Goethe, so was it not with Adler—that after having burnt his Hegelian manuscripts he became for the first time a thoroughgoing Hegelian. But on the other hand, deceived by this striking outward sign of decision, he managed to hide from himself in self-deception that he continued to be a Hegelian. Lyrically, subjectively, fully and firmly convinced that once for all and forever he had broken with the Hegelian philosophy, by burning his Hegelian manuscripts, that by a revelation he was saved forever from the prolixity of the Hegelian philosophy. But, lo, when he then had occasion to explain what he understood by the revelation and how he understood himself in what had happened to him, he recurs to the old Hegelian volatilization. If one were to call his attention to this, it would not be unthinkable that A. would reply: "How can you come with such an absurd objection, that at bottom I might be a Hegelian? I assure you by all that is holy I burnt my Hegelian manuscripts that night. Now believe me!" In that way Magister A. puts the Hegelian philosophy in an extremely comical situation, for the fact that one who is fully and firmly convinced that he has had a revelation uses that philosophy to volatilize this same conception.[11] But thereby A. has the merit of making evident indirectly-satirically the contradiction in the Hegelian philosophy. For when one takes away the eighteen hundred years, the roguish trick, and puts the Hegelian philosophy in the situation of contemporaneousness, then its method of procedure becomes clear, that it fraudulently *explains away* a revelation instead of *denying* it openly. And the extraordinary merit of the comical is reserved for Magister Adler, to be in every way man enough for the whole thing: man enough to have a revelation, and man enough to explain it away.

3

MAGISTER ADLER'S ADVANTAGE

The good, the admirable quality in Magister Adler is that he is moved, is profoundly affected, that thereby his life has acquired a very different rhythm from that of the cab-horse with which most men, religiously understood, go sluggishly through life. Whether it be a panting press of business or a worldly interest, or whatever the distraction may be, it is certain that most men, religiously understood, go through life in a sort of abstraction and absent-mindedness, that never are they sensible of their own ego, of their pulse, of their own heart-beat, in self-concern; they live too objectively to be sensible of any such thing, and on hearing anything said about it they quiet themselves with the explanation that all such things are hysteria, hypochondria, etc. Most men live in relation to their own self as if they were constantly out, never at home; the occurrences and undertakings of their life flutter indefinitely about this self; they sometimes perhaps shut their door . . . in order to be at home, but they do not shut out the distracting thought, and so are themselves "out." The admirable quality in Magister A. consists in the fact that in a serious and strict sense one may say that he was fetched home by a higher power; for before that he was certainly in a great sense "out" or in a foreign land, at the time when he was a Hegelian and objective. In a worldly sense, the misfortune of the Prodigal Son consists not exactly in the fact that he journeyed into a foreign land, but that he wasted his substance there: spiritually and religiously understood, perdition consists in journeying into a foreign land, in being "out," in being objective, so that one gets no impression of oneself by remaining at home with the inward self-concern of conscience.

All religiousness consists in inwardness, in enthusiasm, in strong emotion, in the qualitative tension by the springs of subjectivity. When one beholds people as they are for the most part, one cannot deny that they have some religiousness, some concern to be enlightened and instructed about religious things, but without allowing these things to affect them too closely. For, observing more nearly, one easily discovers that in their religiousness they relate themselves to their self at a certain distance; they make good resolutions *for the future*, but not for the *present*, not for the present instant, to begin right away; contemporaneously with the resolution they do not carry it out, contemporaneously with the resolution they have rather the notion that there is still some time, if it were only half an hour, before they need to begin. They make sacred promises, they resolve . . . tomorrow, etc., but what is really the decisive point, *to be entirely present to themselves in self-concern*, is something with which they are totally unacquainted. Therefore they well may have religious notions, sometimes also may find edification, yet I find no better comparison for their religiousness than the exercises in the field of maneuvers. As these exercises are related to battle or to being in battle (where there is danger, which in the field of maneuvers is absent), so is distance-religiousness related to inward religiousness.[12]

Most men in their religiousness are present at the most *in a bygone time or in a time to come*, but not *in a present time*. They think about the religious, hear it talked about, deal with it in the medium of fantasy, have it with them in the form of the wish, of longing, of presentiment, in the form of the illusory resolution and purpose, but the impression of the religious, that it is to be used now, now at once, now at the very instant, they do not get. They think about the immortality of the soul. In this consciousness they repose at a distance, but for this thought they have no use in concern and self-concern; they think about it in this wise: It is always well to know that you are immortal, for the sake of the chance that you may die; but that, however, may be many years off. So they do not think the thought of death at the same instant with the thought of immortality, they do not reflect that every instant when one has not this consciousness of immortality one is not really immortal. They are like the man full-fed who labors for the food for the coming day, not like the famished man who at once has use for what he can scrape together. At bottom their lives are lived in other categories which give them a deceptive sense of security. While they are busied about or occupied with the religious they do not comprehend that the religious is *the one thing needful*, they regard it as *also needful*, for the sake especially of hard times; they understand very well that a man may die of hunger if he doesn't get anything to live off of, but they do not comprehend that man lives by every word which proceeds out of the mouth of God. When men who live thus religiously at a distance talk about religion (and priests of that quality are of course not altogether rare, indeed they are even of a better sort than card-playing parsons or horsy and newspaper parsons) one notices at once by their talk that they are not in it, just as though while existing they are not really existing, are not present to themselves. Therefore, though the hearers do not sleep through the sermon, which nowadays is rather rare, yet they are *distrait*, for in the discourse itself there is an interval, a space, between the need and the satisfaction of the need, between the means of salvation and the instantaneous use of them, which is the interval of illusion, of time lost, of delay. One notices in the discourse that there is not that fresh outpouring of an experienced religion which now at the moment of the discourse arises to a present life; one notices that it is not as though the speaker needed to defend himself against the wealth of past experience; against the overwhelming power of present experience; one notices rather that it is as if every time he wiped the sweat from his brow he went home and fetched a new factor, as if when he had to say anything he must go away and fetch it. He on the contrary who is present to himself in religious experience has what he is to say at hand, in his mouth and in his heart—indeed, just as nowadays one has in well-equipped buildings water on every floor and never needs to go down and fetch it from the courtyard but only to turn on the spiggot, so has such a religious man always the essentials with him in the present.

To be entirely present to oneself is the highest thing and the highest task for the personal life, it is the power on account of which the Romans called the gods *presentes*. But this thing of being entirely present to oneself in self-concern is the highest in religion, for only thus can it absolutely be comprehended that one absolutely is in need of God every instant, so that everything belonging to time past or to time to come or generally to indefinite time, such as evasions, excuses, digressions, etc., grows pale and vanishes, as the other sort of jugglery, which also belongs to indefinite time of the gloaming and the twilight, retreats and vanishes before the bright light of day. When one is not present to oneself, then one is absent in the past or in the future time, then one's religiousness is recollection of an abstract purpose, then one dwells perhaps piously in the piety of an ancient and vanished age, or builds, religiously understood, the objective religiousness like the Tower of Babel—but this night shall thy soul be required of thee.[13]

So it is with most men—but it is different with Magister Adler. He truly is shaken, he is in mortal danger, he lies (to employ an expression used by another author* over 70,000

* How scrupulous it is of S.K. to dissociate himself thus from his pseudonym!

fathoms of water; what he discovers must be used at once, the help he cries for must at once be employed—or the same instant he sinks. He is absolutely subjective, inwardly wounded, and must therefore remain present to himself in his need. Indeed, Magister A. is so far from the sure ground of indolence and illusion that rather he is so tossed out into the extremity of mortal danger that the words, "today," "tonight," "this very instant," are about to destroy him, so inwardly is he fighting in the instantaneous situation of mortal danger between the intense struggle of self-preservation and the surrender of inwardness.

But Magister A. possesses an advantage in being thus shaken, a qualitative advantage, and verily I shall not in envy depreciate the value of this advantage. As it is an advantage to be truly in love, to be truly enthusiastic, so also it is an advantage, religiously understood, to be shaken and therewith to have found the place of which it is said, *Hic Rhodus, hic saltus*. For where is that place, religiously understood? It is neither at Gerizim nor at Jerusalem, neither in thinking nor in learning, but at the most tender and subjective point of inwardness. When one is deeply affected there, then is one rightly situated at that place. And this deep experience is in turn the trading capital and the true riches. With envy I shall certainly not talk of this advantage of Magister A., but neither with curiosity. There is such a thing as cowardly, effeminate religiosity which will not itself venture out for decision upon the deep, but rather with curiosity likes to feel the shudder with which one who is himself secure sees another struggling out upon the deep. A cowardly and effeminate religiosity which itself writhes at seeing the dreadful experiences which prove what a prodigious power the religious is, but prefers to see the proof adduced by another. As the shades in the underworld sucked the blood of the living in order to live a while longer, so the cowardly and effeminate religious people, conscious that at bottom their religiosity is a hypocritical and rouged-up thing, would therefore like to try occasionally to work up some strong impressions . . . at second hand. Such religious people are not better by a hair's breadth than the idle people who long to see an execution, or a great conflagration, etc., in order to see without danger to themselves the death struggles of men. But precisely because such religious people exist, and only too many of them, especially in our effeminate, shrewd, refined Christendom, it is necessary that the man deeply moved does not abandon himself to them in his inwardness, that in holy wrath he may know how to get behind these cowardly effeminates in order to push them out into the current, instead of abandoning himself to be a diversion and a spectacle. But for this Magister A. lacks reflection and coolness and schooling and holy upbringing, and hence one cannot deny that, even if everything were all right with him in other respects, he nevertheless does harm, for the fact that, instead of helping others out into decision, he presents a diversion to the cowardly and effeminate who love voluptuous shudders. But his advantage over most men is and remains none the less something qualitative, and something to be highly regarded especially in our age. The more that culture, training, and discretion get the upper hand, and the more that men come to live comparatively, all the more common becomes a certain lawyer-like dexterity in handling spiritual determinants. For every situation one knows evasions and exceptions and limitations and excuses; now audaciously, now dispiritedly, one pleads the example of others, so that one constantly avoids a decisive impression of spirit. Culture and training and discretion and life in the flock work precisely to the end of making men, religiously understood, *distrait*, absent-minded.

The advantage of Magister A. is recognizable also in his writings, and the good that is in them must be attributed to this advantage.[14] And the good which is in them is precisely that there is something stirring about them. He is sometimes moving by a noble childlikeness, he alarms by a harrowing description, he sometimes aims and hits with such precision that this is identical. What he has to say is not said by an indifferent man and not fetched from afar; no, he himself is *in* the hasty movement, *in* the danger, *in* the effort, or *in* the repose of comfort, *in* the hope; and what he says he has ready to hand, it is outburst, quite genuinely an outburst of feeling and emotion, and one may say that not rarely has he overwhelmed the reader with his outbursts.—In his style therefore there is sometimes a lyrical seething[15] which, though aesthetically appraised it is sometimes foolish, is nevertheless religiously worthy. There is in it an impatience which outbids itself in expression—and then breaks off abruptly, and thereby precisely makes the impatience still more evident. At the head of a cavalry troop of predicates, each one braver than the other, he hurls himself upon the reader. Aesthetically appraised his style has no merit, and I cannot find a single expression in all his books which I can venture to recommend as correct, there is always something accidental (which lies in the fact that he is *himself* only in the instant of reality and that he comes, in an anguishing sense too close to reality), either sometimes too much or sometimes too little, either an abundance in which he remains so to speak defeated in the sortie, or a scantiness which indicates that imagination will not stretch so far and which has the effect that one sees him struggling for breath;[16] but religiously his presentation makes its impression. What Frater Taciturnus presumably must know very well how to do, since he, though he used a style of a very different sort, lets Quidam of the experiment express himself in this style, examples of which one finds in wild forms in Adler. Building rhetorically upon the antecedent clauses, he lets the consequent clauses be nothing, an abyss from which the reader (if he reads aloud) will shrink away and fall back as it were upon the antecedents; rushing forward on a run as though the wealth would never be exhausted, and precisely in the same second breaking off, which is like the trick of stopping a horse in full career. Most riders fall off on that occasion, whereas ordinarily one makes a transition to a full stop, a shift in the modulation, a veering of the concepts, in one word, the unexpected stopping, etc. Like all southern nations (the Jews, of instance) and like the vocal organs of passionate nations, so does every passionate person speak in such a way that his voice continually breaks—so also it is possible to produce this effect stylistically.

However, this would carry me too far. And how many men are there who even have merely a notion how prose can be used lyrically, and that I engage to do, namely to produce a lyrical effect in prose better than it can be done in verse—in prose where people first learn to read and to require thought in every word, whereas verse contains always a little filling of lime. I break off, for what I have to say concerns only authors. In this respect all the Pseudonyms have a linguistic value for the fact that they have cultivated lyrical prose. Adler has also learned something from them, as is easily seen; for it is not true as the flattering reviewer in the *Church Times* relates, that he began contemporaneously with the Pseudonyms, but he began after them, and the style in his four latest books is notably different from that in his *Sermons*, when he was not yet strongly under their influence. On the other hand, it is true, as this reviewer says, that one sometimes finds passages in A. (in the last four books) which strongly remind one of the Pseudonyms; but I see no merit in this, whether in copying another, or in forgetting that one by having had a revelation has entirely different things to think about than linguistic exercises.

4

THE FUNDAMENTAL FAULT IN MAGISTER ADLER WHICH OCCASIONS THE INCONGRUITY

The fundamental fault consists in the fact that Magister Adler's theological, Christian-theological culture and school-

*ing, is defective and confused and stands in no relation to his
lyrical enthusiasm, whereas, presumably led astray by his
conception of what it is to be a theological candidate, a priest
and a philosopher, he believes he is in a position to be able to
explain something and therefore precipitates himself into
literary production, instead of seeking an education and self-
discipline.*[17]

If it is true that even to be beautiful is an excuse for many
things, that to be in love may be urged as an excuse for much
imprudence, to be enthusiastic as an excuse for much impetu-
osity, to have made a great discovery as an excuse for running
through the streets of Syracuse naked—well then, so the fact
of being deeply moved and shaken, religiously understood,
ought to be an excuse for many imperfections, and in relation
to Magister A. a critic ought to beware of being peevish and
Philistine. However, imprudence, offense, in short, whatever
has to be excused, or the fact that there is something to be
excused, must not be taken to imply that there is something
wrong with respect to the good, with respect to the excellence
which serves as an excuse; no, the offense must consist in
something accidental which is different from this. Running
naked through the streets of Syracuse has thus nothing whatever to do with the discovery, which therefore remains
absolutely just as good as before. Hence it is quite right that
the discovery serves as an excuse for the offense, that because
of that one quite forgets that Archimedes was naked, as he
himself did. Only prudery could dwell long on the offensive-
ness of the act, and only a crazy Philistinism triumphant in a
small town could turn everything round about and reach the
conclusion: It is certain that Archimedes ran naked through
the streets—*ergo* he has made no great discovery.[18] On the
other hand, it would be something different if there had been
doubt about Archimedes' discovery; for a misunderstanding,
a mistake (instead of a great discovery), affords no excuse for
an offense. This too is really the Philistine's train of reason-

ing; for Philistinism has no conception of the great, the sublime, and therefore no notion of the excuse afforded by the great. Philistinism in interpreting the distinguished man would say as did the merchant Bearend, according to a well-known story, when a bird dropped something on the table: "If I had done that," said he, "you would have heard a great row." So it is that the Philistine, too, leaves out the point: he says, "If I had done that"—yes, quite right, but the Philistine is no Archimedes. However, as was said, if there are any ir-regularities with respect to the discovery, then has Archimedes no excuse.

Now, as we have seen, it was Magister Adler's advantage that he was deeply moved, shaken in his inmost being, that hence his inwardness came into being, or he came into being in accordance with his inwardness. But to be thus profoundly moved is a very indefinite expression for something so con-crete as Christian awakening or conversion, and yet one dare say nothing more of Magister A. To be shaken (pretty much in the sense that one speaks of shaking a person to make him wake up) is the more universal foundation for all religious-ness; the experience of being shaken, of being deeply moved, the coming into being of subjectivity in the inwardness of emotion, the pious pagan and the pious Jew have in common with the Christian. Upon this common basis of more universal emotion the qualitative difference must be erected and make itself felt, for the more universal emotion has reference only to something abstract: to be moved by something higher, something eternal, by an idea. And one does not become a Christian by being moved by something indefinitely higher, and not every outpouring of religious emotion is a Christian outpouring. That is to say: emotion which is Christian is checked by the definition of concepts, and when emotion is transposed or expressed in words in order to be communicated, this transposition must occur constantly within the definition of the concepts.

With regard to all inwardness which reflects upon the

purely human, the merely human (*so with regard to all inwardness within the sphere of immanence*), the fact of being deeply moved, of being shaken is to be taken in the sense of shaking a man till he awakes.[19] If this emotion expresses itself, breaks out in words, the transposition occurs in feeling and imagination within such concepts and definitions of concepts which every man may be said to discover in using the words; the transposition is not limited by specific, qualitative concepts which have an historical validity outside the individual and higher than every human individual and paradoxically higher than every human individual, a paradoxical historical validity.—Let us take, for example, falling in love, understood purely in an erotic sense. With regard to the purely erotic experience of being in love there is no specific, qualitative difference between the experience of a Greek, a Jew, or a Christian. The lyrical outburst of love is within the merely human qualification and not within the distinction of the specific, qualitative concepts. The lyrical is appraised with regard to its ability to express the purely human, though with delicate distinctions of feeling in individuation according to race and personality, which differences nevertheless are a vanishing quantity in the immanent, eternally conceived, human equality.

It is different with the definition of a Christian awakening to a religious interest *which lies in the sphere of transcendence.* The emotional seizure of the individual by something higher is far from defining a Christian adequately, for by emotion may be expressed a pagan view, pagan conceptions of God. In order to express oneself Christianly there is required, besides the more universal language of the heart, also skill and schooling in the definition of Christian concepts, while at the same time it is of course assumed that the emotion is of a specific, qualitative sort, the Christian emotion.—But since Christian thought through the centuries has gradually absorbed in a more universal way the whole world-development, its conceptual language having passed over into a volatilized traditional use (which lies on a line with being a Christian of sorts by virtue of living in geographical Christendom), it may come about that one who only in a more universal way is emotionally gripped by something higher expresses himself in the language of the Christian concepts—of course, this is a result which might well be expected. The fault or irregularity is then a double one: that a person thus moved begins to talk in a language which stands in no relation to his emotion, since the language is specifically, qualitatively concrete, and his emotion is more universal; and that he naturally speaks this language in a confusing way. For when one is not in a stricter sense seized by a Christian emotion, and on the other hand is not familiar with, is not strictly disciplined in the language of the concepts in which he expresses his emotion—then he is like one who talks too fast and does not articulate clearly . . . it is twaddle. And in the field of the Christian religion this is not only unfortunate but it is dreadful; for the danger indeed is not merely that of saying something unclear, something foolish, but unconsciously it may be blasphemous.—For a Christian awakening what is required, on the one hand, is being grasped in a Christian sense and, on the other hand, conceptual and terminological firmness and definiteness.[20]

If then Magister A. is regarded as an awakened man in the sense of the Christian religion, his misfortune is just this, that he is not sufficiently and thoroughly acquainted with the language of Christian concepts, that he does not have them under his control. For what chiefly seems to have secured his character as a Christian, the fact that he had had a revelation from the Saviour, seems to be something in which he is not secure, not being in agreement with himself about what is to be understood by a revelation. Since Christianity has been volatilized in the same degree that it has been spread abroad, and since the qualitative emphasis has been lost by the fact that we all of us are Christians, it occurs not so seldom that one without more ado assumes that every religious emotion in the case of an individual who lives in geographical Christendom is *eo ipso* a Christian awakening, and from the fact that he so promptly uses the whole language of the Christian concepts which he was accustomed to use as a conversational language. Before he was religiously moved (in a more general sense) he had been a Christian after a sort, and precisely this is his misfortune, he is therefore not capable of testing himself rightly as to whether his emotion is really a Christian emotion, and after being gripped by emotion he uses again the Christian language of concepts as a careless conversational language. If it is factual that the language of Christian concepts has become in a volatilized sense the conversational language of the whole of Europe, it follows quite simply that the holiest and most decisive definitions are used again and again without being united with the decisive thought. One hears indeed often enough Christian predicates used by Christian priests where the names of God and of Christ constantly appear and passages of Scripture, etc., in discourses which nevertheless as a whole contain pagan views of life without either the priest or the hearers being aware of it.

Hence in case Magister A. had been a layman (lawyer, physician, military officer, etc.), things would perhaps have gone better with him. After being moved by a mighty religious impression, in consideration that he was not a theologian, he would have sought repose·in order to become himself thoroughly conscious of what had occurred, sought schooling on the part of teachers of Christian orthodoxy, and perhaps in this way he would have succeeded in attaining the necessary sense of proportion before he began to express himself. But Magister A. was a theological candidate, he was even a priest, he was a philosopher—must he not then long ago have been preeminently in possession of the schooling in concepts which is necessary for ability to express his emotion with assurance? So it might appear perhaps; but, alas, the knowledge acquired for the theological examination—if one does not bring along to the university what purely religiously must be held in infinite esteem, a deep veneration for the Christian faith instilled in childhood and by upbringing, so that in later moment of decision he will resolutely and frank-heartedly stand up for the choice he had made, rather forego everything else than to alter the least tittle of the Christian faith—alas, the knowledge acquired for the theological examination, though it might be worth ever so much regarded as knowledge, avails but little for standing fast in time of battle.[21] As a priest he had very little opportunity for a schooling since he was so fully occupied with Hegel—and as a Hegelian he was initiated, initiated with complete devotion and conviction, into the total confusion of the Christian faith. But to be *ex animi sententia* a votary of a particular philosopher and his philosophical view, to have with that and in that experienced the culmination of his life and of his life's development—that for a man is pretty much the same as love towards a woman. And certain it is that, if there has been reality in this love, it helps but little to burn all the letters "he wrote to her." He must labor methodically and slowly. If there had been reality in being a Hegelian, it was of no avail to burn the Hegelian manuscripts. And that this was a reality for Magister A. I do not doubt. It would have been the saddest thing of all if even his study of Hegel had been idle talk.

I shall now show briefly how the incongruity between his subjective emotion and his imperfect education in Christian concepts expresses itself in the decisive points of Magister A.'s appearance as an author. The incongruity naturally consists again in the fact that it is dialectical how far his awakening may be called Christian. For of this one can judge only by attending to his utterances, but these precisely are confusing for the fact that they are in the language of the Christian concepts which he has not mastered.

(a) *Here we are*[22] at Magister Adler's *first claim, the preface to his Sermons, or rather the content of it.*[23]

Magister A. is gripped by something higher, but now when he would express his condition in words, would communicate it, *he confounds the subjective with the objective, his subjectively altered condition with an external event*, the experience that there rose up a light before him with the notion that outside of him there came about something new, *the fact that the veil fell from his eyes with the notion that he had a revelation.* Subjectively his emotion reached the highest pitch, he choose the highest expression to indicate it, and by a mental deception he used the objective determinant that he had had a revelation.

To illustrate his confusion in the use of the concept revelation I shall take an example which reflects pure humanity, an example from the sphere of immanence. He who is truly in love can say also that he discovers love, and this from Harold's time [from of yore] every lover can say. Falling in love is a determinant of pure, downright inwardness, it has no other dialectic than that which belongs to inwardness itself, it has no dialectic determinant outside itself, it is the simple identity of subject-object. Love is falling in love, the primitivity of falling in love is the genesis of love. Love does not exist as something objective but comes into being every time a man loves, and it exists only in the lover; not only does it exist only *for* the lover but it exists only *in* the lover.

It is otherwise with every relation within the sphere of transcendence, and then again otherwise with the Christian concept of revelation. Christianity exists before any Christian exists, it must exist in order that one may become a Christian, it contains the determinant by which one may test whether one has become a Christian, it maintains its objective subsistence apart from all believers, while at the same time it is in the inwardness of the believer. In short, here there is no identity between the subjective and the objective. Though Christianity comes into the heart of never so many believers, every believer is conscious that it has not arisen in his heart, is conscious that the objective determinant of Christianity is not a reminiscence, as love is of the fact of falling in love, is not an apparently objective something which nevertheless is subjective, like love which as an objective something is an illusion and loving is the reality. No, even if no one had perceived that God had revealed himself in a human form in Christ, he nevertheless has revealed himself. Hence it is that every contemporary (simply understood) has a responsibility if he does not perceive it.

So Magister A. is deeply affected. That in the first moment of emotion one is easily exposed to the confusion of confounding the change within oneself with a change outside oneself, of confounding the fact that one sees everything changed with the notion that something new must have come into being, this is a thing well enough known, I do not need to dwell upon it. Though Magister A. had for a long time been ensnared in this confusion it would be foolish to blame him—partly because it is nobody's business, partly because it is human. The question is only whether in this condition he expresses himself. If once one is ensnared in this confusion, it is only too easy to support this confusion with a plausible poetical invention and get dramatically an occurrence, a scene, explaining how it came about. Not only every religiously awakened individual, but everyone who in a marked degree possesses inwardness, has also an inclination and dexterity for turning his monologue into a dialogue, that is, for talking to himself in such a way that this self becomes like another self which has reality apart from himself, that is so say, duplicating himself.[24] Instead of being content with the experience that a light suddenly rose up before him, it comes easy to say that it was as though the Saviour appeared to him and bade him, etc. The confusion is undeniably very suspicious, but the principal thing is to hold back the expression until one has come to one's senses.

If from an earlier time Magister A. had had a strict and serious schooling in the concepts, had had a veneration for the dogmatic, qualitative concept of "a revelation," he would have had something to resist with, something to hold on to, something that might prevent the precipitate utterance. But, unfortunately, Magister A. is a Hegelian. So there can be no hope that something might save him from the confusion, since the whole of his philosophic learning must precisely confirm him in the notion that altogether correctly and with philosophical precision he expresses his subjective change by the invention that he had had a revelation. By confounding the subjective with the objective Magister Adler is ensnared in the notion that he has had a revelation, by having had a revelation he likely thinks that he has broken entirely with the Hegelian philosophy which has in its system no room for a qualitative revelation.[25] But, on the other hand, how has the Hegelian philosophy treated the concept of a revelation? It has not bluntly denied it, but it has volatilized it so far that at last it becomes a determinant of subjectivity, the simple identity of subject-object. It is precisely in this confusion Magister A. is, but then he has the support of the Hegelian philosophy in saying of himself that he has had a revelation. The confusion is not brought to a stop, for A. has not been schooled earlier in the definition of Christian concepts, and now he gives himself no time for it. He is subjectively ensnared, and in this condition he thinks that he breaks with the Hegelian philosophy, but he has no other education in the concepts more essential than he finds in Hegel's philosophy, and the topsy-turvy, the double confusion appears in its second power in the fact that he breaks with this philosophy—and it is precisely that which triumphs.

However, Adler spoke out the word, he proclaimed solemnly that he had had a revelation, that at night *the Saviour* had bade him get etc.—*et semel emissum volat irrevocabile verbum*, at least a greater self-conquest is required to retract what has been spoken than to refrain from speaking it.

(b) *Magister Adler's answer to the ecclesiastical authority*. The word spoken meets, however, with the serious opposition of the authority. Magister A. is required to explain himself more particularly,[26] and now we have the same situation raised to the second power.

This confusion of Adler's in the situation raised to a higher power was already shown in Chapter III, § 1, together with the exposition that the incongruity consists precisely in the fact that he lacks schooling in the Christian concepts, and therefore explains and explains, substituting the qualitatively most diverse determinants in place one of another, and yet thinks that he is in identity with himself.

(c) *Magister Adler's four last books.* Time and repose was what Magister A. then needed, a strict, fundamental schooling in the language of Christian concepts, in order to get the proper sense of proportion.[27] Magister A. himself gives expression to this need: "that with a longer time to revise the ideas quietly he will in the future find himself in a position to give them a more appropriate form"—and thereupon he begins a new, voluminous literary productivity, in which, however, he does not seem to have got any farther along, so far as qualitative education is concerned. The fact that he himself seems to perceive that he stands in need of a pause, the fact that instead of acting in virtue of this perception he continues his productivity, is thoroughly characteristic psychologically, and unfortunately is an indication that it will be hard enough for him to give himself time for serious reflection. The fact that a man who puts the opposite course of action into effect uses the adage that for the future he hopes to change—rather indicates that there will not likely be much of a change. The urge he might feel for a change gets no power over him, precisely because it is constantly proclaimed, so that, at last, all that remains is the urge to say it once in a while or very often—whereas he does the contrary. It is strange that Holberg has not made use of this characteristic trait in depicting "the bustling man"; it would have been thoroughly characteristic of the bustling man to have had an adage: "It cannot be endured, the press of business;

but beginning from New Year's Day I shall retire completely from business life." It is quite certain that this line, when the spectator by the aid of the situation must also be dramatically aware that it was an adage, would precisely characterize the incessant movement of the bustling man and prove that he was incorrigible. When a student has for a long time been reading for his professional examination it becomes with every year less probable that he will ever take it, only when it becomes an adage, "Next time I will"—it is clear enough that he will not take any examination. Trop (the hero of the play) is precisely for this reason hopeless and given up because he possesses his hope in the form of an adage.

Magister A. hopes indeed in the future, but if one were to ask him where the last four books have a place in a sustained literary effort or in the development of a personal life, where A. now is, intellectually understood (which is something different from asking him about a particular utterance, the particular explanation of a Biblical passage, the particular study, etc.), then one may say that he has been productive at the wrong place, his productivity sails before a false wind.[28] *For instead of giving himself time, gaining repose, coming to his senses*, going to school; instead of acquiring respect for what after all it means to have had a revelation, and coming to an understanding with himself and to a qualitative decision, *in short, instead of keeping silent and acting and laboring, he becomes so productive in a literary way about all this*,[29] *that he has not yet attained repose*, that "he is fatigued, that he is shaken, pale, that he is on the point of making the leap, that with a longer time for working quietly to revise the ideas he hopes, etc." First and last the task is to get out of the tension, to understand himself in the fact of revelation,[30] instead of which he becomes productive literarily about his condition, and *moreover deceives himself with a dreadfully grandiose means of diversion*: a voluminous literary activity about detached particulars, individual texts from Scripture, individual thoughts, prolix productivity on detached sheets of paper.

Here we have it again:[31] Magister A. lacks education in the definition of Christian concepts, his lyrical emotion bears no proportion to this, as is shown from the fact that he has so little respect for the concept "revelation" that he can let his declaration that he has had a revelation remain dubious, indeed it would seem that he has quite forgotten the whole story and has become literarily productive about everything else one can possibly conceive. And furthermore the incongruity is another, that he lacks ethical firmness to procure for himself repose, in order "by having a longer time to revise quietly the ideas, etc."

Everyone who knows something about the dangers of reflection, and about the dangerous course followed in the course of reflection, knows also that it is a suspicious circumstance when a man, instead of getting out of a tension by resolution and action, becomes literarily productive about his situation in the tension. Then no work is done to get out of the situation, but the reflection fixes the situation before the eyes of reflection, and thereby fixes (in a different sense of the word) the man [in the German slang sense of reckoning on his fall]. The more abundantly thoughts and expressions proffer themselves to a writer, the more quickly the productivity advances —in the wrong direction—all the more dangerous it is, and all the more is it hidden from the person concerned that his labor, his most exacting labor, perhaps also, for a third person who has the total view, his very interesting labor—is a labor to get himself deeper and deeper involved. For he does not work himself loose, he works himself fast,[32] and makes himself interesting by reflecting about the tension. And one notes clearly enough that Magister A. is unacquainted with, and with the use of, the innumerable prudential methods which he who is experienced upon the ocean of reflection knows very well and practices constantly, to test the direction of the productivity, to regulate the speed, to determine the place where one is, by stopping an instant, by devising quite arbitrary, trivial, and mechanical measures for determining the powers of the mind, by forcing reflection into an entirely opposite direction in order to see whether any illusion is in play, etc. No, Magister A. goes on producing at *one* speed, which quite consistently increases the productivity with every step in advance; and so in production he is as it were far out upon the ocean of reflection, where no one can directly call out to him, where all sea-marks are dialectical, he steers at a considerable speed—in the wrong direction.

If then Magister A. had had from an earlier time an impression of a strict ethical view, had had a serious schooling in ethics, this surely would be of advantage to him now. But Magister A.'s life-development was such[33] that it must quite naturally culminate in Hegel's philosophy, which, as is well known, has no ethic. It may happen to the most serious ethicist when he is far out upon the sea of reflection that once for an instant he makes a mistake, but he will quickly discover it, for he tests his life to see where he is. It may happen even to the most serious ethicist that for an instant he is ensnared in an illusion, but he will soon discover it. When a serious man says to himself, "You must give yourself time, collect yourself for reflection, in order that for the future you may be able to present the ideas in a more appropriate form," and he notices that he remains nevertheless in the same old path, then he discovers that his reflection was humbug, he takes the thing up seriously, instantly he defines the limit, that the indeterminateness of time may not deceive him, he starves himself with trivial labors in order that he may not deceive himself and waste his time upon literary productivity, which is interesting to him really because he has an apprehension that there is something else he should be doing. It is so true what Paul Moler once said as the fruit of experience: "In almost absolute idleness one may yet escape boredom so long as a practical duty is neglected through idleness, for one is in a way preoccupied by the constant strife in which one is involved with oneself; but so soon as the duty ceases, or one has not the least remembrance of it, boredom ensues." The teacher who prescribes a lesson from hour to hour is amused so long as he is on the alert to look after his pupils, but when he has resolved to neglect the lesson hour his amusement ceases. In this instance the reminder of his conscience is something unpleasant which serves to give relish to something unpleasant. A poet who is writing a tragedy when it is part of his life-plan to study for an examination does it with greater enthusiasm than he would later when he has relinquished that plan. And so also perhaps it is the obscure consciousness he has that now instead of being literarily productive he ought to be doing something else which makes Magister A. so productive and makes his productivity interesting, while he, instead of becoming clear to himself by his productivity, rather defends himself against what ethical simplicity would bid him do.

So then Magister A. has no decisive ethical presuppositions, the Hegelian philosophy has taught him to dispense with ethics; so that there is nothing to bring him to a halt and let him see that his latest productivity, be it never so clever, is a mistake which does not lead him to understand himself more clearly in respect to what is the decisive event in his life, to have had a revelation, but rather leads him farther from it. The Hegelian philosophy, far from being able to explain this to him, must simply confirm him in the notion that the direction of his productivity is the right one.

The Hegelian philosophy has no ethics, it has therefore never dealt with the future, which is essentially the element or medium of ethics. The Hegelian philosophy contemplates the past, the six thousand years of world-history, and then is busy in pointing out every particular development as a transitory factor in the world-historical process. *Charmant*! But the late Professor Hegel of blessed memory had when he lived, as every man has or at least ought to have, an ethical relation to the future. Of this the Hegelian philosophy knows nothing. Hence it comes about quite simply that every living person who by the help of the Hegelian philosophy would understand himself in his own personal life falls into the most foolish confusion. As a Hegelian he will be able to understand his life only when it is too late, when it is past, when he is dead—but unfortunately he now is alive. With what then must he properly fill his life while he is living? With nothing; for really he must wait for the moment of death to understand with the averted glance of this moment the meaning of his past life. But when the past life was filled with nothing, what is there really left for him to understand? But suppose a man lives nevertheless, lives forward in the direction of life's course, and thus does after all fill a section of his life with something, then as a Hegelian he must as quickly as possible construe his past as a factor in his life, and then, so long as his glance is turned backward, he ceases for a moment to be an existing individual with an ethical direction towards the future.[34] If he is entirely absorbed in desiring to understand his own life as a factor, then he regards himself essentially as dead.

Let us now think of Magister A. He has gone astray in reflection, he is absorbed in reflection about his situation in a tension, instead of working out of it. Thus indeed an ethicist will view his productivity. But a Hegelian[35] must confirm him in the notion that his procedure is the right one, since he is in fact engaged in construing this situation of his as a factor in the development of his life.[36] But to construe it as a factor is not to get out of it, and on the other hand he must be well out of it before there can be any question of construing it as a factor. In general the ethical at once inverts everything: the main thing is to act, to strive, to get out of the wrong situation—at the most there may be conceded incidentally a little half-hour to construe individual experiences of the past as a factor in one's life. Adler is ensnared in self-reflection, but then too he is so far from having anything to help him out of it that he also has within him Hegelian reminiscences which must confirm him in the notion that this after all is the profound thing and the highest wisdom.

It is perfectly unbelievable what confusion the Hegelian philosophy has wrought as a sorry consequence of the fact that as a philosopher a man is such a hero, and in a purely personal aspect a Philistine. Among philosophers subsequent to Hegel who have appropriated the Hegelian method there are to be found astonishing examples. One such philosopher writes a new book and becomes conscious of himself as a factor within the endeavor which began with his first book; but this is not enough, for his whole endeavor (which as a whole is not yet in existence) he becomes conscious of as a factor in the whole endeavor of philosophy, and then again as a factor in Hegel, and of Hegel as a factor in the world-historical process from ancient times, through China, Persia, Greece, Judaism, Christianity, the Middle Ages. This to my notion is the most inhuman whim any philosopher can have, also it is a story à la Munchausen, that a poor individual man wants to make us believe he can do such things.

But this baleful inclination to construe has become a fixed idea by which philosophers become self-important, sometimes even adding to the confusion by indicating future factors. The ethical view of being in the future, and the metaphysical view of construing everything as a factor, contend with one another for life and death. Every living man, if he is not thoughtless and *distrait*, chooses decisively; but if he chooses the metaphysical view, he commits, spiritually understood, suicide.

As in general, so here, A. has indirectly a merit in satirizing Hegel unconsciously. A tame, domesticated professor, leading a still life, can skulk through better with the illusion of living backwards. He himself is No. 0, and therefore presumably is busy only with the past and with construing it as a factor.[37] But an itinerant scholastic (the word itinerant being used almost in the sense of confused), a lyrically exalted dithyrambic poet—well, up to this point he may be right in saying that he has broken with Hegel, but when he goes on and gets himself stuck in reflection, and then moreover wants to be thought-conscious that his present condition is a factor in his life-development—then he produces in the Hegelian philosophy, quite literally, a state of flatulence, which is not at all to its advantage.

5

MAGISTER ADLER AS AN EPIGRAM UPON CHRISTENDOM OF OUR DAY

How Magister A. satirized the Hegelian philosophy indirectly by breaking with it conspicuously but nevertheless conniving with it unconsciously and then by the confusion of his life bringing the Hegelian philosophy into a situation where it must show itself to be as self-contradictory as it is, has often been demonstrated. The fact too that he is an epigram upon the Christendom of our day will also be pointed out and utilized.

Magister A. was in fact born and confirmed in geographical Christendom and belonged to it . . . so he was a Christian (as we all of us are Christians), he was a candidate in theology . . . so he was a Christian (as we all of us are Christians); he became a Christian priest—and then for the first time he had a curious experience: owing to a deep impression upon his life he came more seriously into contact with the decision . . . to become a Christian. Just then when he had come nearer to being a Christian than ever before during all the time he was a Christian, just then he was deposed. And his deposition was quite proper, for then for the first time the State Church had an opportunity to become aware how it stood with his Christianity. But the epigram remains nevertheless that as a pagan he became a Christian priest, and that when he had undeniably come somewhat nearer to being a Christian he was deposed.

By a single occurrence of this sort one has undeniably an opportunity of acquiring an insight into what after all must be understood by the notion that we are all Christians of a sort; one gets a suspicion whether after all it is not an illusion about the many Christians in geographical Christendom. This certainly is not said by way of judgment—far be from me all preoccupation with externals. It is a different matter whether the individual by himself might not be able to learn something for himself from the whole business about Magister A. This certainly is my opinion; and, though I am doubtful how far one really can say that Magister A. has had a Christian awakening, it seems to me that the catastrophe of his life must be able to exert some awakening effect upon every one, whatever be the result for Magister A.[38] At all events, it is undeniable that, while at one time in the world to become a Christian was a decision from which most men shrank, now the thing of becoming a Christian of sorts is an enchanting delight in which one is confirmed in so many ways that there well may be needed a special sort of awakening which will be able to pluck one out of the illusion, if one is ensnared in it after the example of a man who can even become a Christian priest though he is ensnared in the delusion that he is a Christian and essentially is only a pagan.

Perhaps this is not so—I know nothing about it and want to know nothing. But let us imagine it, that many live on in a way as Christians and really are pagans, owing to the fact that existence, the world around them, has transformed itself into a great illusion which again and again and in every way confirms them in the notion that they are Christians. Let us imagine that these many in a more advanced age constitute each of them a family. These fictitious Christians bring up in turn their children—what will the next generation of Christians become?

In general it is certainly characteristic of our time that the concept of *upbringing*, at least in the sense of former times, is vanishing more and more from man's speech and from his

life. In former times men set a high value upon the significance of bringing up, understanding by this a harmonious
development of that which was to support the various gifts
and talents and peculiarities of personality ethically in the
direction of character. In our times one seems to want to do
away impatiently with this upbringing and therewith empha-
sizes *instruction*. One wants the young to learn quickly and
as early as possible much and all sorts of things, to learn what
one almost palpably can ascertain is knowledge and is something. Formal culture, the ethical culture of character, is not
such a something, and yet it requires much time and much
diligence. In our time one seems to think that if only one
takes pains in all ways to see that the child learns something,
learns languages, mathematics, religion, etc., then for the
rest the child can pretty much bring up himself. In every age
and in every land this is certainly a great misunderstanding,
but it is especially dreadful in Christendom. For if a person
is not to be simply disappointed in Christianity, one of two
things must be done: *either* one must keep the child from
his earliest childhood, so long as he is under tutelage, far
from every relationship with Christianity, one must allow
him to grow up without any Christian knowledge whatsoever,
in order that at a mature age he may get a decisive impression
of Christianity and choose for himself; *or* the parents must
assume responsibility for giving him from his earliest childhood by a strict Christian upbringing a decisive impression
of the Christian faith. But let him grow up from childhood
with the view of his environment of what it is to be a Christian of sorts as a matter of course, and with that one has done
everything a man can possibly do to deceive him with regard
to the absolutely qualitative decision in human life. He then
is a Christian in about the same sense that he is a man, and
as little as it could occur to him in later life to reflect seriously
whether after all he really is a man, just so little will it
ordinarily occur to him to make an accounting of himself as
to whether after all he is now really a Christian.

I will now imagine—for it is abhorrent to my soul to meddle in the God-relationship of any man, even so far as to know that there actually lives such a man as I describe—I will imagine the father of a family. He is capable in his business, not without cleverness, rather a little of everything, hospitable and sociable in his home, he is no reviler of religion (which, though it is dangerous, might perhaps be still better for the children, for it provides elasticity), neither is he in the strictest sense indifferent, he is in a way a Christian, he would think it strange, far-fetched and remarkable to make any further fuss about the matter, either inwardly or outwardly; he is in a way a Christian, through the reading of one or another recent work he is in agreement with the view that Christianity represents the highest culture of the soul, together with the opinion that every cultured man is a Christian. In his home life, whether there be company or no, he never has occasion to express himself religiously about religious matters. If it happens occasionally that one or another religious individual calls attention to himself and becomes the subject of the day and the subject also of conversation in the home of that *paterfamilias*, the judgment upon such a man and upon his conduct is not a religious judgment but an aesthetic one, it stigmatizes such form and substance as bad form, as something that cannot be tolerated in cultured circles.—This man's wife is a lovable woman, free from all modern womanish whims, goodhearted as a mother and wife. She has also at a single instant in her life felt a need for deeper religious reflection. But since such matters and such concerns had never been broached between her and her husband, and since she has perhaps an exaggerated respect for the requirements of a husband so superior to her with respect to culture, she feels that it might betray a lack of culture or be offensive were she to talk about religious subjects. Therefore she keeps silent and with womanly devotion submits herself entirely to her husband, gracefully appropriating an attitude which is so becoming to her husband as a man; and these two harmonize as rarely a couple in Christendom do.

Under the eyes of these parents the children grow up. Nothing is spared to enrich them with knowledge, and while the children grow up in knowledge and information they pick up naturally the cultured manners of their parents, so that this family is really an exceedingly pleasant home to come into. It follows as a matter of course that the children are Christians, they were born in fact of Christian parents, so this is just as natural as that a person is a Jew who is born of Jewish parents*—where in all the world could the children get any other notion? That there are Jews, pagans, Mohammedans, fetish worshipers, they know well enough from history and from their scientific religious instruction, but they know it also as something with which they are entirely unconcerned.[39]

Let us take the oldest child. He has now reached the age when he is to be confirmed. It is a matter of course that the boy answers "Yes" to the question put to him. How in the world could anything else occur to this boy? Has anybody ever heard tell that somebody answered "No," or has the boy ever been told that he might answer "No"? On the other hand, one may perhaps have heard his father say not to

* The notion of being a Christian because one is born of Christian parents is the fundamental delusion from which a multitude of others stem. One is a Jew by being born of Jewish parents; quite right, because Judaism is essentially connected with and founded upon a natural determinant. But Christianity is a determinant of spirit, so that in it there is neither Jew nor pagan nor a *born* Christian, for the determinant of spirit is higher than the natural determinant. On the other hand, one cannot well *become* a Jew, for one must be born a Jew. One cannot be a Christian and yet not a Christian; on the other hand, one can be a Jew and yet not be a Jew, because the natural determinant is preponderant; for though one is not a believing Jew, he is just as fully a Jew; but a Christian who is not a believing Christian is not a Christian at all. The determinant "Christian" is precisely that of which it must be said in the most absolute terms, one is not born to this determinant—exactly the contrary, it is precisely what one must *become*.

answer too loudly nor too softly, but to do it in a becoming and polite way; he remembers perhaps to have heard his father say that the whispered yes was something rather affected in church. To that extent it is a matter of course that he must answer "Yes"—to the extent that, instead of having his attention called to the significance of the answer, it was called to the purely aesthetic side of the formality. So then he answers "Yes"—neither too loudly nor too softly, but with the frank and modest decorum which is so becoming to a boy. His father is somewhat more serious than usual on the day of confirmation, yet his seriousness has rather a festal than a religious character and therefore harmonizes with the cheerfulness which makes its appearance when they have come home from the church, where the father is not only as agreeable as ever but employs his talents to make that day a festival. The mother is moved, she even wept in church. But motherly tenderness and worldly concern for the child's future fate is not restricted to Christianity. The boy therefore on the day of his confirmation got a more solemn impression of his father and a more touching impression of his mother; he will remember that day with gratitude and gladness as a beautiful recollection; but he gets no decisive Christian impression. The boy gets the impression that this day must be rather a significant day in life—but not so significant as the day he becomes, for example, a university student and matriculates.

The youth is confirmed, and now little by little begins for him the busy time, since he has to get ready for his examination as an officer—we may assume that he will follow that course. So he passes his examination with distinction; he goes to the university, distinguishes himself further, the parents are delighted with their son, whom now, however, they see more rarely, since he has moved away from home and is always busy. He is fortunate, at the age of twenty-six he is already captain.—Our young captain falls in love. She is a lovable and charming girl, corresponding entirely to the parents' wish, and the family, already so agreeable, acquires a new enchantment by receiving her into their circle, and by the comfortable feeling which was diffused over the home life when it was implied that the older generation is now about to be rejuvenated in the new one. The captain is really in love. But to be really in love is after all no specific determinant of Christianity; surely lovers have lived just as well in Greece as in Christendom, indeed the erotic determinant is not properly Christian. The wedding day is appointed. One finds that a church wedding is the most solemn. The captain's father holds the opinion that a church wedding, with the impression of the lofty vaulting of the church, with the tones of the organ, with the whole environment, and with having the priest in his proper environment, attunes the soul quite otherwise than to sneak off to the priest in a carriage to be married upon a silver salver. To this was added the opinion expressed by the captain's father, that over all mysteriousness there hangs a nemesis, that every unforeseen fatality acquires an almost ridiculous power over one. Thus in case the carriage goes wrong or overturns and there is a disorderly mob— if the affair were publicly known and official, if the unfortunates were on the way to a church wedding, well, that would always be an unpleasant delay; but if it were secret, it ought to be secret, if it was a quiet wedding it ought to occur in perfect quietness.—So then the captain stood before the altar with his young bride—a charming couple. And the priest asks, "Hast thou taken counsel with God and with thine own conscience, etc." What shall the captain answer? Well, after all, it goes without saying that the captain, who, erotically understood, is really in love, doesn't wait to be asked twice whether he wants to have the girl. So he answers "Yes" —not too loudly and not too softly, but precisely with the noble, self-confident yet modest tone which is so becoming to a young man. Whether this indeed might be just entirely a precise answer to the priest's question does not occur to the captain; he is fortunate in his love, he is happy, confident and honestly convinced that he will make the girl as happy as he can.—So the marriage couple are united. The notes of the organ roar a worldly farewell, the crowd looks wonderingly, almost enviously, at the charming couple, and everyone who can see more closely sees love shining from the captain's eyes. Indeed, there is reason to be envious of him, reason for the family to be proud of him: he is young, happily developed, beautiful in a manly way, honest enough to be truly in love, happy in his love, faithful to a sincere resolution.

Suppose now that this had taken place in geographical Christendom—who then has been more deceived in respect to Christianity than precisely our captain! For one who has never heard anything about Christianity is not deceived, but one who without having the least decisive impression of Christian truth has from the first been confirmed in the notion that he is a Christian—he is deceived. Where in all the world might it occur to him to be concerned about how far he is a Christian, or even to be concerned about becoming that which from his earliest recollection he was in a way assured that he is? And in this assurance everything has confirmed him; his parents have said nothing about the Christian faith, they thought, "That the priest must do," and the priest thought, "To instruct the young about religion, that I can do for sure; but to give them a decisive impression, that must be the parents' affair." So he has grown up, been confirmed, become lieutenant, captain—and now a Christian husband.

In case one who was not a priest[40] should ask our captain whether he were a Christian, the captain undoubtedly would smile. There would be nothing rude or offensive in this smile, as though by the smile he would give the questioner to understand what a stupid person he was; no, for this the captain is too cultured, for he really is a cultured young man. But he would smile involuntarily, because the question would seem to him just as strange as though somebody were to ask him whether he were a man. In case that evening at the tea-table in our captain's house the story was told about Socrates, that he is reported to have said that he did not know definitely whether he was a man, our captain would perhaps say, "That undoubtedly is very ironical, and one cannot help smiling at it; but on the other hand there is something whimsical in expressing such a doubt which concerns the very first and simplest and most necessary presuppositions in life; thus today there was a man who asked me seriously whether I were a Christian."[41]

Let us imagine the opposite: that one by a strict Christian upbringing has already received as a child a decisive impression of Christianity. If this is to come about, the parents themselves must be essentially Christians, so that the child gets the constant impression of how his parents for daily use lead a religious life, concerning themselves with Christianity both for their own edification and in order to express it by their conduct. So then the child grows up, and during the age which is most receptive and in which memory is most faithful the decisive impressions of Christianity are imprinted indelibly upon his soul and κατά δύναμιν modify his character. For, as was said, might not the observation that one nowadays so rarely meets a man of strong character have some connection with the fact that people have no conception what upbringing is, that they confound it with learning (*discere*), confound learning with learning to obey, to bow before the mighty and daily impression of ethics and religion?

And now that such a child, because he had had a serious Christian upbringing, must be a Christian, would again be an illusion; and next to the notion of being a Christian because one is born of Christian parents, comes the erroneous inference: his parents were pious Christians, *ergo* he is a Christian. No, the unforgettable and profound impression due to upbringing is only a presupposition.

Then this child too goes out into the world. Undeniably he has presuppositions with respect to becoming a Christian; humanly speaking, everything has been done for him that was humanly possible. But there is not yet a decision; for even though his "Yes" on the day of confirmation was the result of upbringing, it still is not the decisive act.

Now in the course of years entirely different sides of life, entirely different factors of the soul, will presumably advance their claims; the young man will be sensible of impressions which are quite unknown to him. For the strict Christian upbringing is a presupposition, and such a one as he must grow up in order properly to accept it. As parents at an age when the children are growing most rapidly have their clothes made a little larger, made to grow up to, so one may say seriously of one who has received a strict Christian upbringing that his parents have given him a garment which is made to grow up to, but also a garment which no one can outgrow.[42] He will now make acquaintance with the world, and then perhaps for a time it will seem to him as though his parents had deceived him; for what he gets to see now that he makes his appearance youthfully upon the dancing-floor of youth, all the joy of life, this lightheartedness—this his parents had as it were hidden from him. He will stand wondering and confused: with the grave conception due to a strict Christian upbringing of what it means to be a man, he stands now in the midst of this worldliness—and in the main it seems good to him. Yes, he will undoubtedly feel as one who has been deceived. As for the captain, he presumably will never discover that he was deceived; he precisely was initiated and educated into that medium in which he permanently belongs. But the other, he as a child has heard nothing about the glory the world has to offer, or he has heard of it only as a strict admonition against it; with the presuppositions of his strict Christian upbringing he stands as a stranger, indeed, as one deceived, in all this worldliness, which now when he must examine it himself seems quite different from the description given him as a child.

Yet, humanly speaking, for this young man was done everything that could be done: his life must so lie before him that he cannot avoid a catastrophe, he must come to a decision whether he will become a Christian, or actually give up Christianity. And if it is true as Socrates says that the most frightful thing of all is to live in error, then must that young man be accounted fortunate.[48] In every Christian land where Christianity has so permeated all relationships that everyone as a matter of course (i.e. without the decision of inwardness) is in a way a Christian, it is important first and last to pose the problem ... of becoming a Christian, and that the problem be not confused by theological debates. However, on this subject I can refer to *The Concluding Postscript* by Johannes Climacus.

Whether it is a pure illusion for a man to imagine he is a Christian, or whether it may rather be that by a strict Christian upbringing he has got a decisive impression of Christianity, he faces exactly the same problem: to become a Christian. To this intent cautions and admonitions may well be needed in a Christian land. But such an admonition is contained precisely in Magister A.'s life. What difficulties lie in the way of becoming a Christian; in what sense a Christian upbringing is after all only a presupposition; how precarious such an upbringing may be; what responsibility the parents assume in undertaking it, but also conversely by not undertaking it—about all such things one finds of course no illumination in Magister A.'s life or in the catastrophe involved in it. He quite gives the impression of a pagan who has suddenly come into touch with Christianity. But precisely for this reason his life is an admonition for many, or may be; for in fact he was a Christian of a sort, as all men are Christians, he was confirmed, became a theological candidate, a Christian priest in geographical Christendom—and yet the catastrophe revealed how his being a Christian is to be understood. Here it is an occurrence which is the admonition, and also the admonition is indirect, it depends upon the individual whether he for himself will allow himself to be admonished; it is not as when a religiously exalted person thunders and condemns, which so easily may exasperate men instead of profiting them.[44]

No, Magister A. exerts an effect by his life, and he exerts also an indirect effect. His significance for our time will surely not consist so much in what he became through the catastrophe, or in the literary productivity which derives from it, as in the fact that by the catastrophe he indirectly reveals how in geographical Christendom one may in a way become a Christian, and even a Christian priest, without having the least impression of Christianity in the way of . . . becoming a Christian.

This treatise was written before the events which have now altered the shape of Europe. If in reference to a time long gone by one might say justly that as a whole it lacked action, it may seem that now on the contrary we have got only too much action. But this only seems so. Everyone who has a well-developed notion of what it is to act will on closer inspection easily see that in all of Europe almost nothing at all is done that can be called action, that everything that comes to pass resolves itself into a mere occurrence, or that something comes about, something prodigious, but without there being any active personality who knows definitely beforehand what he wills, so that afterwards he can say definitely whether what came about was what he would or no. So in France—a republic of that sort does not properly belong to history, nor does it come absolutely under the rubric action; it finds its place more properly in a newspaper under the heading: *Advertisement*. In the greater part of Europe it is just the same. Everywhere and altogether what comes to pass is an occurrence, in many places an imitation, which not even re-garded as imitation is action, for there is no individual who imitates a foreign institution and then in the situation of his country is after all active. No, imitation consists pre-cisely in the fact that there comes about, God knows how, a sort of commotion—and so nothing really comes about. But there is nobody that rules, nobody that acts, nobody that could say with truth, It is this and this I willed, and now there has come about what I willed, or it has not come about. Hence the introduction of a change or a novelty must, at the moment when it is introduced, begin with an untruth, it must take several days for people to imagine and make others imagine that what had come about was what one willed. Since for the single individual there is something insipid in finding that "one fair morning," God knows how, he has become something or another—therefore one must try to help oneself out with divers untruths, that what he has now become he willed to be from his earliest childhood, etc., etc. As in the case of a man who in an exalted moment at a ball falls in love with a girl he is not acquainted with and knows hardly who she is—he feels the need or the temptation for shame's sake to begin with a little untruth about having loved her from his earliest childhood, about already having once before made love to her, etc., etc. So the race also falls into the embarrassment of having to help itself out with a little untruth, in order to get the story started again. Yet one still has a little recollection of what it must be to be a free rational being. To secure this conception one must poetize that what has come about is what one willed—unless one assumes with Hegel that it came about by necessity. But that a revolution of affairs came about in such a way (i.e. by necessity) is again the same old evil tendency to shove off from oneself the responsibility—in this case indeed it is raised to so high a degree, carried out on such a scale, that in the end existence must acknowledge the paternity of what comes to pass in the world of free rational beings, pretty much as in nature, so that these meaningless and inhuman revolutions are to be regarded as natural phenomena, so that revolutions simply *are* and republics come into existence in the same sense that there is cholera.*

If one were to say that then the *extraordinarius* begins with an untruth, indeed makes God a party to the untruth, it may be replied that all true communication of truth must always begin with an untruth. In part, this has its ground in the fact that it is indeed impossible to tell the whole truth in one minute or even a shorter time; on the contrary a long, long time may perhaps be needed for it. In part, this first untruth is merely reduplication, that the true communication

* The following paragraph (which is to be found in *Papirer* IX B 3 b) was written at the same time as the *Postscript*, evidently with the intention of adding it to the text. The translator can find no place for it more appropriate than this.

of truth is cautious and aware of the fact that it might indeed be possible that the recipient of the communication was in the untruth, in which case the direct communication of the truth would be untruth. This is "reflection," the critical moment in the communication of truth. Thus the ignorance of Socrates was in fact untruth; but it was only for the sake of truth, i.e. it is precisely reduplication's expression for the fact that he truly would communicate truth, that he was profoundly aware that those who were to receive the communication were possibly in the untruth of delusions of all sorts, so that it would not do to communicate truth quite directly, expectorating it cheerfully or declaiming it or lecturing it. To mention the highest instance, Christ's own life shows this; for when one is God it is indeed an untruth (in the sense that truth is merely direct) to come in the form of a lowly servant; and, viewed from the other side (since he had come for the sake of suffering and dying), it would have been an untruth to accept for one sole instant the favor of the people and occasion this misunderstanding. However, I shall carry this out no farther. But in the case of the *extraordinarius* precisely this must be a part of his dreadful responsibility, that in a stricter sense he has to begin with an untruth. And an untruth to begin with is in the case of the *extraordinarius* not to be avoided. Dialectically this lies in the nature of the case. If this untruth is not present, then the *extraordinarius* is not the *extraordinarius*, this title is then taken in vain, it is a direct superlative in contrast to the ordinary. But this is an altogether undialectical definition of the extraordinary.

As for the present treatise, the reader, I hope, will constantly get from reading it the impression that it is ethico-religious and has nothing to do with politics, that it investigates ethico-religiously how it comes about that a new point of departure is created in relation to the established order; that it comes about by the fact that *the point of departure is* FROM ABOVE, *from God*, and *the formula is this paradox that an individual is employed.* Humanly understood, an individual, according to all reason, is infinitely nothing in comparison with the established order (the universal), so it is a paradox that the individual is the stronger. This can be explained only by the fact that it is God who makes use of him, God who stands behind him; but just for this reason one sees God again, just because the situation is a paradox. When there are hundreds of men, what comes to pass is explained simply by the activity of the hundreds of men, but the paradox compels us (insofar as freedom can be compelled) to take notice of God, that he is taking part in it.

Politically the whole thing, even when it comes to decision, goes far more easily: the less paradox, the simpler it is. Politically one has nothing to do with God, suffers no inconvenience from the thought that he takes part: *the starting point is from below*, FROM *that which is lower* than the established order; for even the most mediocre "establishment" is preferable to and higher than the vaguest of all vague conceptions, "the multitude," which, if you please, accounts for the fact that nowadays this absurdity finds a place in the State, that there exists a monster of fairyland with many heads, or, more correctly and truly, with a thousand legs, or, according to circumstances, with a hundred thousand: "the multitude," an absurd monster or a monstrous absurdity, which nevertheless is physically in possession of power, of outcries and of noise, and besides that has an extraordinary virtuosity in making everything commensurable for the decision of the hands upraised to vote or the fists upraised to fight. This abstraction is an inhuman something, the power of which is, to be sure, prodigious, but it is a prodigious power which cannot be defined in human terms, but more properly as one defines the power of a machine, calling it so and so many horsepower: the power of the multitude is always horsepower.

This abstraction, whether you will call it the public or the multitude or the majority or the senseless people—this abstraction is used politically to bring about movement. Just as in whist or other social games there is some stake for which men play, so is this abstraction the stake for which men play politically. Truth and such like things, God in heaven, etc., death, judgment and more of this sort, the politician regards in about the same way as when one finds it tiresome to play cards for nothing. No, cards must be played for money, and politically the game must be played for the multitude, as to whether one can *à tout prix* get the most on his side, or the most who go over to his side with their many legs. So when one of the players sees that he has got the most he hurries to put himself at the head to lead this monster—or rather there is not even any player, this is rather too much a characterization of personality; the whole thing is like a game where there is no player, or like a speech where yet there is no speaker, as in ventriloquism. But certain it is that in an evening hour, or possibly for several evenings in succession, there is a monstrous multitude on its legs, which for the organism of the State is certainly a very suspicious situation which can only be likened to wind. This human mass becomes at last enraged by friction, and now demands—or rather it demands nothing, it does not itself know what it wills, it takes the threatening attitude only in the hope that something after all will come to pass, in the hope that the weaker side (the established government, the ruler) will perhaps become so much alarmed that it will go ahead and do something which neither the multitude nor those at the head of it, the stronger ones, the courageous ones (if there be any such), have the courage to speak out in definite words. The fact of being the stronger therefore does not mean to act, but by an abstract possibility, by a sound of nature (such as is heard in Ceylon), to frighten the weaker into doing something—as Louis Philippe went off in alarm and by running away gave France a republic, or brought France into a situation out of which (who ever would have thought of it!) a republic came about. In alarm the king goes off and does something—and what the king does, that the human multitude then adores, maintaining that *it* had done it.

While the individual who truly connects himself with a religious movement must watch out and be ready to fight lest the dreadful thing should come to pass that this monstrous abstraction should wish to help him by going over with its legs to his side (for to conquer by the help of this is, religiously, to help untruth to conquer); while the religious individual must suffer indescribably under the weight of his responsibility and of doubly reflected contention in loneliness (for he contends alone—but at the same time contends for life and death to be permitted to be alone), it goes far easier for the political hero, and easiest of all for one who is not so much as a political hero. But if there be such a hero, he only takes care to assure himself of these thousands before venturing anything, and when he is assured of them he ventures— that is, he does not in fact venture anything, for physically he is by far the stronger, and he contends physically.

But for this reason also almost every political movement, instead of being an advance to the rational, is a retrogression to the irrational. Even a poor government which yet is organic is better than the senseless situation when such an abstraction rules the State. The existence of this abstraction in the State (like an unwholesome fluid in the blood) puts finally an end to the rational State. Wherever this abstraction is set upon the throne there really is no government. One is obedient only to the man whom he himself has boosted up, pretty much as the idolater worships and serves the god he himself has made, i.e. one obeys himself. With the discontinuance of the rational State the art of statesmanship will become a game. Everything will turn upon getting the multitude pollinated, and after that getting them to vote on his side, with noise, with torches and with weapons, indifferent, absolutely indifferent, as to whether they understand anything or no.

Since such is the case and since everything in these times is politics, I do not wonder that many may find that the present treatise deals with nothing, is concerned with difficulties which absolutely do not exist. Well—be it so then, it deals in fact with God and with the God-relationship in the individual.

APPENDIX

Corrections made by S.K. to the first draft (*Papirer* VII B 235) subsequent to the 28 additions and erasures registered in the text of this draft. For the sake of brevity, w., l., & p. (word, line, & page) indicate the plural as well as the singular. The inconspicuous numerals in the text can easily be ignored by readers who are not interested in this technical register which cost me so much labor.

INTRODUCTION

1.	VII B 243,	2.	2 w. added.
2.	" " "	3.	2 w. " , 9 l. omitted.
3.	" " "	4.	3 w. " , 16 l. omitted.
4.	" " "	5.	5 l. omitted.
5.	" " "	6.	6 l. "
6.	" " "	7.	3 l. " which S.K. had added.
7.	" " "	8.	10 l. "
8.	" " "	9.	11 l. "
9.	" " "	10.	2½ l. "
10.	" " "	11.	31 l. omitted. A note.
11.	" " "	12.	8 l. omitted, 3 l. added.
12.	" " 247,	1.	8 l. "
13.	IX B 1.		Parenthesis of 3 l. omitted.
14.	VII B 244.		3½ l. sub. for 9 p. & 2 notes.
15.	" " 248,	6.	5 l. sub. for 4½ l.
16.	" " "	8.	5 l. omitted.
17.	VIII B 9b.		21 l. omitted.
18.	VII B 248,	9.	7 l. sub. for 4 l.
19.	" " "	10.	The word "French" added.

CHAPTER I

1.	VIII B 13.		1 l. omitted.
2.	" " 9 c.		10 l. omitted.
3.	" " 13,	10.	1 w. added.
4.	VII B 249,	6.	8 l. added.
5.	" " "	7.	4 w. added.
6.	" " "	8.	1 w. added.
7.	" " "	9.	4 w. added.

8.	VII B 249,	10.	13 l. omitted.
9.	" " "	11.	6 l. omitted, 1 w. changed.
10.	?		13 l. omitted.
11.	" " "	12.	Note of 7 l. omitted.
12.	" " "	13.	8 l. omitted.
13.	" " "	14.	1 l. omitted.
14.	" " "	15.	6 l. omitted, 10 w. added.
15.	" " "	17.	19 l. omitted.
16.	" " "	18.	Note of 7 l. omitted.
17.	" " "	19.	Latin encomium to S.K. by the Rector of his school as a recommendation to the university—omitted where it was used later more generally.
18.	IX B 7,	4.	Reference to Adler & Mynster generalized.
19.	IX B 9,	9.	Note of 10 l. omitted.
20.	IX B 7,	7.	14 w. added.
21.	VII B 249,	23.	Note of 1 p. omitted.
22.	" " "	25.	3 l. sub. for 5.
23.	" " "	26.	5 l. omitted.
24.	" " "	27.	5 l. sub. for 13.
25.	VIII B 9,	4 a.	Footnote of 3 p. omitted—in which S.K. had made 9 corrections!
26.	VII B 252,	1.	7 l. sub. for 7.
27.	VIII B 9,	13.	6 l. omitted.
28.	VII B 252,	5.	9 l. omitted.
29.	" " "	6.	9 l. omitted.
30.	" " "	9.	Note of 12 l. omitted.
31.	" " "	13.	6 l. omitted.
32.	" " "	14.	15 l. & note omitted.
33.	" " "	15.	2 l. changed & note of 1 p. omitted.
34.	" " "	16.	13 l. omitted.
35.	" " "	18.	5 l. omitted.
36.	" " "	19.	2 l. sub. for 4.
37.	" " "	20.	2 l. sub. for 4.

CHAPTER II

1.	VII B 253,	1.	1 p. & 12 l. omitted.
2.	" " "	2.	7 l. omitted.

3.	VII B 253, 3.	21 l. & note omitted, 24 l.
4.	VII B 253, 4.	23 l. omitted.
5.	VIII B 5, 2 b & c.	Note of 2 p. & 5 l. omitted.
6.	IX B 4 b.	3 l. omitted.
7.	VIII B 9, 5 d.	Note of 4 l. omitted.
8.	" " 5 e.	3 l. omitted.
9.	VII B 253, 6.	6 l. omitted.
10.	" " " 7.	4 l. sub. for 18.
11.	" " " 8.	1 l. sub. for 4.
12.	" " " 9.	2 l. & note of 8 l. omitted.
13.	" " " 10.	4 w. changed.
14.	VIII B 9, 5 f.	Several lines changed, and note of 4 l. omitted.
15.	" " " 5 h.	6 l. changed, note of 24 l. omitted.
16.	" " " 5 i.	14 l. omitted.
17.	" " " 5 l.	15 l. omitted.

CHAPTER III

1.	VII B 253.	Slightly changed.
2.	" " 255.	Abbreviated.
3.	" " 257, 2 & 3.	6 l. sub. for 1 p. & note.
4.	" " " 4.	1 w. changed, note of 14 l. omitted.
5.	" " " 5.	3 l. omitted.
6.	" " " 6.	12 l. omitted.
7.	" " " 7.	4 l. sub. for $1\frac{1}{2}$ p.
8.	VII B 257, 8.	4 l. sub. for 7.
9.	" " " 9.	4 l. sub. for 12.
10.	" " " 10.	4 l. sub. for 12.
11.	" " " 11.	3 l. sub. for 16.
12.	" " " 12.	$1\frac{1}{2}$ p. sub. for $2\frac{1}{2}$.
13.	" " " 13.	29 l. sub. for 2.
14.	" " " 14.	2 l. sub. for 2.
15.	" " " 15.	14 l. omitted.
16.	" " " 16.	16 l. omitted.
17.	" " " 17.	4 l. omitted & note of 17 l.
18.	" " " 18.	2 w. added.
19.	" " " 19.	4 l. sub. for 14.
20.	" " " 20.	10 l. omitted (already erased!).

21. VII B 257, 21.   12 l. sub. for 21.
22. " " " 22.   2 p. omitted.
23. " " 259.   Paragraph rewritten—1 p. instead of 9 l.
24. " " 261, 1.   5 l. omitted.
25. " " " 2.   2 w. added.
26. " " " 3.   1 l. sub. for 8.
27. " " " 4.   Note of 11 l. omitted.
28. " " " 5.   1 l. added.
29. " " " 6.   2 l. added.
30. " " " 7.   6 l. added, 1 p. & 8 l. omitted.
31. " " " 17.   1 l. added.
32. " " " 18.   7 l. added.
33. " " " 24.   13 l. omitted, 6 added.
34. " " " 25.   2 l. altered.
35. " " " 26.   2 l. altered.
36. " " 264, 1.   16 l. omitted.

CHAPTER IV

1. VII B 265, 1.   1 w. changed.
2. " " 266, 1.   6 l. omitted.
3. " " " 2.   28 l. omitted.
4. " " " 3.   12 l. omitted & 2 added.
5. " " " 5.   10 l. omitted & 4 added.
6. " " " 6.   1½ l. sub. for 2 l.
7. " " " 7.   20 l. omitted.
8. " " " 8.   7 l. retained which S.K. omitted.
9. " " " 9.   Parenthesis added.
10. IX B 5, 2 f.   8 l. sub. for 8 l.
11. " " " " g.   13 l. omitted.
12. VII B 266 12.   12 l. omitted.
13. " " " 13.   31 l. omitted.
14. " " " 14.   4 l. sub. for 11 l.
15. " " " 15.   6 l. sub. for 5 l.
16. " " " 16   41 l. sub. for 16 l.
        & VII A 150.
17. VII B 266, 17.   9 l. omitted.
18. IX B 5, 2 k.   1 l. omitted.
19. VII B 266, 19.   1 l. & note of 5 l. omitted.

20.	VII B 266, 20.	15 l. omitted.
21.	IX B 5, 2 *o.*	1 l. omitted.
22.	" " " " *q.*	1 w. omitted.
23.	" " " " *r & s.*	11 w. omitted.
24.	VII B 266, 22.	5 l. sub. for 11.
25.	" " " 23.	14 l. sub. for 3 p.
26.	VII B 266, 24.	7 l. sub. for 18.
27.	IX B 5, 2 *ae.*	7 w. omitted.
28.	" " " " *ee.*	12 l. omitted.
29.	VII B 266, 25.	Note of 12 l. omitted.
30.	IX B 5, 2 *ff.*	5 l. sub. for 4 l.
31.	" " " " *gg.*	A few w. changed.
32.	" " " " *jj.*	2 l. omitted.
33.	" " " " *kk.*	A few w. omitted.
34.	VII B 266, 27.	2 l. sub. for 19 l.
35.	IX B 5, 2 *ll.*	Parenthesis omitted.
36.	VII B 266, 28.	39 l. sub. for 26.
37.	" " " 29.	7 l. sub. for 6.
38.	" " " 30.	8 l. sub. for 4.
39.	IX B 5, 2 *nn.*	1½ l. omitted.
40.	VII B 266, 31.	Note of 28 l. omitted.
41.	" " " 32.	11 l. omitted.
42.	" " " 33.	9 l. sub. for 6.
43.	" " " 34.	6 l. sub. for 12 l.
44.	" " " 35.	Paragraph added.

INDEX

This Index is composed in large part of key words which suggest important aspects of Kierkegaard's thought, and which will be immediately familiar to readers of other Kierkegaard works.

Revised December, 1966

harper ✦ torchbooks

HUMANITIES AND SOCIAL SCIENCES

American Studies: General

American Studies: Colonial

American Studies: From the Revolution to 1860

---

† The New American Nation Series, edited by Henry Steele Commager and Richard B. Morris.

‡ American Perspectives series, edited by Bernard Wishy and William E. Leuchtenburg.

* The Rise of Modern Europe series, edited by William L. Langer.

¶ Researches in the Social, Cultural, and Behavioral Sciences, edited by Benjamin Nelson.

§ The Library of Religion and Culture, edited by Benjamin Nelson.

Σ Harper Modern Science Series, edited by James R. Newman.

° Not for sale in Canada.

△ Not for sale in the U. K.

MILLARD MEISS: Painting in Florence and Siena after the Black Death: *The Arts, Religion and Society in the Mid-Fourteenth Century. 169 illus.* TB/1148

ERICH NEUMANN: The Archetypal World of Henry Moore. △ *107 illus.* TB/2020

DORA & ERWIN PANOFSKY : Pandora's Box: *The Changing Aspects of a Mythical Symbol. Revised Edition. Illus.* TB/2021

ERWIN PANOFSKY: Studies in Iconology: *Humanistic Themes in the Art of the Renaissance.* △ *180 illustrations* TB/1077

ALEXANDRE PIANKOFF: The Shrines of Tut-Ankh-Amon. *Edited by N. Rambova. 117 illus.* TB/2011

JEAN SEZNEC: The Survival of the Pagan Gods: *The Mythological Tradition and Its Place in Renaissance Humanism and Art.* 108 illustrations TB/2004

OTTO VON SIMSON: The Gothic Cathedral: *Origins of Gothic Architecture and the Medieval Concept of Order.* △ *58 illus.* TB/2018

HEINRICH ZIMMER: Myth and Symbols in Indian Art and Civilization. *70 illustrations* TB/2005

Business, Economics & Economic History

REINHARD BENDIX: Work and Authority in Industry: *Ideologies of Management in the Course of Industrialization* TB/3035

GILBERT BURCK & EDITORS OF FORTUNE: The Computer Age: *And Its Potential for Management* TB/1179

THOMAS C. COCHRAN: The American Business System: *A Historical Perspective, 1900-1955* TB/1080

THOMAS C. COCHRAN: The Inner Revolution: *Essays on the Social Sciences in History* △ TB/1140

THOMAS C. COCHRAN & WILLIAM MILLER: The Age of Enterprise: *A Social History of Industrial America* TB/1054

ROBERT DAHL & CHARLES E. LINDBLOM: Politics, Economics, and Welfare: *Planning and Politico-Economic Systems Resolved into Basic Social Processes* TB/3037

PETER F. DRUCKER: The New Society: *The Anatomy of Industrial Order* △ TB/1082

EDITORS OF FORTUNE: America in the Sixties: *The Economy and the Society* TB/1015

ROBERT L. HEILBRONER: The Great Ascent: *The Struggle for Economic Development in Our Time* TB/3030

FRANK H. KNIGHT: The Economic Organization TB/1214

FRANK H. KNIGHT: Risk, Uncertainty and Profit TB/1215

ABBA P. LERNER: Everybody's Business: *Current Assumptions in Economics and Public Policy* TB/3051

ROBERT GREEN MC CLOSKEY: American Conservatism in the Age of Enterprise, 1865-1910 △ TB/1137

PAUL MANTOUX: The Industrial Revolution in the Eighteenth Century: *The Beginnings of the Modern Factory System in England* ○ △ TB/1079

WILLIAM MILLER, Ed.: Men in Business: *Essays on the Historical Role of the Entrepreneur* TB/1081

RICHARD B. MORRIS: Government and Labor in Early America △ TB/1244

HERBERT SIMON: The Shape of Automation: *For Men and Management* TB/1245

PERRIN STRYKER: The Character of the Executive: *Eleven Studies in Managerial Qualities* TB/1041

PIERRE URI: Partnership for Progress: *A Program for Transatlantic Action* TB/3036

Contemporary Culture

JACQUES BARZUN: The House of Intellect △ TB/1051

CLARK KERR: The Uses of the University TB/1264

JOHN U. NEF: Cultural Foundations of Industrial Civilization △ TB/1024

NATHAN M. PUSEY: The Age of the Scholar: *Observations on Education in a Troubled Decade* TB/1157

PAUL VALÉRY: The Outlook for Intelligence △ TB/2016

RAYMOND WILLIAMS: Culture and Society, 1780-1950 ○ △ TB/1252

RAYMOND WILLIAMS: The Long Revolution.○ △ *Revised Edition* TB/1253

Historiography & Philosophy of History

JACOB BURCKHARDT: On History and Historians. △ *Introduction by H. R. Trevor-Roper* TB/1216

WILHELM DILTHEY: Pattern and Meaning in History: *Thoughts on History and Society.* ○ △ *Edited with an Introduction by H. P. Rickman* TB/1075

J. H. HEXTER: Reappraisals in History: *New Views on History & Society in Early Modern Europe* △ TB/1100

H. STUART HUGHES: History as Art and as Science: *Twin Vistas on the Past* TB/1207

RAYMOND KLIBANSKY & H. J. PATON, Eds.: Philosophy and History: *The Ernst Cassirer Festschrift. Illus.* TB/1115

ARNOLDO MOMIGLIANO: Studies in Historiography ○ △ TB/1288

GEORGE H. NADEL, Ed.: Studies in the Philosophy of History: *Selected Essays from History and Theory* TB/1208

JOSE ORTEGA Y GASSET: The Modern Theme. *Introduction by Jose Ferrater Mora* TB/1038

KARL R. POPPER: The Open Society and Its Enemies △
Vol. I: *The Spell of Plato* TB/1101
Vol. II: *The High Tide of Prophecy: Hegel, Marx and the Aftermath* TB/1102

KARL R. POPPER: The Poverty of Historicism ○ △ TB/1126

G. J. RENIER: History: *Its Purpose and Method* △ TB/1209

W. H. WALSH: Philosophy of History: *An Introduction* △ TB/1020

History: General

L. CARRINGTON GOODRICH: A Short History of the Chinese People. △ *Illus.* TB/3015

DAN N. JACOBS & HANS H. BAERWALD: Chinese Communism: *Selected Documents* TB/3031

BERNARD LEWIS: The Arabs in History △ TB/1029

BERNARD LEWIS: The Middle East and the West ○ △ TB/1274

History: Ancient

A. ANDREWES: The Greek Tyrants △ TB/1103

ADOLF ERMAN, Ed.: The Ancient Egyptians: *A Sourcebook of Their Writings. New material and Introduction by William Kelly Simpson* TB/1233

MICHAEL GRANT: Ancient History ○ △ TB/1190

SAMUEL NOAH KRAMER: Sumerian Mythology TB/1055

NAPHTALI LEWIS & MEYER REINHOLD, Eds.: Roman Civilization. *Sourcebook I: The Republic* TB/1231

NAPHTALI LEWIS & MEYER REINHOLD, Eds.: Roman Civilization. *Sourcebook II: The Empire* TB/1232

History: Medieval

P. BOISSONNADE: Life and Work in Medieval Europe: *The Evolution of the Medieval Economy, the 5th to the 15th Century.* ○ △ *Preface by Lynn White, Jr.* TB/1141

HELEN CAM: England before Elizabeth △ TB/1026

NORMAN COHN: The Pursuit of the Millennium: *Revolutionary Messianism in Medieval and Reformation Europe* △ TB/1037

G. G. COULTON: Medieval Village, Manor, and Monastery TB/1022

CHRISTOPHER DAWSON, Ed.: Mission to Asia: *Narratives and Letters of the Franciscan Missionaries in Mongolia and China in the 13th and 14 Centuries* △ TB/315

HEINRICH FICHTENAU: The Carolingian Empire: *The Age of Charlemagne* TB/1142

F. L. GANSHOF: Feudalism △ TB/1058

DENO GEANAKOPLOS: Byzantine East and Latin West: *Two Worlds of Christendom in the Middle Ages and Renaissance* TB/1265

EDWARD GIBBON: The Triumph of Christendom in the Roman Empire *(Chaps. XV-XX of "Decline and Fall," J. B. Bury edition).* § △ *Illus.* TB/46

W. O. HASSALL, Ed.: Medieval England: *As Viewed by Contemporaries* △ TB/1205

DENYS HAY: Europe: The Emergence of an Idea TB/1275

DENYS HAY: The Medieval Centuries ° △ TB/1192

J. M. HUSSEY: The Byzantine World △ TB/1057

ROBERT LATOUCHE: The Birth of Western Economy: *Economic Aspects of the Dark Ages.* ° △ *Intro. by Philip Grierson* TB/1290

FERDINAND LOT: The End of the Ancient World and the Beginnings of the Middle Ages. *Introduction by Glanville Downey* TB/1044

G. MOLLAT: The Popes at Avignon: 1305-1378 △ TB/308

CHARLES PETIT-DUTAILLIS: The Feudal Monarchy in France and England: *From the Tenth to the Thirteenth Century* ° △ TB/1165

HENRI PIRENNE: Early Democracies in the Low Countries: *Urban Society and Political Conflict in the Middle Ages and the Renaissance. Introduction by John H. Mundy* TB/1110

STEVEN RUNCIMAN: A History of the Crusades. △
Volume I: *The First Crusade and the Foundation of the Kingdom of Jerusalem. Illus.* TB/1143
Volume II: *The Kingdom of Jerusalem and the Frankish East, 1100-1187. Illus.* TB/1243

FERDINAND SCHEVILL: Siena: *The History of a Medieval Commune. Intro. by William M. Bowsky* TB/1164

SULPICIUS SEVERUS et al.: The Western Fathers: *Being the Lives of Martin of Tours, Ambrose, Augustine of Hippo, Honoratus of Arles and Germanus of Auxerre.* △ *Edited and trans. by F. O. Hoare* TB/309

HENRY OSBORN TAYLOR: The Classical Heritage of the Middle Ages. *Foreword and Biblio. by Kenneth M. Setton* TB/1117

F. VAN DER MEER: Augustine The Bishop: *Church and Society at the Dawn of the Middle Ages* △ TB/304

J. M. WALLACE-HADRILL: The Barbarian West: *The Early Middle Ages, A.D. 400-1000* △ TB/1061

History: Renaissance & Reformation

JACOB BURCKHARDT: The Civilization of the Renaissance in Italy. △ *Intro. by Benjamin Nelson & Charles Trinkaus. Illus.* Vol. I TB/40; Vol. II TB/41

JOHN CALVIN & JACOPO SADOLETO: A Reformation Debate. *Edited by John C. Olin* TB/1239

ERNST CASSIRER: The Individual and the Cosmos in Renaissance Philosophy. △ *Translated with an Introduction by Mario Domandi* TB/1097

FEDERICO CHABOD: Machiavelli and the Renaissance △ TB/1193

EDWARD P. CHEYNEY: The Dawn of a New Era, 1250-1453. * Illus. TB/3002

G. CONSTANT: The Reformation in England: *The English Schism, Henry VIII, 1509-1547* △ TB/314

R. TREVOR DAVIES: The Golden Century of Spain, 1501-1621 ° △ TB/1194

G. R. ELTON: Reformation Europe, 1517-1559 ° △ TB/1270

DESIDERIUS ERASMUS: Christian Humanism and the Reformation: *Selected Writings. Edited and translated by John C. Olin* TB/1166

WALLACE K. FERGUSON et al.: Facets of the Renaissance TB/1098

WALLACE K. FERGUSON et al.: The Renaissance: *Six Essays. Illus.* TB/1084

JOHN NEVILLE FIGGIS: The Divine Right of Kings. *Introduction by G. R. Elton* TB/1191

JOHN NEVILLE FIGGIS: Political Thought from Gerson to Grotius: 1414-1625: *Seven Studies. Introduction by Garrett Mattingly* TB/1032

MYRON P. GILMORE: The World of Humanism, 1453-1517. * Illus. TB/3003

FRANCESCO GUICCIARDINI: Maxims and Reflections of a Renaissance Statesman (Ricordi). *Trans. by Mario Domandi. Intro. by Nicolai Rubinstein* TB/1160

J. H. HEXTER: More's Utopia: *The Biography of an Idea, New Epilogue by the Author* TB/1195

HAJO HOLBORN: Ulrich von Hutten and the German Reformation TB/1238

JOHAN HUIZINGA: Erasmus and the Age of Reformation. △ *Illus.* TB/19

JOEL HURSTFIELD, Ed.: The Reformation Crisis △ TB/1267

ULRICH VON HUTTEN et al.: On the Eve of the Reformation: *"Letters of Obscure Men." Introduction by Hajo Holborn* TB/1124

PAUL O. KRISTELLER: Renaissance Thought: *The Classic, Scholastic, and Humanist Strains* TB/1048

PAUL O. KRISTELLER: Renaissance Thought II: *Papers on Humanism and the Arts* TB/1163

NICCOLÒ MACHIAVELLI: History of Florence and of the Affairs of Italy: *from the earliest times to the death of Lorenzo the Magnificent. Introduction by Felix Gilbert* △ TB/1027

ALFRED VON MARTIN: Sociology of the Renaissance. *Introduction by Wallace K. Ferguson* TB/1099

GARRETT MATTINGLY et al.: Renaissance Profiles. △ *Edited by J. H. Plumb* TB/1162

MILLARD MEISS: Painting in Florence and Siena after the Black Death: *The Arts, Religion and Society in the Mid-Fourteenth Century.* △ *169 illus.* TB/1148

J. E. NEALE: The Age of Catherine de Medici ° △ TB/1085

ERWIN PANOFSKY: Studies in Iconology: *Humanistic Themes in the Art of the Renaissance.* △ *180 illustrations* TB/1077

J. H. PARRY: The Establishment of the European Hegemony: 1415-1715: *Trade and Exploration in the Age of the Renaissance* △ TB/1045

J. H. PLUMB: The Italian Renaissance: *A Concise Survey of Its History and Culture* △ TB/1161

A. F. POLLARD: Henry VIII. ° △ *Introduction by A. G. Dickens* TB/1249

A. F. POLLARD: Wolsey. ° △ *Introduction by A. G. Dickens* TB/1248

CECIL ROTH: The Jews in the Renaissance. *Illus.* TB/834

A. L. ROWSE: The Expansion of Elizabethan England. ° △ *Illus.* TB/1220

GORDON RUPP: Luther's Progress to the Diet of Worms ° △ TB/120

FERDINAND SCHEVILL: The Medici. *Illus.* TB/1010

FERDINAND SCHEVILL: Medieval and Renaissance Florence. *Illus.* Volume I: *Medieval Florence* TB/1090
Volume II: *The Coming of Humanism and the Age of the Medici* TB/1091

G. M. TREVELYAN: England in the Age of Wycliffe, 1368-1520 ° △ TB/1112

VESPASIANO: Renaissance Princes, Popes, and Prelates: *The Vespasiano Memoirs: Lives of Illustrious Men of the XVth Century. Intro. by Myron P. Gilmore* TB/1111

History: Modern European

FREDERICK B. ARTZ: Reaction and Revolution, 1815-1832. * Illus. TB/3034

MAX BELOFF: The Age of Absolutism, 1660-1815 △ TB/1062

ROBERT C. BINKLEY: Realism and Nationalism, 1852-1871. * Illus. TB/3038

ASA BRIGGS: The Making of Modern England, 1784-1867: *The Age of Improvement* ° △ TB/1203

CRANE BRINTON: A Decade of Revolution, 1789-1799. * Illus. TB/3018

D. W. BROGAN: The Development of Modern France. ° △
Volume I: *From the Fall of the Empire to the Dreyfus Affair* TB/1184
Volume II: *The Shadow of War, World War I, Between the Two Wars. New Introduction by the Author* TB/1185

J. BRONOWSKI & BRUCE MAZLISH: The Western Intellectual Tradition: *From Leonardo to Hegel* △ TB/3001

GEOFFREY BRUUN: Europe and the French Imperium, 1799-1814. * Illus. TB/3033

ALAN BULLOCK: Hitler, A Study in Tyranny. ° △ *Illus.* TB/1123

4

Intellectual History & History of Ideas

PHILIP P. WIENER: Evolution and the Founders of Pragmatism. △ *Foreword by John Dewey* TB/1212

BASIL WILLEY: Nineteenth Century Studies: *Coleridge to Matthew Arnold* ○ △ TB/1261

BASIL WILLEY: More Nineteenth Century Studies: *A Group of Honest Doubters* ○ △ TB/1262

Literature, Poetry, The Novel & Criticism

JAMES BAIRD: Ishmael: *The Art of Melville in the Contexts of International Primitivism* TB/1023

JACQUES BARZUN: The House of Intellect △ TB/1051

W. J. BATE: From Classic to Romantic: *Premises of Taste in Eighteenth Century England* TB/1036

RACHEL BESPALOFF: On the Iliad TB/2006

R. P. BLACKMUR et al.: Lectures in Criticism. *Introduction by Huntington Cairns* TB/2003

JAMES BOSWELL: The Life of Dr. Johnson & The Journal of a Tour to the Hebrides with Samuel Johnson LL.D.: *Selections.* ○ △ *Edited by F. V. Morley. Illus. by Ernest Shepard* TB/1254

ABRAHAM CAHAN: The Rise of David Levinsky: *a documentary novel of social mobility in early twentieth century America. Intro. by John Higham* TB/1028

ERNST R. CURTIUS: European Literature and the Latin Middle Ages △ TB/2015

GEORGE ELIOT: Daniel Deronda: *a novel. Introduction by F. R. Leavis* TB/1039

ADOLF ERMAN, Ed.: The Ancient Egyptians: *A Sourcebook of Their Writings. New Material and Introduction by William Kelly Simpson* TB/1233

ÉTIENNE GILSON: Dante and Philosophy TB/1089

ALFRED HARBAGE: As They Liked It: *A Study of Shakespeare's Moral Artistry* TB/1035

STANLEY R. HOPPER, Ed : Spiritual Problems in Contemporary Literature § TB/21

A. R. HUMPHREYS: The Augustan World: *Society, Thought and Letters in 18th Century England* ○ △ TB/1105

ALDOUS HUXLEY: Antic Hay & The Giaconda Smile. ○ △ *Introduction by Martin Green* TB/3503

ALDOUS HUXLEY: Brave New World & Brave New World Revisited. ○ △ *Introduction by Martin Green* TB/3501

HENRY JAMES: The Tragic Muse: *a novel. Introduction by Leon Edel* TB/1017

ARNOLD KETTLE: An Introduction to the English Novel. △
Volume I: *Defoe to George Eliot* TB/1011
Volume II: *Henry James to the Present* TB/1012

RICHMOND LATTIMORE: The Poetry of Greek Tragedy △ TB/1257

J. B. LEISHMAN: The Monarch of Wit: *An Analytical and Comparative Study of the Poetry of John Donne* ○ △ TB/1258

J. B. LEISHMAN: Themes and Variations in Shakespeare's Sonnets ○ △ TB/1259

ROGER SHERMAN LOOMIS: The Development of Arthurian Romance △ TB/1167

JOHN STUART MILL: On Bentham and Coleridge. △ *Introduction by F. R. Leavis* TB/1070

KENNETH B. MURDOCK: Literature and Theology in Colonial New England TB/99

SAMUEL PEPYS: The Diary of Samuel Pepys. ○ *Edited by O. F. Morshead. Illus. by Ernest Shepard* TB/1007

ST.-JOHN PERSE: Seamarks TB/2002

V. DE S. PINTO: Crisis in English Poetry, 1880-1940 ○ TB/1260

GEORGE SANTAYANA: Interpretations of Poetry and Religion § TB/9

C. K. STEAD: The New Poetic: *Yeats to Eliot* △ TB/1263

HEINRICH STRAUMANN: American Literature in the Twentieth Century. △ *Third Edition, Revised* TB/1168

PAGET TOYNBEE: Dante Alighieri: *His Life and Works. Edited with Intro. by Charles S. Singleton* TB/1206

DOROTHY VAN GHENT: The English Novel: *Form and Function* TB/1050

E. B. WHITE: One Man's Meat. *Introduction by Walter Blair* TB/3505

BASIL WILLEY: Nineteenth Century Studies: *Coleridge to Matthew Arnold* △ TB/1261

BASIL WILLEY: More Nineteenth Century Studies: *A Group of Honest Doubters* ○ △ TB/1262

RAYMOND WILLIAMS: Culture and Society, 1780-1950 ○ △ TB/1252

RAYMOND WILLIAMS: The Long Revolution. ○ △ *Revised Edition* TB/1253

MORTON DAUWEN ZABEL, Editor: Literary Opinion in America Vol. I TB/3013; Vol. II TB/3014

Myth, Symbol & Folklore

JOSEPH CAMPBELL, Editor: Pagan and Christian Mysteries *Illus.* TB/2013

MIRCEA ELIADE: Cosmos and History: *The Myth of the Eternal Return* § △ TB/2050

MIRCEA ELIADE: Rites and Symbols of Initiation: *The Mysteries of Birth and Rebirth* § △ TB/1236

THEODOR H. GASTER: Thespis: *Ritual, Myth and Drama in the Ancient Near East* △ TB/1281

C. G. JUNG & C. KERÉNYI: Essays on a Science of Mythology: *The Myths of the Divine Child and the Divine Maiden* TB/2014

DORA & ERWIN PANOFSKY: Pandora's Box: *The Changing Aspects of a Mythical Symbol.* △ *Revised edition. Illus.* TB/2021

ERWIN PANOFSKY: Studies in Iconology: *Humanistic Themes in the Art of the Renaissance.* △ *180 illustrations* TB/1077

JEAN SEZNEC: The Survival of the Pagan Gods: *The Mythological Tradition and its Place in Renaissance Humanism and Art.* △ *108 illustrations* TB/2004

HELLMUT WILHELM: Change: *Eight Lectures on the I Ching* △ TB/2019

HEINRICH ZIMMER: Myths and Symbols in Indian Art and Civilization. △ *70 illustrations* TB/2005

Philosophy

G. E. M. ANSCOMBE: An Introduction to Wittgenstein's Tractatus. ○ △ *Second Edition, Revised* TB/1210

HENRI BERGSON: Time and Free Will: *An Essay on the Immediate Data of Consciousness* ○ △ TB/1021

H. J. BLACKHAM: Six Existentialist Thinkers: *Kierkegaard, Nietzsche, Jaspers, Marcel, Heidegger, Sartre* ○ △ TB/1002

CRANE BRINTON: Nietzsche. *New Preface, Bibliography and Epilogue by the Author* TB/1197

MARTIN BUBER: The Knowledge of Man. △ *Ed. with an Intro. by Maurice Friedman. Trans. by Maurice Friedman and Ronald Gregor Smith* TB/135

ERNST CASSIRER: The Individual and the Cosmos in Renaissance Philosophy. △ *Translated with an Introduction by Mario Domandi* TB/1097

ERNST CASSIRER: Rousseau, Kant and Goethe. *Introduction by Peter Gay* TB/1092

FREDERICK COPLESTON: Medieval Philosophy ○ △ TB/376

F. M. CORNFORD: Principium Sapientiae: *A Study of the Origins of Greek Philosophical Thought. Edited by W. K. C. Guthrie* TB/1213

F. M. CORNFORD: From Religion to Philosophy: *A Study in the Origins of Western Speculation* § TB/20

WILFRID DESAN: The Tragic Finale: *An Essay on the Philosophy of Jean-Paul Sartre* TB/1030

A. P. D'ENTRÈVES: Natural Law: *An Historical Survey* △ TB/1223

MARVIN FARBER: The Aims of Phenomenology: *The Motives, Methods, and Impact of Husserl's Thought* TB/1291

HERBERT FINGARETTE: The Self in Transformation: *Psychoanalysis, Philosophy and the Life of the Spirit* ¶ TB/1177

PAUL FRIEDLÄNDER: Plato: *An Introduction* △ TB/2017

ÉTIENNE GILSON: Dante and Philosophy TB/1089

WILLIAM CHASE GREENE: Moira: *Fate, Good, and Evil in Greek Thought* TB/1104

7

ERICH NEUMANN: Amor and Psyche: *The Psychic Development of the Feminine* △ TB/2012

ERICH NEUMANN: The Archetypal World of Henry Moore. △ *107 illus.* TB/2020

ERICH NEUMANN: The Origins and History of Consciousness △ Vol. I *Illus.* TB/2007; Vol. II TB/2008

C. P. OBERNDORF: A History of Psychoanalysis in America TB/1147

RALPH BARTON PERRY: The Thought and Character of William James: *Briefer Version* TB/1156

JEAN PIAGET, BÄRBEL INHELDER, & ALINA SZEMINSKA: The Child's Conception of Geometry º △ TB/1146

JOHN H. SCHAAR: Escape from Authority: *The Perspectives of Erich Fromm* TB/1155

MUZAFER SHERIF: The Psychology of Social Norms TB/3072

Sociology

JACQUES BARZUN: Race: *A Study in Superstition. Revised Edition* TB/1172

BERNARD BERELSON, Ed.: The Behavioral Sciences Today TB/1127

ABRAHAM CAHAN: The Rise of David Levinsky: *A documentary novel of social mobility in early twentieth century America. Intro. by John Higham* TB/1028

THOMAS C. COCHRAN: The Inner Revolution: *Essays on the Social Sciences in History* TB/1140

ALLISON DAVIS & JOHN DOLLARD: Children of Bondage: *The Personality Development of Negro Youth in the Urban South* ¶ TB/3049

ST. CLAIR DRAKE & HORACE R. CAYTON: Black Metropolis: *A Study of Negro Life in a Northern City.* △ *Revised and Enlarged. Intro. by Everett C. Hughes* Vol. I TB/1086; Vol. II TB/1087

EMILE DURKHEIM et al.: Essays on Sociology and Philosophy: *With Analyses of Durkheim's Life and Work.* ¶ *Edited by Kurt H. Wolff* TB/1151

LEON FESTINGER, HENRY W. RIECKEN & STANLEY SCHACHTER: When Prophecy Fails: *A Social and Psychological Account of a Modern Group that Predicted the Destruction of the World* ¶ TB/1132

ALVIN W. GOULDNER: Wildcat Strike: *A Study in Worker-Management Relationships* ¶ TB/1176

FRANCIS J. GRUND: Aristocracy in America: *Social Class in the Formative Years of the New Nation* △ TB/1001

KURT LEWIN: Field Theory in Social Science: *Selected Theoretical Papers.* ¶ △ *Edited with a Foreword by Dorwin Cartwright* TB/1135

R. M. MAC IVER: Social Causation TB/1153

ROBERT K. MERTON, LEONARD BROOM, LEONARD S. COTTRELL, JR., Editors: Sociology Today: *Problems and Prospects* ¶ Vol. I TB/1173; Vol. II TB/1174

ROBERTO MICHELS: First Lectures in Political Sociology. *Edited by Alfred de Grazia* ¶ º TB/1224

BARRINGTON MOORE, JR.: Political Power and Social Theory: *Seven Studies* ¶ TB/1221

BARRINGTON MOORE, JR.: Soviet Politics—The Dilemma of Power: *The Role of Ideas in Social Change* ¶ TB/1222

TALCOTT PARSONS & EDWARD A. SHILS, Editors: Toward a General Theory of Action: *Theoretical Foundations for the Social Sciences* TB/1083

JOHN H. ROHRER & MUNRO S. EDMONDSON, Eds.: The Eighth Generation Grows Up: *Cultures and Personalities of New Orleans Negroes* ¶ TB/3050

ARNOLD ROSE: The Negro in America: *The Condensed Version of Gunnar Myrdal's An American Dilemma* TB/3048

KURT SAMUELSSON: Religion and Economic Action: *A Critique of Max Weber's The Protestant Ethic and the Spirit of Capitalism.* ¶ º *Trans. by E. G. French. Ed. with Intro. by D. C. Coleman* TB/1131

PHILIP SELZNICK: TVA and the Grass Roots: *A Study in the Sociology of Formal Organization* TB/1230

GEORG SIMMEL et al.: Essays on Sociology, Philosophy, and Aesthetics. ¶ *Edited by Kurt H. Wolff* TB/1234

HERBERT SIMON: The Shape of Automation: *For Men and Management* △ TB/1245

PITIRIM A. SOROKIN: Contemporary Sociological Theories. *Through the First Quarter of the 20th Century* TB/3046

MAURICE R. STEIN: The Eclipse of Community: *An Interpretation of American Studies* TB/1128

FERDINAND TÖNNIES: Community and Society: *Gemeinschaft und Gesellschaft. Translated and edited by Charles P. Loomis* TB/1116

W. LLOYD WARNER & Associates: Democracy in Jonesville: *A Study in Quality and Inequality* TB/1129

W. LLOYD WARNER: Social Class in America: *The Evaluation of Status* TB/1013

RELIGION

Ancient & Classical

J. H. BREASTED: Development of Religion and Thought in Ancient Egypt. *Intro. by John A. Wilson* TB/57

HENRI FRANKFORT: Ancient Egyptian Religion: *An Interpretation* TB/77

G. RACHEL LEVY: Religious Conceptions of the Stone Age and their Influence upon European Thought. △ *Illus. Introduction by Henri Frankfort* TB/106

MARTIN P. NILSSON: Greek Folk Religion. *Foreword by Arthur Darby Nock* TB/78

ALEXANDRE PIANKOFF: The Shrines of Tut-Ankh-Amon. △ *Edited by N. Rambova. 117 illus.* TB/2011

ERWIN ROHDE: Psyche: *The Cult of Souls and Belief in Immortality Among the Greeks.* △ *Intro. by W. K. C. Guthrie* Vol. I TB/140; Vol. II TB/141

H. J. ROSE: Religion in Greece and Rome △ TB/55

Biblical Thought & Literature

W. F. ALBRIGHT: The Biblical Period from Abraham to Ezra TB/102

C. K. BARRETT, Ed.: The New Testament Background: *Selected Documents* △ TB/86

C. H. DODD: The Authority of the Bible △ TB/43

M. S. ENSLIN: Christian Beginnings △ TB/5

M. S. ENSLIN: The Literature of the Christian Movement △ TB/6

JOHN GRAY: Archaeology and the Old Testament World. △ *Illus.* TB/127

JAMES MUILENBURG: The Way of Israel: *Biblical Faith and Ethics* △ TB/133

H. H. ROWLEY: The Growth of the Old Testament △ TB/107

GEORGE ADAM SMITH: The Historical Geography of the Holy Land. º △ *Revised and reset* TB/138

D. WINTON THOMAS, Ed.: Documents from Old Testament Times △ TB/85

The Judaic Tradition

LEO BAECK: Judaism and Christianity. *Trans. with Intro. by Walter Kaufmann* JP/23

SALO W. BARON: Modern Nationalism and Religion JP/18

MARTIN BUBER: Eclipse of God: *Studies in the Relation Between Religion and Philosophy* △ TB/12

MARTIN BUBER: For the Sake of Heaven TB/801

MARTIN BUBER: Hasidism and Modern Man. △ *Ed. and Trans. by Maurice Friedman* TB/839

MARTIN BUBER: The Knowledge of Man. △ *Edited with an Introduction by Maurice Friedman. Translated by Maurice Friedman and Ronald Gregor Smith* TB/135

MARTIN BUBER: Moses: *The Revelation and the Covenant* △ TB/837

MARTIN BUBER: The Origin and Meaning of Hasidism △ TB/835

MARTIN BUBER: Pointing the Way. △ *Introduction by Maurice S. Friedman* TB/103

MARTIN BUBER: The Prophetic Faith TB/73

MARTIN BUBER: Two Types of Faith: *the interpenetration of Judaism and Christianity* º △ TB/75

9

10

√B 126401E
√T
$ 2.25